AF328504

Verne Dawson

LUND HUMPHRIES | CONTEMPORARY PAINTERS

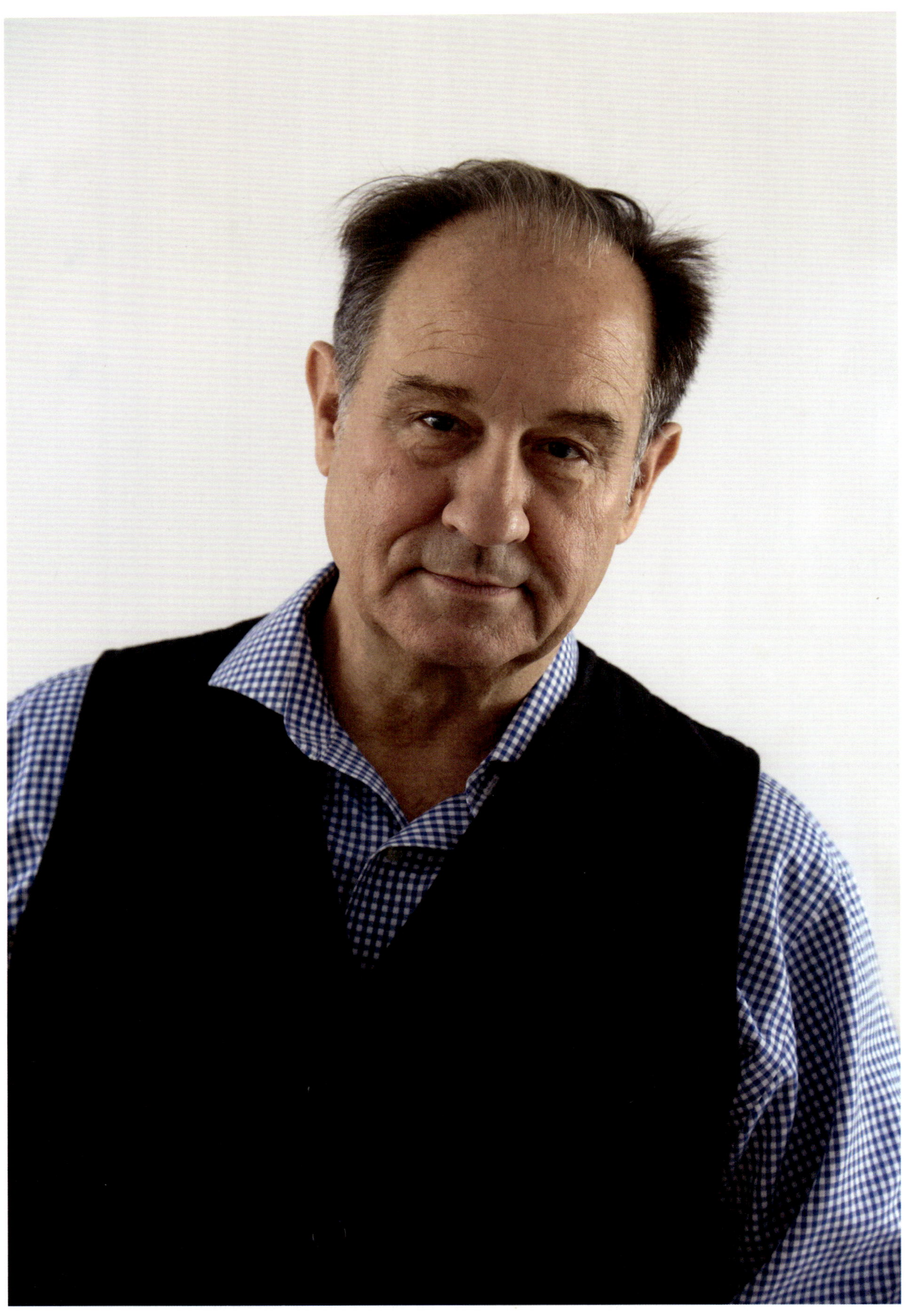

John Hutchinson

Verne Dawson

LUND HUMPHRIES | CONTEMPORARY PAINTERS

Contemporary Painters Series
Series Editor: Barry Schwabsky

The Contemporary Painters Series is a new, curated series of accessible, authoritative
and highly illustrated monographs on the world's leading living painters, which locates
painting as a vibrant and vital part of contemporary art.

The series is edited by American art critic Barry Schwabsky, supported by an
international advisory board with a specialist interest in contemporary painting.
It aims to redefine 'painting' in the contemporary context as work which is done within
the conventions and history of painting, but which may incorporate other materials
or techniques.

Advisory Board
Paco Barragán, independent curator and arts writer and Contributing Editor of ARTPULSE
Tony Godfrey, freelance writer and curator based in the Philippines
David Pagel, Los Angeles-based art critic, curator and writer
Ida Panicelli, former Editor-in-Chief of *Artforum*
Simon Rees, Director of the Govett-Brewster Art Gallery/Len Lye Centre, New Zealand
Beatrix Ruf, former Director of the Stedelijk Museum, Amsterdam
Philip Tinari, Director of the Ullens Center for Contemporary Art, Beijing
Gilda Williams, art critic, writer, lecturer and London correspondent for *Artforum*
John Yau, poet, art critic and curator

Also available in the series:
Etel Adnan by Kaelen Wilson-Goldie
Lois Dodd by Faye Hirsch
Neo Rauch by Michael Glover
Philip Taafe by John Yau
Thomas Nozkowski by John Yau

Contents

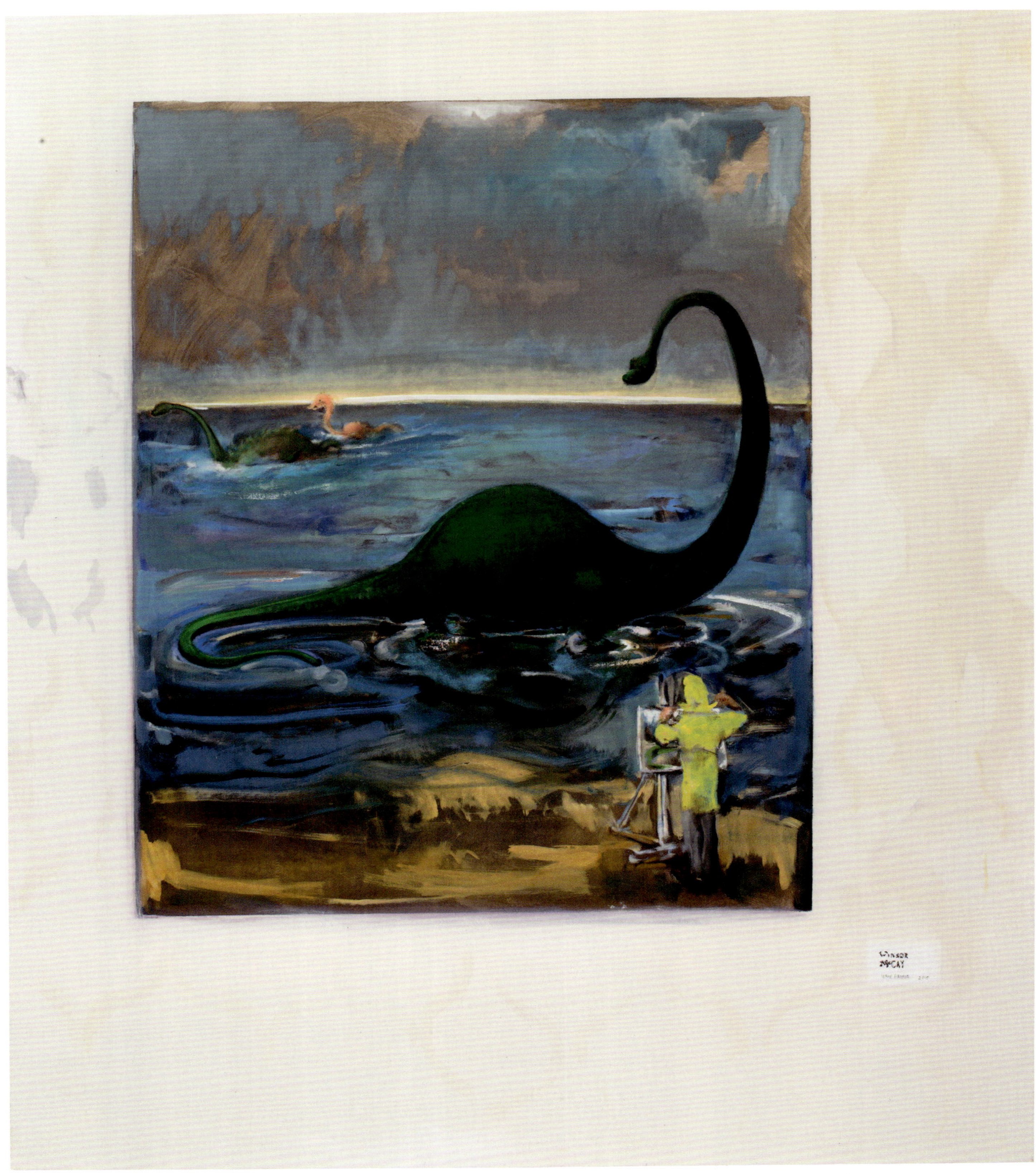

1. Winsor Mckay   2015

Oil on canvas
215.9 x 193 cm (85 x 76 in)
Ringier Collection, Switzerland

Foreword

Verne Dawson's art looks to the past and to what may be to come. This 'archaic future', as John Hutchinson calls it, can have the atmosphere of fairy tale, but it just might be a kind of utopian or dystopian science fiction. In any case, the paintings carry a subtext. Their often whimsical imagery and its homespun style – like that of some impossibly refined folk artist – can lend them a comforting air of familiarity, yet there is also a sense of disquiet that should put us on alert: Dawson is telling us things we do not know or have perhaps forgotten, and might prefer to ignore. He has said that his subject is 'man's integration into the natural world or lack thereof. This is predicated on the belief that even now, we are capable of creating a paradise on this earth.'[1] Strange but true: it is that very optimism, the ecstatic certainty that paradise is possible and that we belong to it, that makes Dawson's work so unsettling, because it means that we cannot settle quietly into the self-created discontents of our unhappy civilization. For this artist, the age-old tools and materials of painting are a means to stay in touch with a millennial knowledge of the human in its corporeal, social, earthly and celestial environs.

This book is the fruit of Hutchinson's long-standing interest in and commitment to Dawson's work, which he exhibited no less than four times – in solo shows in 2004, 2008 and 2016, and a group show in 2004 – during his 25 years as Director of the Douglas Hyde Gallery, Trinity College, Dublin. Hutchinson presents Dawson as an artist who has 'taken the vernacular storytelling traditions that were part of the culture of the American South where he grew up and made them visual.' The emphasis is on aspects of the work that may not be evident to the casual viewer, to its subject matter rooted, as Hutchinson says, in multitudinous references to astronomy, myths, landscapes and the counterculture. He shows us these ostensibly folksy images, surprisingly tinged at times with a rococo grace, as products of considerable erudition, albeit often culled from unusual and academically discountenanced sources. Hutchinson locates Dawson in a line of American visionary painters such as Albert Pinkham Ryder (1847–1917), Arthur B. Davies (1862–1928) and Louis Eilshemius (1864–1941), eccentrics who went against the grain of the dominant culture. And yet, while sharing those artists' stubborn integrity, his work is slyer, more self-aware than theirs. As Hutchinson says, 'It is the tension between apparent innocence and their less obvious knowingness that so often brings [Dawson's] pictures to life.' He goes on to point out that this is just as true of his stylistic choices as of his subject matter. In laying out the sources of this tension, Hutchinson brings the reader closer to the life of Dawson's art.

Barry Schwabsky

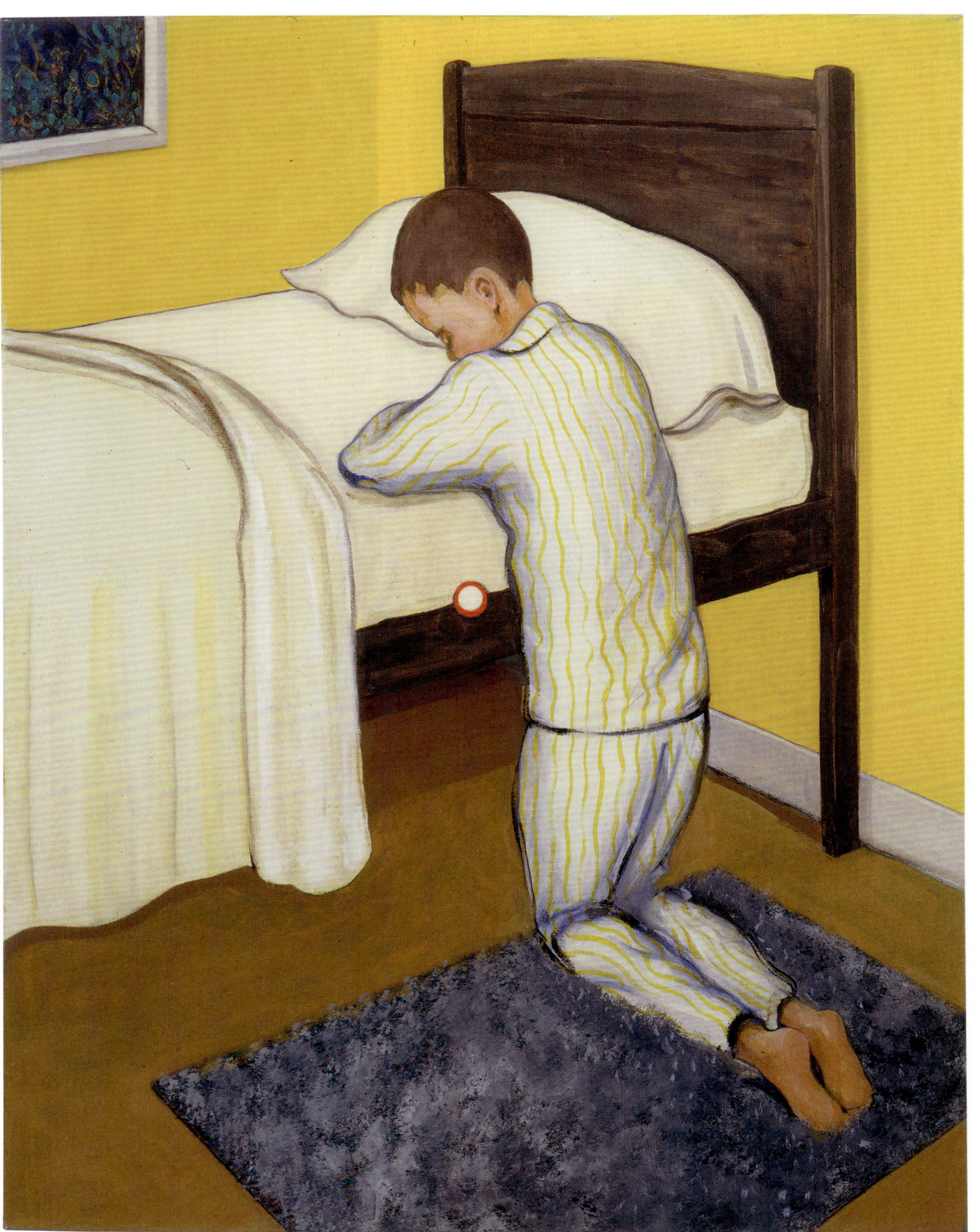

1 Stories of an Archaic Future

In a small early painting, *Praying Boy*, begun in 1990 and returned to a decade later (fig.2), Verne Dawson (b.1955) depicts a young boy in pyjamas kneeling beside his bed and saying his prayers. Plainly and simply painted, it would verge on the sentimental were it not for an important element: the tiny white circle, ringed with red, at the very heart of the picture. It is not at all clear what it means or why it is there, but it recalls the moment in *Time Bandits* (Terry Gilliam, 1981), a fantasy film greatly enjoyed by Dawson, in which Kevin, the young protagonist, finds to his surprise that his bedroom wardrobe contains a 'time hole', through which emerge a gang of dwarves with a map of the universe. His extraordinary adventure then begins to unfold.

The empty 'hole' in Dawson's picture evokes thoughts and speculations, some worldly and others metaphysical. This is not surprising, for Verne Dawson is a born storyteller and many of his paintings, such as *Little Red Riding Hood* and *Big Bear* (figs 3 and 4), have fairy tales and myths as their subjects. His images are preponderantly narratives, occasionally fragmentary but always allusive, drawing on fantasy, innocent belief and a subversive willingness to look at the world in an archaic way. Furthermore, underlying most of them is a search for meaning, transformation and, perhaps, transcendence.

There are elements of escapism and despair in Dawson's world view, but rarely cynicism. His style contains traces of self-consciousness, but he does not use distance or irony as ways of disguising unfashionable earnestness and idealism. He employs tropes and motifs from outsider and 'folk art' while not being part of those traditions, and he draws our attention to symbols and allegories that we may not fully understand, yet we sense that they are interesting and meaningful. It is significant, too, that the simplicity and utopianism of his work serve to position his images in a countercultural context; Dawson has taken the vernacular storytelling traditions that were part of the culture of the American South where he grew up and made them visual. From an artistic point of view this is unusual, because in the late 1970s and early 1980s, when he first began to study art, figuration and narrative painting were at odds with the dominant art movements of the time. This made little difference to him, for he was determined to find a way of telling stories in paint.

★

In 'Experience and Poverty',[2] written in 1933, philosopher and critical theorist Walter Benjamin (1892–1940) mourns the disappearance of storytelling. He begins with a

2. Praying Boy   *1990/2000*

Oil on canvas
Two parts, each 76.2 x 61 cm (each 30 x 24 in)
Private collection

"""

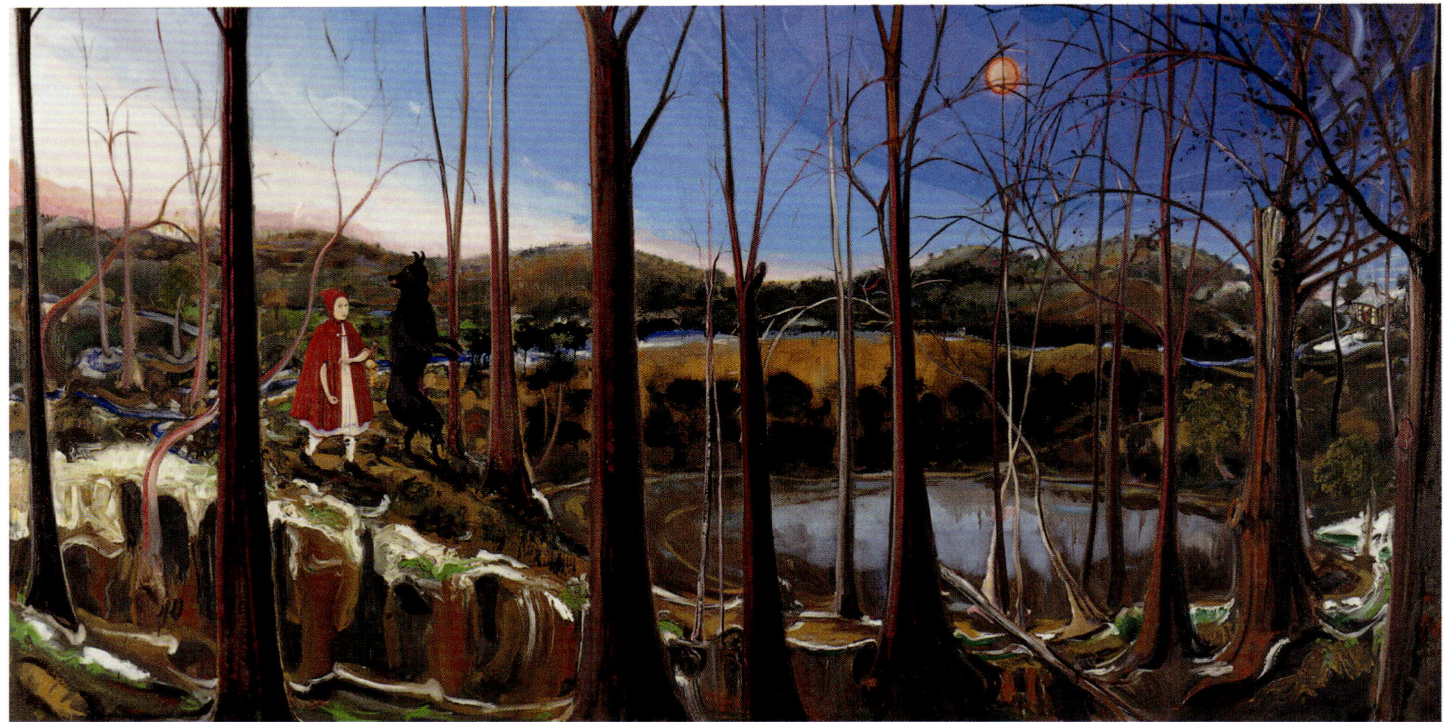

3. Little Red Riding Hood   2006

Oil on canvas
182.9 x 365.8 cm (72 x 144 in)
Ringier Collection, Switzerland

short tale about an old man on his deathbed who tricks his sons into believing that there is treasure buried in their vineyard. The sons dig it up but find nothing. In time, however, the vines bear magnificent fruit, and they come to realize that their father has passed on to them the valuable lesson that riches lie in hard work, not in gold. Benjamin then poses some questions. Where, he asks, has all this lived experience gone? And where are the people who really know how to tell a story? Experience, he suggests, is no longer considered to be of much value, and with the rapid development of technology a 'completely new poverty' has begun to afflict mankind, a poverty that is directly connected to the oppressive spread of ideas that are divorced from actual experience. People have 'devoured' everything, and this has exhausted them. Tiredness is followed by sleep, and only dreams may make up for the sadness and discouragement of the day.

Three years later, in 'The Storyteller',[3] Benjamin returns to the theme. He observes that the best tales are those that most closely reflect their oral source, and that the art of storytelling is dying out, partly because people no longer have the ability to exchange experiences in this way, and partly because the very communicability of lived experience is vanishing. Storytelling, according to Benjamin, always offers counsel and thus has no place in the modern world. Wisdom itself, which he defines as 'counsel woven in to the fabric of life' and also having its origins in storytelling, is coming to an end.

The rise of the novel, he explains, is one of the primary reasons for the decline of storytelling. While the origins of the traditional story lie in shared experience, the modern novel is founded on the isolation of the solitary self. Another reason, perhaps even more resonant and plausible in the 21st century, is the growing dominance of information, predominantly of the new media, which threatens storytelling even more. Storytelling, Benjamin says, has a validity that needs no external verification; information, on the other hand, must always be subject to authentication. The former is more subjective – aspects of the teller always cling to the story. The telling of stories, in consequence, is an artisan form of communication, with memory creating a chain of tradition that passes something on from one generation to another. The great storyteller is rooted in the vernacular and in the world of craftspeople.

Psychologist Bruno Bettelheim (1903–90), in his classic *The Uses of Enchantment*, first published in 1975,[4] developed further reasons why storytelling is important, especially to children. 'If we hope to live not just from moment to moment, but in true consciousness of our existence, then our greatest need and most difficult achievement is to find meaning in our lives. Our positive feelings give us the strength to develop our rationality; only hope for the future can sustain us in the adversities we unavoidably encounter,'[5] he writes. Children must be helped to make some sense and order out of the disarray of their feelings, and they are often enabled to do so through old fairy tales, which convey both overt and covert meanings, simultaneously speaking to all levels of the human personality and communicating in a way that can reach the undeveloped mind of the child as well as that of the sophisticated adult. They allude to the child's severe inner pressures and concerns in a manner that is unconsciously understood, and without diminishing or belittling his or her challenges. By the same token, explaining to a child why a fairy tale is engaging or captivating runs the risk of destroying the story's enchantment and losing the possibility of helping the child to work through problems and challenges independently.

There is no clear line that separates myths from folk or fairy tales: some of the latter evolved out of the former, while others became part of them. According to Bettelheim, they are all reflections of the accumulated experience of a particular culture or society, created because men and women wished to recall past wisdom for themselves and to transmit it to future generations. While many of these stories are simply entertainment, cautionary tales or fables, some are repositories of deep insights that have long sustained the inner life of humankind. There is one marked difference, however, between myths and fairy tales. A myth, like a fairy tale, may express inner conflicts in symbolic terms and suggest how they can be resolved, but the conflicts may not necessarily be its core concern. In myths, much more than in fairy stories, a hero is commonly presented as an inspirational figure, whose example should be followed in real life. Fairy tales, in contrast, are presented in simple, ordinary ways with no demands made on the listener or reader. In fairy tales, internal feelings and psychic processes, as represented by the protagonists and their experiences in the story, are articulated and rendered comprehensible. Thus, when unconscious thoughts and feelings are allowed to be absorbed into the awareness and worked through in the imagination, at least some of their power forces can be directed into positive purpose and meaning.

Bettelheim also refers to more prosaic interpretations of fairy tales, but he is not especially enthused by them. He observes, somewhat unexpectedly, that the delight and pleasure – the enchantment – we feel when we allow ourselves to respond to a fairy tale is derived less from its psychological meaning than from its literary or storytelling qualities. In other words, a tale's ability to enchant has a clear connection with its quality as a work of art. The effect of its enchantment, Bettelheim emphasizes, depends to a great extent on the child not quite knowing why he is delighted by it.

A fairy tale can help a child to understand the actual world through the visualization of an imaginary one, but the story's disregard for logic, like its non sequiturs and improbable reversals, may reveal hidden drives, desires and fears, and it also has much to say about everyday experience. Nor is Bettelheim especially convinced by Jungian explanations of fairy tales and human inner life in terms of perennial archetypes. He suggests that although structures of the imagination and common human experience may inspire narratives that have certain resemblances, comparisons between them are usually vague and unconvincing. Besides, while similar stories may spring up in distant places, they often have different moods and tones, divergent details and specific regional contexts. The wish to find universal significance in tales and legends has sometimes obscured their more obvious ability to illuminate experiences that are rooted in specific social and material conditions, and their meanings are also contingent on context. It is no accident, Bettelheim writes, that traditional tales and fairy stories have often been associated with arcane forms of knowledge, unconventional science and insoluble riddles, despite their superficial accommodation to the ideology of the children's nursery.

★

Throughout the 18th and 19th centuries, thousands of Scots–Irish migrated to America by ship, inspired by dreams of new and more prosperous lives. Most went to Pennsylvania, and from there they travelled on to Virginia, the Carolinas and across to the South, with many choosing to settle in the Appalachians, called the 'Unending Mountains' by the Cherokee, which were formed about 400 million years ago when Europe and North America were joined as a single continent.

As they often travelled with large families who would eventually need their own farms, the Scots–Irish tended to pass by the areas already settled by Germans and

4. Big Bear 2002

Oil on canvas
152.4 x 121.9 cm (60 x 48 in)
Collection of Chris Ofili

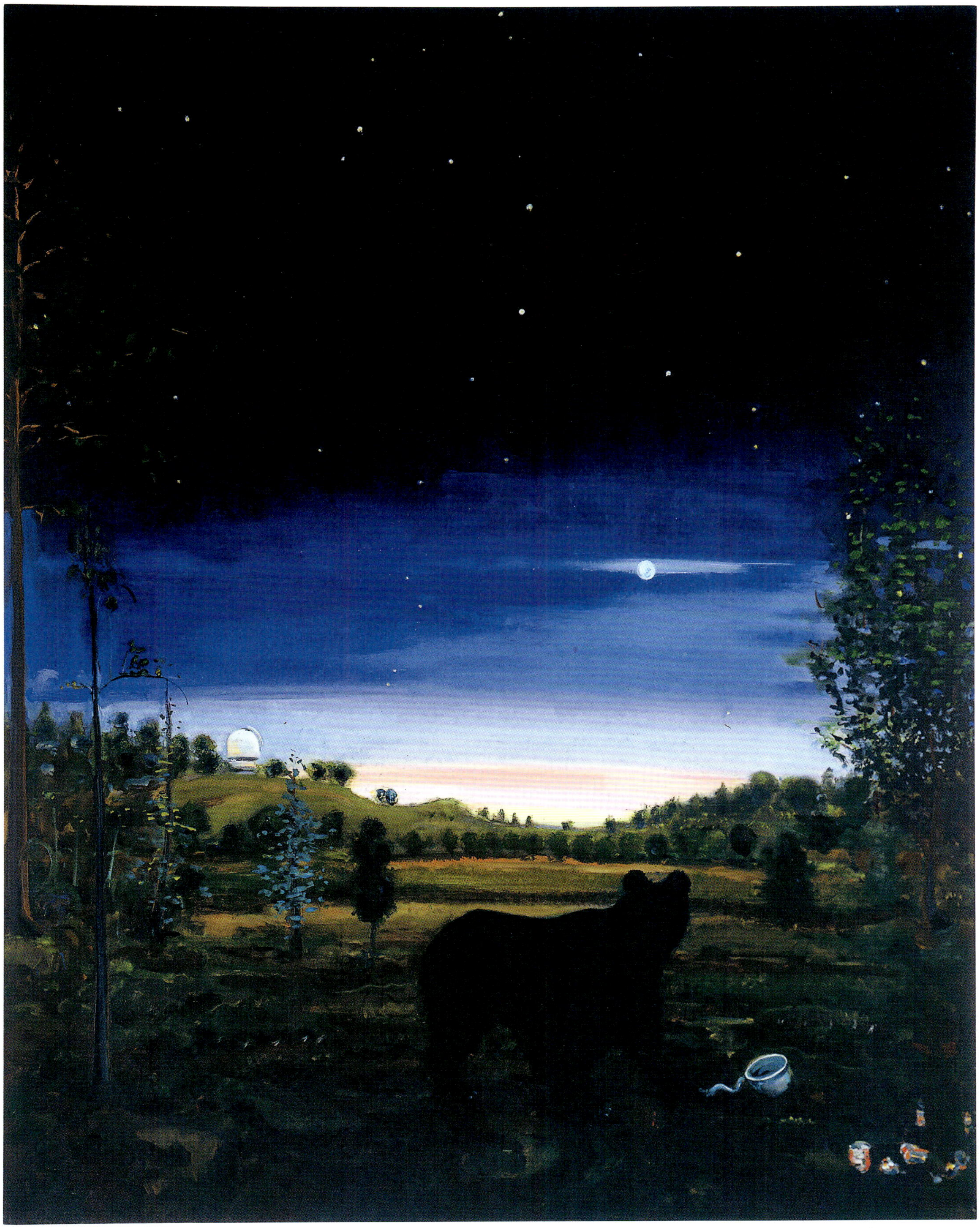

Quakers, moving into the more mountainous southern regions where land could be purchased fairly inexpensively. Life there, however, was tough and demanding, with deprivation and hardship, so the settlers, who often found themselves in conflict with Native American tribes, typically formed tight groups of related families who lived close to each other, worshipped and worked together, and intermarried. Suspicious of outsiders, some of their descendants came to be known as 'hillbillies', a derogatory term that probably has its origins in Scotland and Ireland, and which carried then, as it still does today, associations with poverty, backwardness and violence. An early 20th-century newspaper article, for instance, explained that 'a Hill-Billie is a free and untrammeled white citizen of Tennessee, who lives in the hills, has no means to speak of, dresses as he can, talks as he pleases, drinks whiskey when he gets it, and fires off his revolver as the fancy takes him.'[6]

The Scots–Irish migrants who followed the main route south along the Appalachians, through the Shenandoah Valley into Virginia and the Carolinas, were also hardy adventurers, with those who continued on to settle in the middle and upper Carolinas especially independent and self-reliant. They brought with them a strong sense of cultural identity, which was frequently expressed in music and storytelling. British song collector Cecil Sharp (1859–1924), a visitor to America many decades later, remarked on this. 'North Carolina is amazingly rich in folk songs', he wrote, and it was there that he came across 'some of the most beautiful music I have ever heard in my life'.[7] Having collected hundreds of folk songs in the region, he also noted that the local musical tradition suggested that the North of England and the Lowlands (rather than the Highlands) of Scotland were the areas from which the songs had originally migrated. The Appalachian tunes, he observed, have far more affinity with English folk tunes than with those of the Gaelic-speaking Highlander, while many stories and other tales of mountain folklore can also be traced back to their roots in lowland Scotland.

A Southerner by birth and upbringing, Verne Dawson now spends much of his time in North Carolina on an old farm where he paints and tends to his peach trees. He says that there is an abandoned opal mine nearby and that it is not uncommon to come across quartz crystals sparkling in his informal orchard.[8] The farm is not far from the small town of Saluda, itself some 25 miles south of Asheville, the home, as Dawson remarks, of many New Agers who are convinced that it will survive the forthcoming apocalypse. Saluda, once at the end of a railway line cut through a steep gorge, was then known as Pace's Gap or Pace's Ridge, but is now called after a Native American chief whose name translates as 'corn river'. Close to the Blue Ridge Mountains and known for its beautiful wooded hills and musical traditions – bluegrass and country music, played on guitars, fiddles and banjos (an instrument to which Dawson is devoted) – Saluda is not far from the celebrated Black Mountain College that became famous during the 1930s and 1940s for its distinguished faculty and students, which included Josef and Anni Albers (respectively, 1888–1976 and

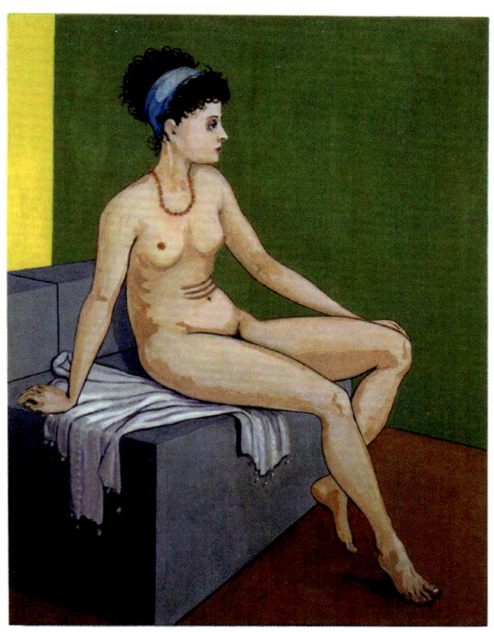

5. Virgin   1986–2001

Oil on canvas
76.2 x 61 cm (30 x 24 in)
Private collection

1899–1994), Walter Gropius (1883–1969), Robert Rauschenberg (1925–2008), Merce Cunningham (1919–2009) and John Cage (1912–92). Unusually for an art college, and with the intention of creating a balance between art, education and shared labour, students were expected to join in farm work, construction projects and kitchen duty.

The area and its culture have long been important to Dawson's life and work, and although he still resides in New York for part of the year, he feels especially at home there. He remarks:

> I now live much of the time in North Carolina, where the languid air, as well as the abundant wit and memory of its residents, are reason enough to live another day. There is a desire in the South, and patience, to hear a story to its end, and an equal effort to make it worth one's while. After all, it is hot, time is not money, and we move slowly to avoid perspiration. These are ideal conditions in which to nurture the long tale.[9]

His commitment to the area was recently reflected by a successful effort to help establish the humble birthplace of the singer Nina Simone (1933–2003), whose music he loves, as a national treasure.

Dawson has written an evocative record of his early life, and most of the following information has been taken from the picturesque 'A Recollection'.[10] He was born in October of 1955; it was the year, as he wryly points out, that Elvis first appeared on television, when Allen Ginsberg's poem 'Howl' was seized by US Customs, and when the first McDonald's fast-food restaurant opened. It was also when the Eisenhower administration began to prepare America for a nuclear attack, Congress ordered the phrase 'In God We Trust' to be added to all US paper currency, Disneyland opened in California and, in Alabama, the civil rights movement began to take shape.

Biddie Doris Clardy, Dawson's mother, grew up on a farm in rural Alabama near the Tennessee border, not far from Huntsville, which was the county seat and at that time a small farming town. It was soon to change. In 1950, the Office of Strategic Services (the then secret security agency of the US Army) began to recruit the best German scientists from the defeated Third Reich, and they were taken to Huntsville. Wernher von Braun (1912–77), the inventor of the V2 rocket, led the Army's rocket development research centre at Huntsville's Redstone Arsenal, where Dawson's father – also called Verne – was assigned. There, among other duties, he drove a jeep for von Braun. Biddie Clardy, then aged seventeen, worked part-time after school behind the lunch counter at Woolworth's, which is where the artist's parents met. In due course, Braun and his colleagues developed the Jupiter rocket, which launched the first American satellites into space. NASA came to be based in Huntsville, the eventual home of rockets of lunar and space exploration, including the manned Apollo flights to the moon. Less benevolently, however, rockets developed at Redstone Arsenal were used for the first nuclear ballistic missile tests in America. From a small

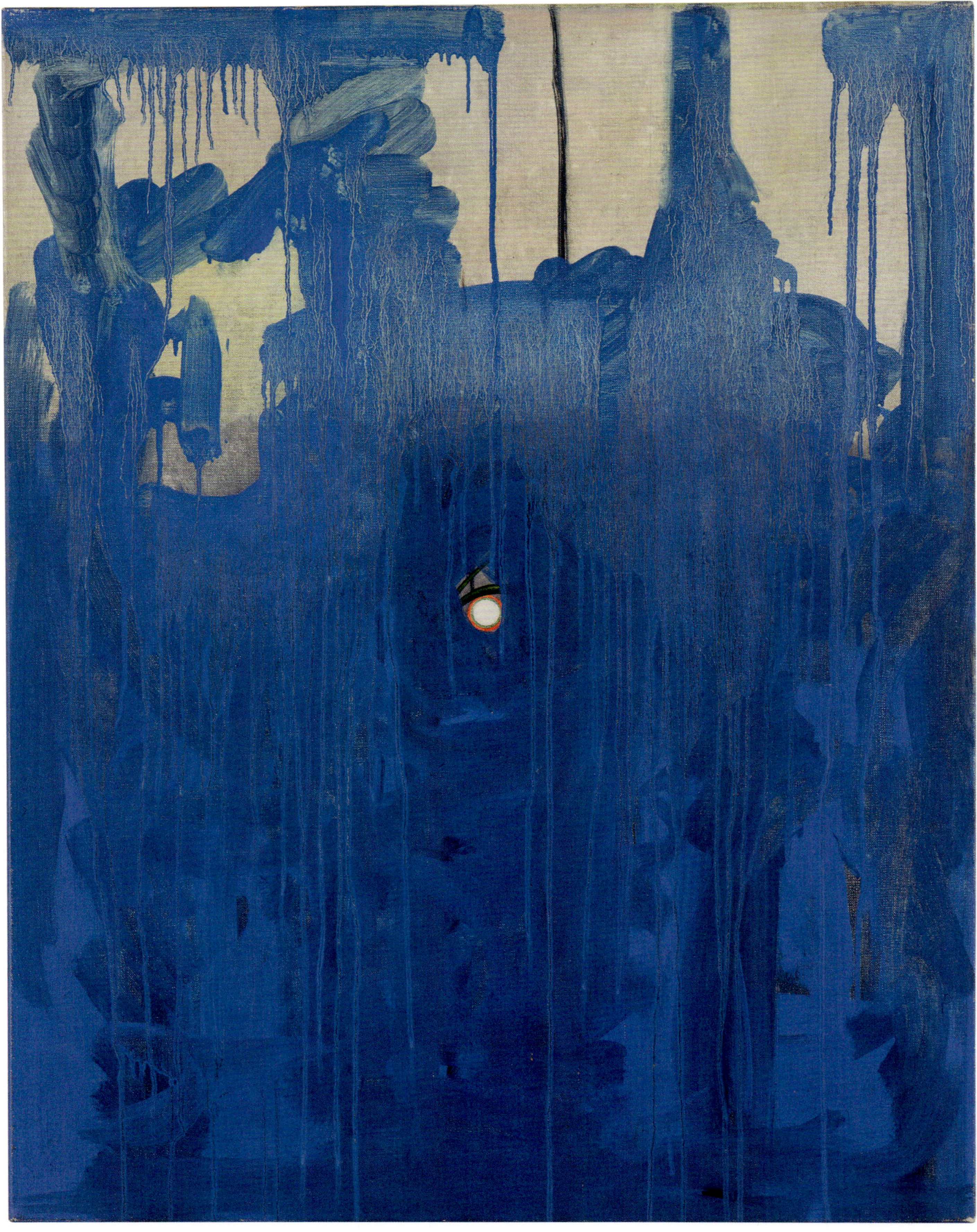

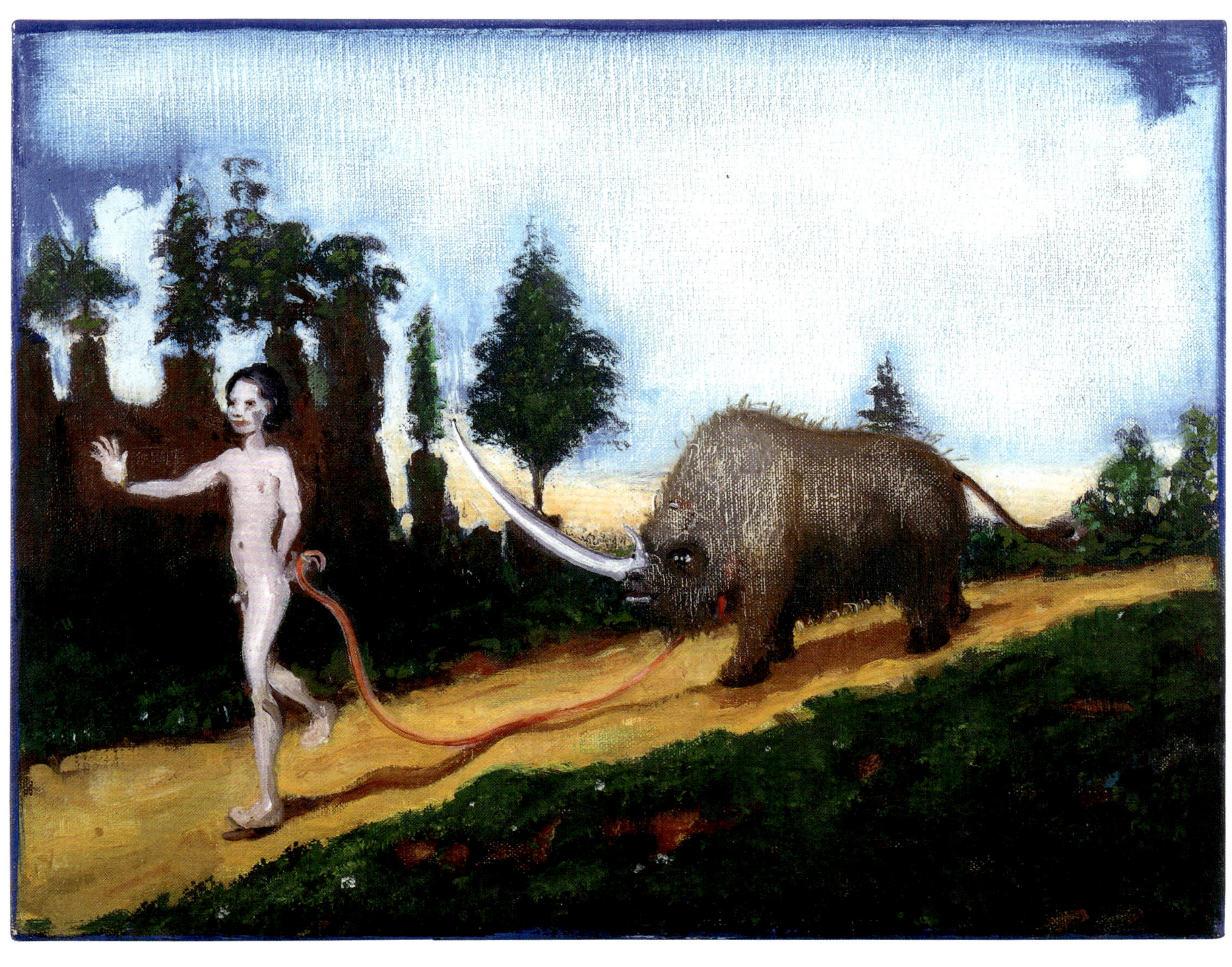

6. The Ivory-Billed Woodpecker   1985–91

Oil on canvas
76.2 x 61 cm (30 x 24 in)
Courtesy Gavin Brown's enterprise, New York/Rome

7. Boy and Wooly Rhinoceros   1999

Oil on canvas
30.5 x 40.6 cm (12 x 16 in)
Private collection

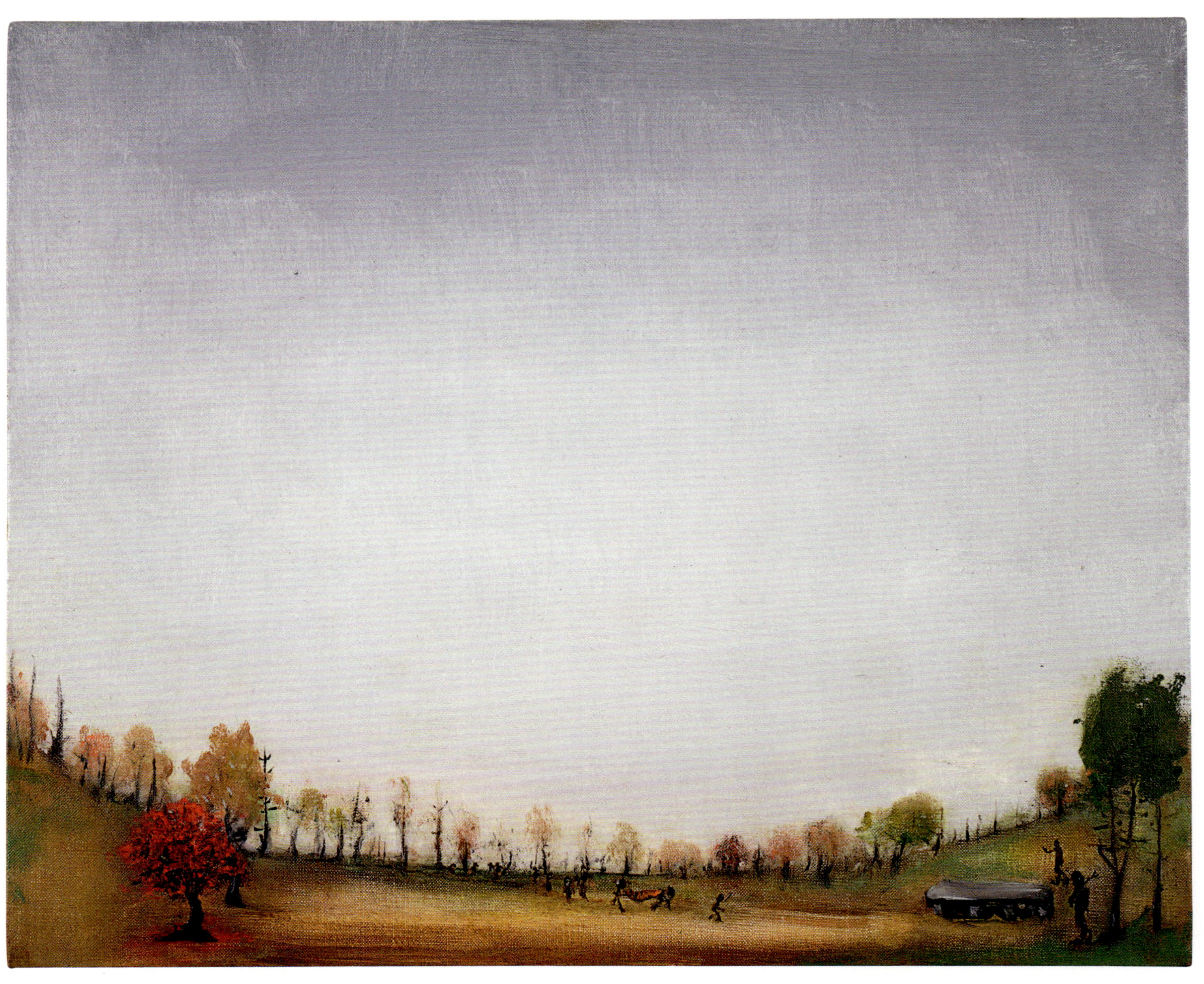

8. Study for Autumn   2001

Oil on canvas
40.6 x 50.8 cm (16 x 20 in)
Ringier Collection, Switzerland

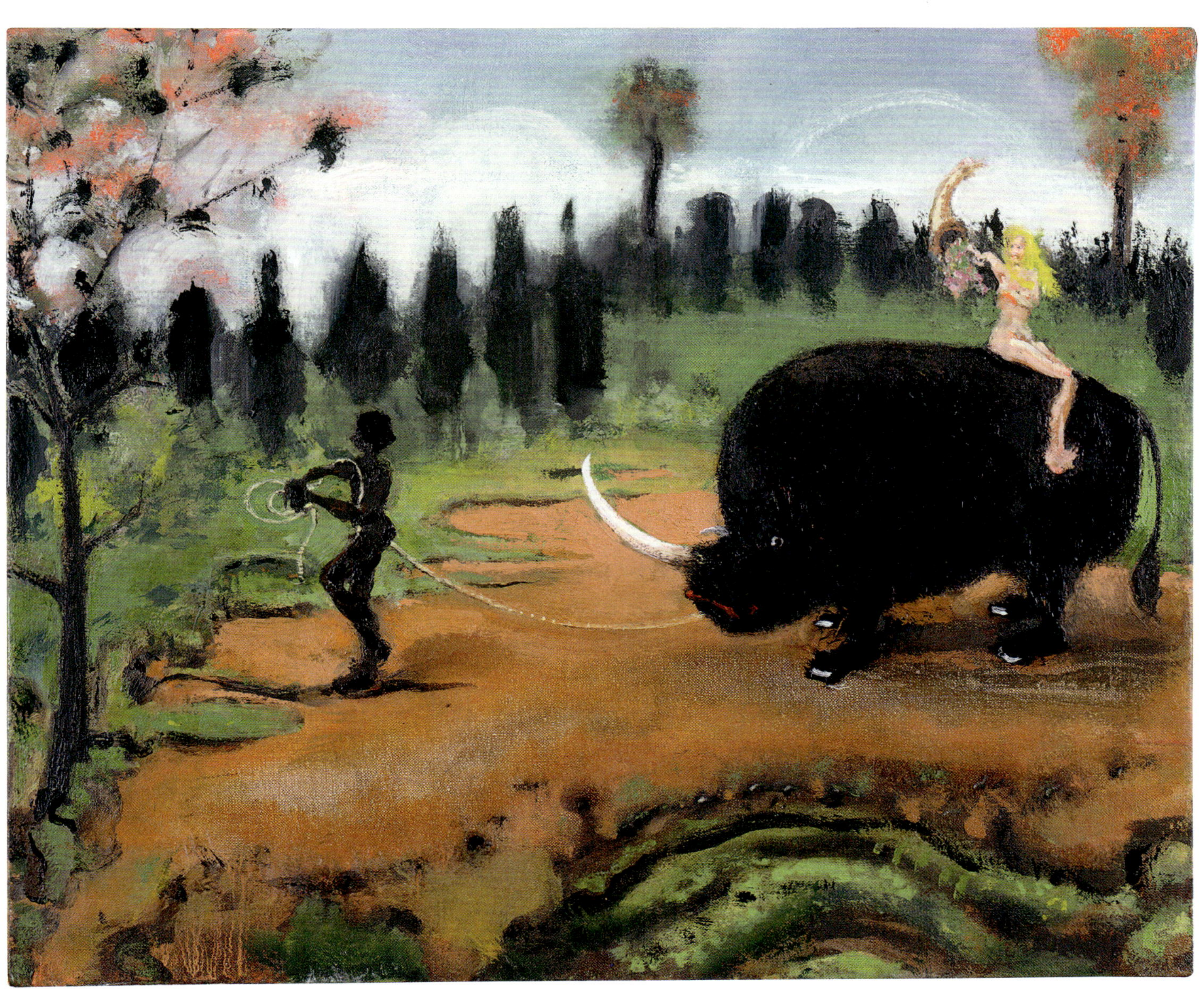

9. **Study for Spring**   2001

Oil on canvas
40.6 x 50.8 cm (16 x 20 in)
Ringier Collection, Switzerland

rural town, Huntsville grew rapidly as it became a research centre for advanced technology, eventually becoming known as 'Rocket City, USA'.

In Huntsville there are a large number of substantial underground caves. The Clardy family used to hold picnics and reunions at Big Spring Park, where it is possible to enter a grotto and drift along an underground river for 6 miles, later to emerge beneath a waterfall in the small park next to the Court House. Years later, it was perhaps not coincidental that Dawson, as a young artist on his first trip abroad, found his way to the Dordogne in southwest France, an area renowned for its caves and sites of prehistoric significance. Many of the caves were still open to the public at that time, so Dawson spent as much time as he could looking at the art in the spectacular underground caverns; even now he thinks of them as the source of deeply formative experiences.

Dawson tells of how, as a boy, he would lie in bed at night listening to the radio. He liked the pop and rock transmitted from stations in distant places like Memphis, Chicago and New Orleans, although later, in his early teens, he was more drawn to music made less far away, in Muscle Shoals, Alabama, by artists such as Otis Redding, Aretha Franklin and Duane Allman. Dawson's grandfather, Henry Nolan Clardy, listened to, played and loved country music. He spent much time with his grandson watching and listening to country stars such as Dolly Parton and Porter Wagoner, Lester Flatt and Earl Scruggs, Johnny Cash, Bill Monroe, Loretta Lynn, George Jones and Tammy Wynette. Somewhat wistfully, Dawson reflects that his grandfather was once a fine fiddle player and square-dance caller, but that in the early 1960s he exchanged his excellent instrument for a Cadillac. Nonetheless, through the examples set by his grandparents, the young Verne came to absorb the traditional values of farming and music. And then, through an acquaintance with a teenage boy who lived on a nearby farm, the possessor of a collection of shoeboxes filled with hundreds of ancient Cherokee artifacts that included tomahawks and arrowheads, bowls and grinding tools, he came to love relics from a lost world.

In contrast, however, Verne Dawson Sr. was determinedly modern and progressive. Working with aviators in the Army and later at an airport, where he had a job in the control tower, his father had an appreciation of technology and industrial design that was 'both infectious and influential'. Meanwhile, their surroundings and environment were beginning to change: 'We always seemed to live at the edge of the past and the present, with a vast woodland in one direction and cracker-box houses proliferating in subdivisions in the other. I remember I witnessed many old-growth forests leveled for instant communities of new homes.' At school, Dawson found himself absorbed in images in such magazines as *Life*, *Look*, *Time*, *Newsweek* and *National Geographic*, becoming entranced by photographs of Amazon tribes, animals on the verge of extinction, galaxies, planets, nebulas and supernovas, nuclear detonations, microscopic views of DNA and atomic structure, famines and film stars. 'What became alarmingly clear to me', he writes, 'was that modern man was actively, passively, intentionally and unintentionally eradicating extensive ancient cultures of man and of the natural world . . . One could only assume that adults couldn't see this or chose not to concern themselves.'

In 1968, at the age of 13, Dawson moved with his family to Alaska, where he was to experience something of the vastness of nature and the wilderness. He fished on the Gulf of Alaska with whales breaching around him, made overnight and inadvertently dangerous treks in the mountains and came to know a primeval world that was strikingly different from the primitive wilderness of the American South. At school with native Alaskans, he became aware of the devastating effects of cultural dislocation and how traditions of the past were being casually and carelessly discarded. Unsurprisingly, when he returned to Alabama several years later, the young Dawson found it impossible to fit in with the normal ways of high-school boys. He had little interest in what he found there – 'the dull classes, the football rallies, the adolescent evangelism' – but unexpected respite came in the form of a part-time job, after school and on Saturdays, at the local public library, an occupation that he later came to rely on for 25 years in New York.

Another formative influence came soon afterwards. As a teenager, concerned about the Vietnam War, Dawson was drawn to the pacifism of the Quakers, the Society of Friends. After corresponding with the Friends' headquarters in Philadelphia, he was put in touch with a Quaker who lived at Koinonia, a religious community in rural Georgia that had been co-founded by Clarence Jordan, a farmer and author of the 'Cotton Patch' translation of the New Testament. Koinonia was a large farm, run on Christian principles, 'a demonstration plot for the Kingdom of God' as it once called itself, that brought together local African Americans with young idealistic intellectuals and some older activists. As soon as he received his driving licence at the age of sixteen, Dawson made the three-hour drive from Alabama to the commune in Americus, Georgia. It was a very hot summer, and on the first morning he was set to work sorting pecan nuts in a shed. Later, when the afternoon heat was at its height, he was moved to the shady plot where worms were raised and then collected in pint containers for sale to fish and bait shops. It was a brief and enjoyable adventure, but Dawson was too young to leave school, and the residents of Koinonia had no wish to house a runaway, so after a few days he drove home again, bringing with him lasting impressions and memories of communal life.

There was little art in the Alabama town where he lived, but the young Verne spent hours poring over art books in the local library, and, by the age of fifteen, had already developed a strong wish to become an artist. An elderly neighbour was another influence: Dawson visited him occasionally to look at the paintings that the old man had inherited decades earlier from his father. Among the American Civil War memorabilia, Robert E. Lee letters and Stonewall Jackson's bed, there were a few pictures by lesser-known French Impressionists, but the most significant painting of all, at least in Dawson's eyes, was a moonlit waterfall scene by Albert

Pinkham Ryder. 'I read everything I could about Ryder, an outsider and real Yankee mystic,' Dawson elaborates. 'Somehow, if he became an artist, I thought, why couldn't I?'

★

An artistic career nevertheless seemed unlikely so, with scant resources and a young man's desire to see the world, Dawson decided to join the US Navy. Stationed in Norfolk, Virginia, he began occasionally to visit New York, travelling up on Friday afternoons on buses filled with sailors from Brooklyn, Manhattan and Queens who were making the eight-hour journey to see their families in the city. From the Port Authority Bus Terminal he would walk to the United Service Organizations Center at Times Square, where he was given vouchers for a hotel and some theatre tickets. His favourite destinations, however, were the museums – the Metropolitan Museum of Art, the Museum of Modern Art, the Guggenheim, the Frick Collection and the Whitney Museum of American Art – and it was during those visits that he discovered more about art schools and how to study art.

An unexpected turn of events led him forward. Less than a year after he had enrolled, Dawson was discharged for sleepwalking; as he now puts it, this was 'a happy occurrence for both parties'. Dawson returned to Alabama and then went to the Gulf Coast, where he lived for a while on a small sailing boat moored in the old bay of Panama City, Florida. Then, in 1976, with no resources other than a modest monthly stipend consequent on his time in the Navy and a little help from his family, Dawson went to live in New York to study at the Art Students League. Another door quickly opened too: the week he arrived in the city, he applied to the New York Public Library and was hired to work in its Oriental Division, where the linguist, polymath and department's director, E. Christian Filstrup (who remains a good friend), led the young artist to a deepening investigation of comparative religion and shamanism, subjects in which he had already shown some interest.

Dawson enjoyed his time at the Art Students League, an institution he had read about in Alabama while leafing through the advertisements in *Art News*. It was informal, democratic and had no entrance requirements. He explains:

> You could just show up, decide what class you wanted to take, pay a reasonable fee and start straight away. You knew you were in good company too: Jackson Pollock had studied there, and so had Georgia O'Keeffe. It was based on a French pedagogical model, with fantastic studios and with the teaching oriented towards figure drawing. My time there was a wonderful experience.

But not everything went well. He left the League and returned to the South when the building he lived in caught fire and he was forced to abandon his apartment.

Later that year he applied to the Cooper Union School of Art in New York, was accepted and, like all students at the School, was awarded a full scholarship. At Cooper Union, first-year students do not choose an academic major in fine arts, but are instead allowed and encouraged to select courses from any of the School's various departments – from engineering to the history of art – an approach that helps to stimulate their particular interests and abilities. The curriculum also emphasizes creative and imaginative development, as opposed to technical proficiency in specific media, in order to develop the social awareness and critical skills that are considered relevant to art in the contemporary world. To some, and perhaps especially to painters, this approach might not be especially well suited, but there were at least a few unexpected benefits for young artists like Dawson. Under the influence of a course called 'Art and Math', taught by a professor of sculpture, Arthur Corwin (1929–2017), Dawson developed a fervent and lasting interest in the relationships between astronomy, folklore and religion. Corwin encouraged his students to examine the ways in which certain numbers, first apparent in religions and folklore, and later manifested in holidays, superstitions and even advertisements, can be seen to be remnants of archaic science and astronomy. Much of Dawson's work, including his series on days of the week and circuses (figs 26–31 and 34–38), has explored subjects that were introduced to him by Arthur Corwin. Another influence, less obvious but equally long-lasting, was that of the experimental film-maker, painter and sculptor Robert Breer (1926–2011), whose anarchic sensibility and willingness to combine incongruous styles and subjects helped to inspire both Dawson's way of thinking about his art and the concepts behind his methods of presentation.

Despite being briefly convinced that he should become a conceptual artist, more traditional art remained his core interest – Dawson had been drawing and painting since childhood, even while in the Navy and living on the sailing boat. At Cooper Union, after a year of Hans Haacke's sculpture class, where students brought in a stream of conceptual art projects every week, Dawson became even more convinced that the preservation of the past, specifically painting, was the challenge with which he wanted to engage. 'It is often said that painting has too much "baggage" for a contemporary artist, a burden of history too heavy to bear', Dawson has written. 'I understand that, particularly if one's aim is to express temporal states. For me, however, painting offered the much-desired possibility to escape time.'[11] In his view, the qualities that make a great painting are the same now as at any time in the past. Fundamental values remain unchanged, and all of them are 'based on that elusive ability to manifest and integrate subject matter, gesture and materials'.

After graduation in 1980, Dawson travelled with a friend to the Dordogne Valley in France, where (as mentioned above) he studied the prehistoric art in the many caves for which the area is renowned. Dawson remembers:

We stayed with this old lady who would drive us to different caves everyday.
She'd drop us off and sit in the car and read the newspaper. We'd go into these

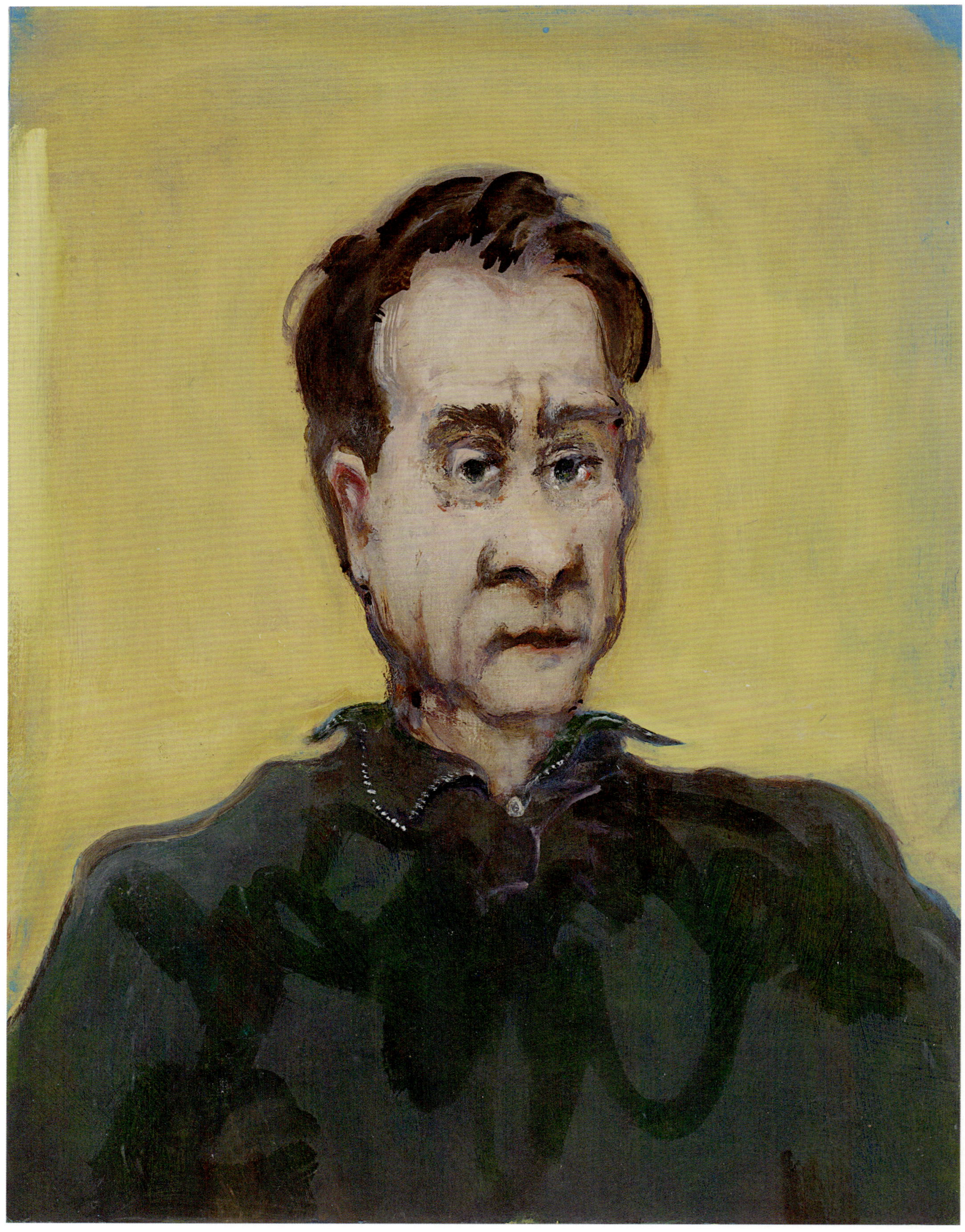

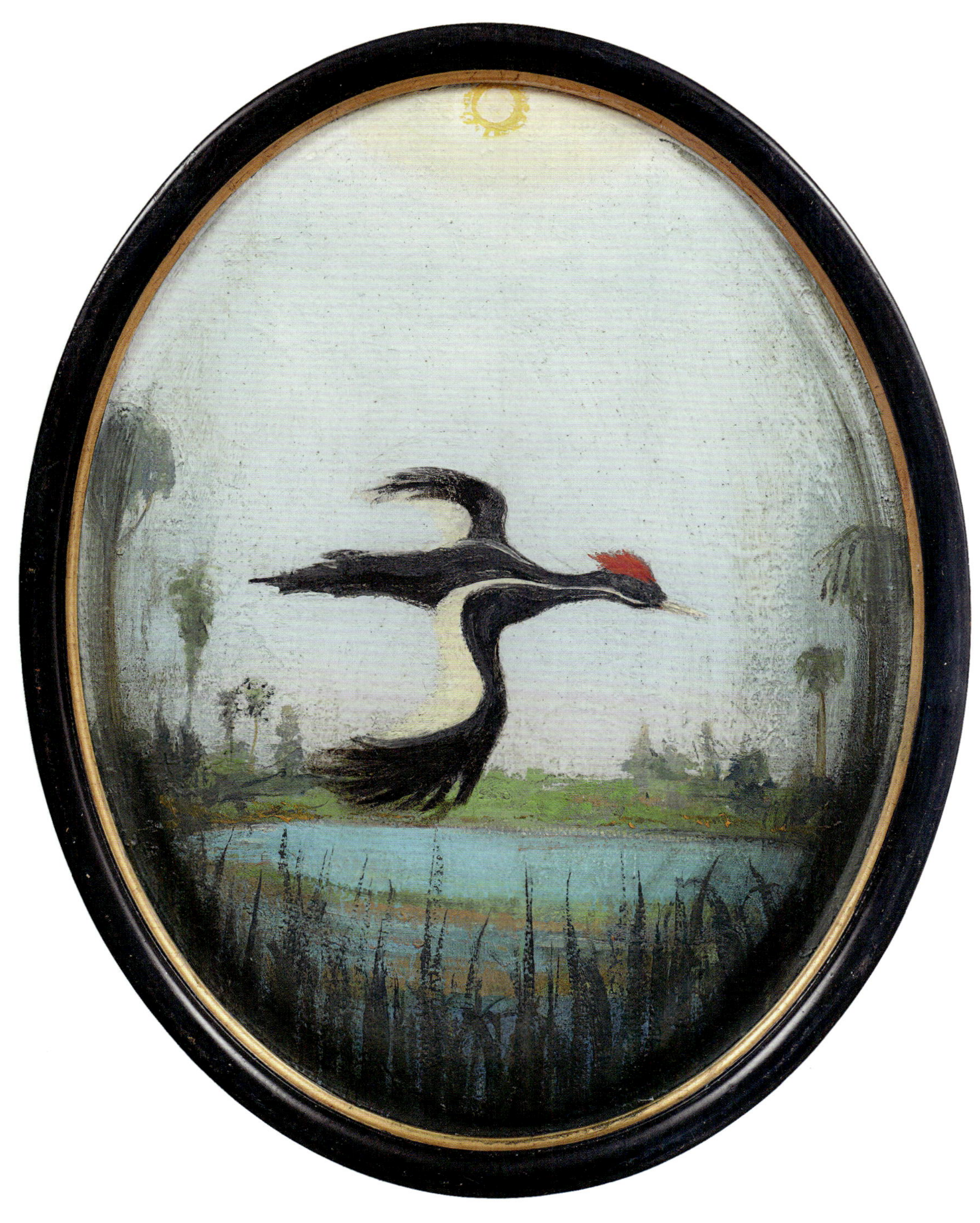

10. Self-Portrait, 2001

Oil on canvas
50.8 x 40.6 cm (20 x 16 in)
Courtesy Victoria Miro, London/Venice

11. Ivory-Billed Woodpecker   1992–2000

Oil on canvas
50.8 x 40.6 cm (20 x 16 in)
Collection of the artist

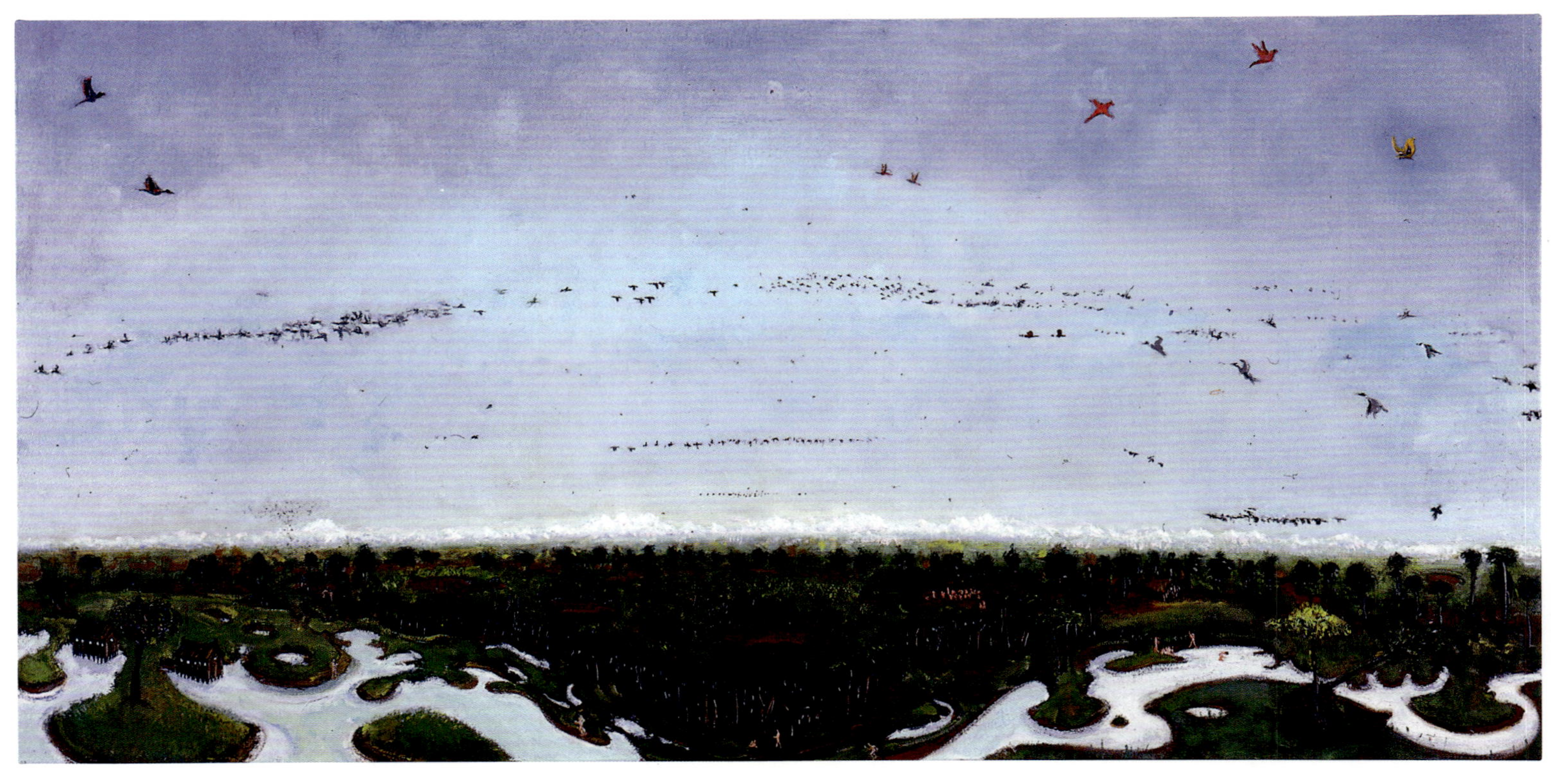

12. Pianura Padana   2000

Oil on canvas
86.4 x 177.8 cm (34 x 70 in)
Private collection

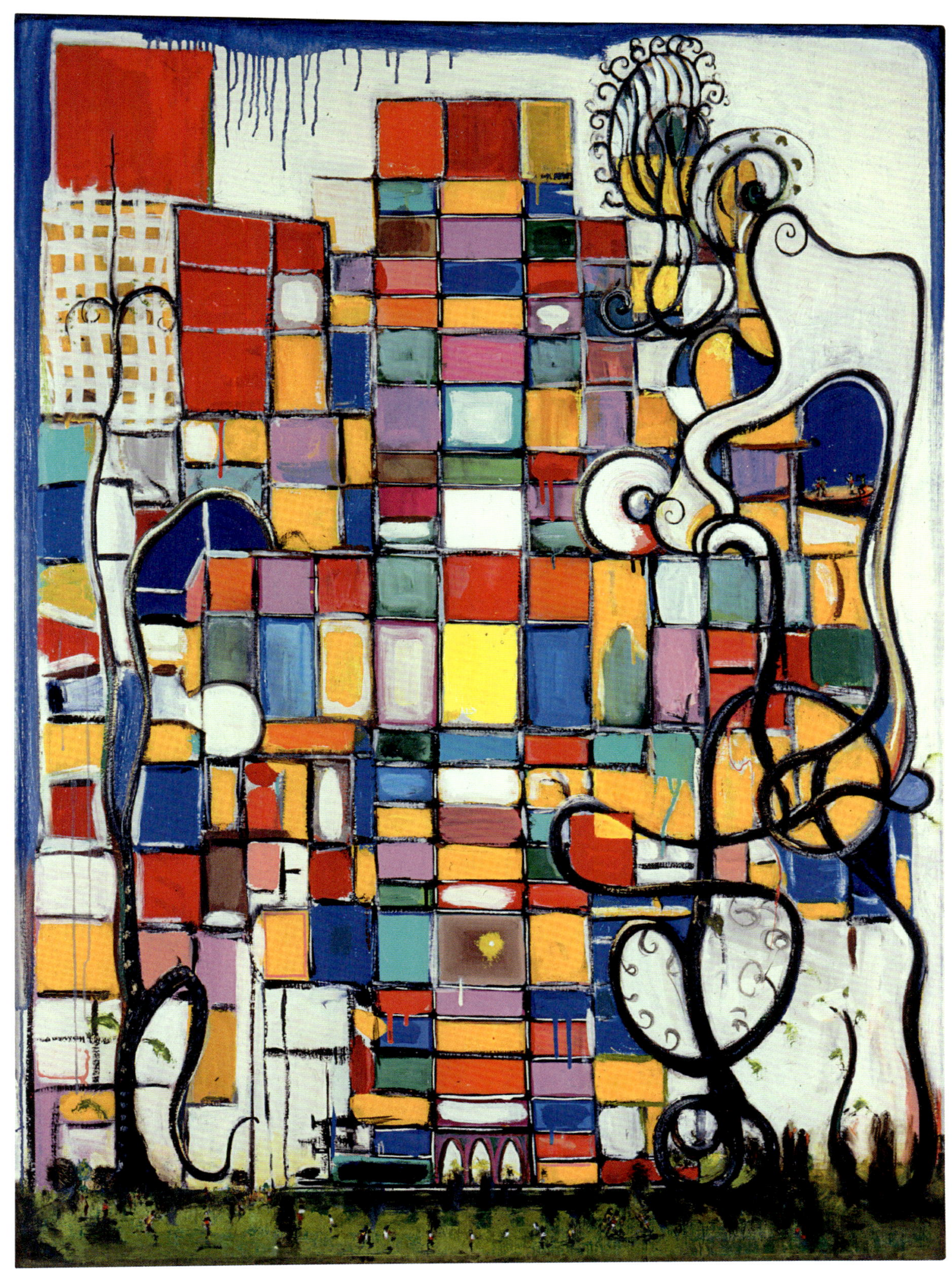

13. High Rise   1994/2003

Oil on canvas
121.9 x 91.4 cm (48 x 36 in)
Hauser & Wirth Collection, Switzerland

caves, most of which are closed now, to see these magnificent etchings, drawings
and paintings. We think of the people who made these as brutes, but when
you see those things, the great skill and the knowledge of anatomy, it becomes
obvious that these were very sophisticated minds at work.[12]

These visits had a profound effect on him, to the extent that he once mused that his
ideal studio might be a Dordogne cave, and they confirmed his intention to practise
'the near-obsolete craft of painting', his tools being 'wooden sticks with animal hair at
the ends', as one writer has ironically put it.[13]

In 1983, Dawson found himself back in New York, without either money or
home. For a few months he lived with friends and took a part-time job in a small
psychoanalytic library in Greenwich Village. Art, however, was still his main interest.
Spurred on by the notion that artists should practise their craft or trade in the context
of a larger community, he went into business as a portrait painter. He discovered a
vacant small shop near Sixth Avenue and 20th Street, and, while it was only a single
room, he was able – with some subterfuge and discretion – to live there too. He made
a sign to hang outside, a painting of a palette and brushes, embellished with the words
'PORTRAIT STUDIO'. Not unexpectedly, business was slow during the three years
he was there, amounting only to a handful of enquiries and two commissions, but
because he had a space that could act as a gallery he also organized some group shows
of work by friends. Flyers were circulated for the exhibitions, and on one occasion
an advertisement was placed in the *East Village Eye* magazine, but there were very
few visitors.

Nevertheless, as a young student and artist in New York Dawson was not without
influential contacts. He was introduced to fellow Southerner Jasper Johns (b.1930), a
painter he still greatly admires, who went to his early shows, wrote him encouraging
notes and asked to visit Dawson's studio. He met Andy Warhol (1928–87) on several
occasions, and, as already noted, one of Dawson's teachers at Cooper Union had
been Robert Breer, whose support and inspiring stories about living in Paris in the
1950s and 1960s were enough to ensure that they remained close until his death. 'He
brought in such wonderful artists to our class,' Dawson remarked. 'Claes Oldenburg,
his old friend; Laurie Anderson, a sweet young woman with a violin at the time;
Vito Acconci, a most dynamic speaker and charismatic person; Stan Brakhage,
Daniel Buren, Elizabeth Murray, Robert Ryman.' Dawson, asked recently about
other connections in the art world, replied, with a touch of humour, that he had met
Vladimir Horowitz and Robert Rauschenberg, danced with Liza Minnelli at Studio
54, taken a drawing class with Jim Dine, helped Jacqueline Kennedy Onassis on
several occasions when he worked in the New York Public Library and seen Samuel
Beckett walk past on Rue Saint-Jacques in Paris.

Throughout this period Dawson continued to work on his own paintings, most
of them now lost, in a variety of modes and styles – he was still finding his way. The

first significant step in his professional career was perhaps his participation in a 1988 group show at White Columns, a well-known alternative space in New York. This led to a solo show the following year at the Althea Viafora Gallery in SoHo. According to the artist, his exhibition was well received and one large painting sold, although it was returned a month later when the buyer recognized some hidden erotic imagery in it. Much to his chagrin, Dawson had to refund the buyer's money and left the gallery shortly afterwards. He was not to have another solo exhibition until 1994 at the newly minted gallery Gavin Brown's enterprise.

In the same year as he had his first exhibition at a commercial gallery, he met Laura Hoptman, an art history graduate student and an aspiring curator of contemporary art. In 1993, Hoptman included Dawson's work in a small exhibition; they have been together ever since. Both partners had different sets of friends, several of whom were to become celebrated artists. Dawson was close to the painter Elizabeth Peyton (b.1965) and to Rirkrit Tiravanija (b.1961), who became widely known for his 'relational' art practice. Hoptman was particularly friendly with artists Gabriel Orozco and Maurizio Cattelan. This group – Peyton, Tiravanija, Orozco and Cattelan – became Dawson and Hoptman's circle in New York. There were others, of course, including Dawson's close friend, the painter Bill Lynch (1960–2013), but he was not part of the core group. More recent companions include the Swiss artist Ugo Rondinone (b.1964) and the poet and performance artist John Giorno (b.1936). It was Peyton and Tiravanija, then married, who introduced Dawson to the young British gallerist Gavin Brown, and, in 1994, Brown asked Dawson to show some works at the Gramercy Park Hotel, at what was the first Armory Show art fair. Brown opened a gallery shortly thereafter, and his core group of artists included Tiravanija, Peyton and Dawson, as well as the painters Peter Doig (b.1959) and Chris Ofili (b.1968).

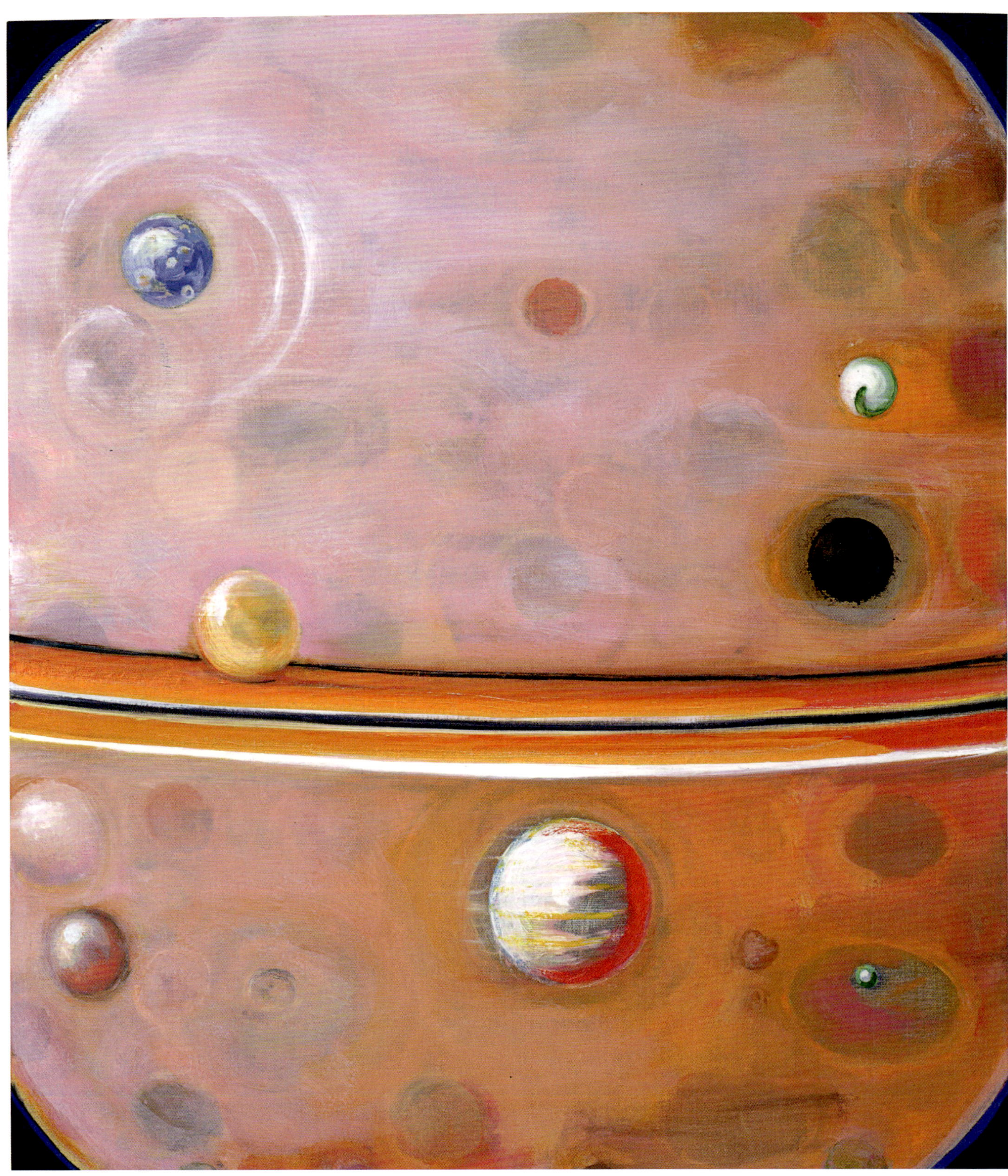

2 Astronomy, Myths, Landscapes and the Counterculture

The Zodiac: Cosmic Sounds was an oddity in the Elektra Records catalogue when it was released in 1967. The label, then independent and cultish, was known mainly for its folk albums and, increasingly, for its startling recordings by new bands and musicians such as Love, Tim Buckley and The Doors. *The Zodiac: Cosmic Sounds* was different. Appearing at a time when both psychedelia and astrology were becoming fashionable in the counterculture, it was a peculiar concept album, subtitled 'Celestial Counterpoint with Words and Music', and it combined psychedelic rock with narration and experimental electronic instrumentation. The record was intended, according to the purple instructions on the extravagantly ornate sleeve, to be played in the dark. There were twelve tracks, one for each astrological sign, and despite its supposedly archaic roots the album was futuristic in tone, its rather banal rock background enhanced by harpsichord, organ, exotic instruments such as a sitar and an early Moog synthesizer. All this served as background to dramatic recitations on the nature of each astrological sign, read in a theatrical deep voice that lacked either humour or irony. The 'songs' were unexpectedly evocative, but only if listened to when stoned or in the right frame of mind.

Although probably of more lasting cultural importance than *The Zodiac: Cosmic Sounds*, and certainly more self-aware, Verne Dawson's paintings of such things as astronomical calendars and the days of the week, all of them informed by his love of prehistory, the study of ancient astronomy called 'archaeoastronomy' and mythical stories, have something in common with that curious and contradictory record, which was at once unique, unconventional and characteristic of its time. Similarly, there are not many contemporary artists who would want or be able to explain, as Dawson once did in a conversation with the anarchic performer Genesis P-Orridge,[14] that the 78 cards of Tarot can be used as an accurate calendar that only needs adjustment every 2,200 years, and that a normal pack of 52 cards is also a calendar: one for each week, in four suits, one for each season. Each suit, he went on to reveal, has 13 cards that represent the year's 13 full moons, one for each month, or more appropriately 'moonth', of a lunar year, and the two jokers do what jokers and tricksters always do – they provide the irrational, occupying the leap days that balance a calendar. Dawson has painted a variety of pictures that incorporate these ideas, many of them tondos that feature cards, planets, figures and landscapes, and reminiscent in canvas shape of the target paintings by Jasper Johns. A key work of the kind is *Celestial Atlas (after 17th-Century Illustrated*

14. *Saturday* 2004

Oil on canvas
76.2 x 66 cm (30 x 26 in)
Lindemann Collection, Miami Beach

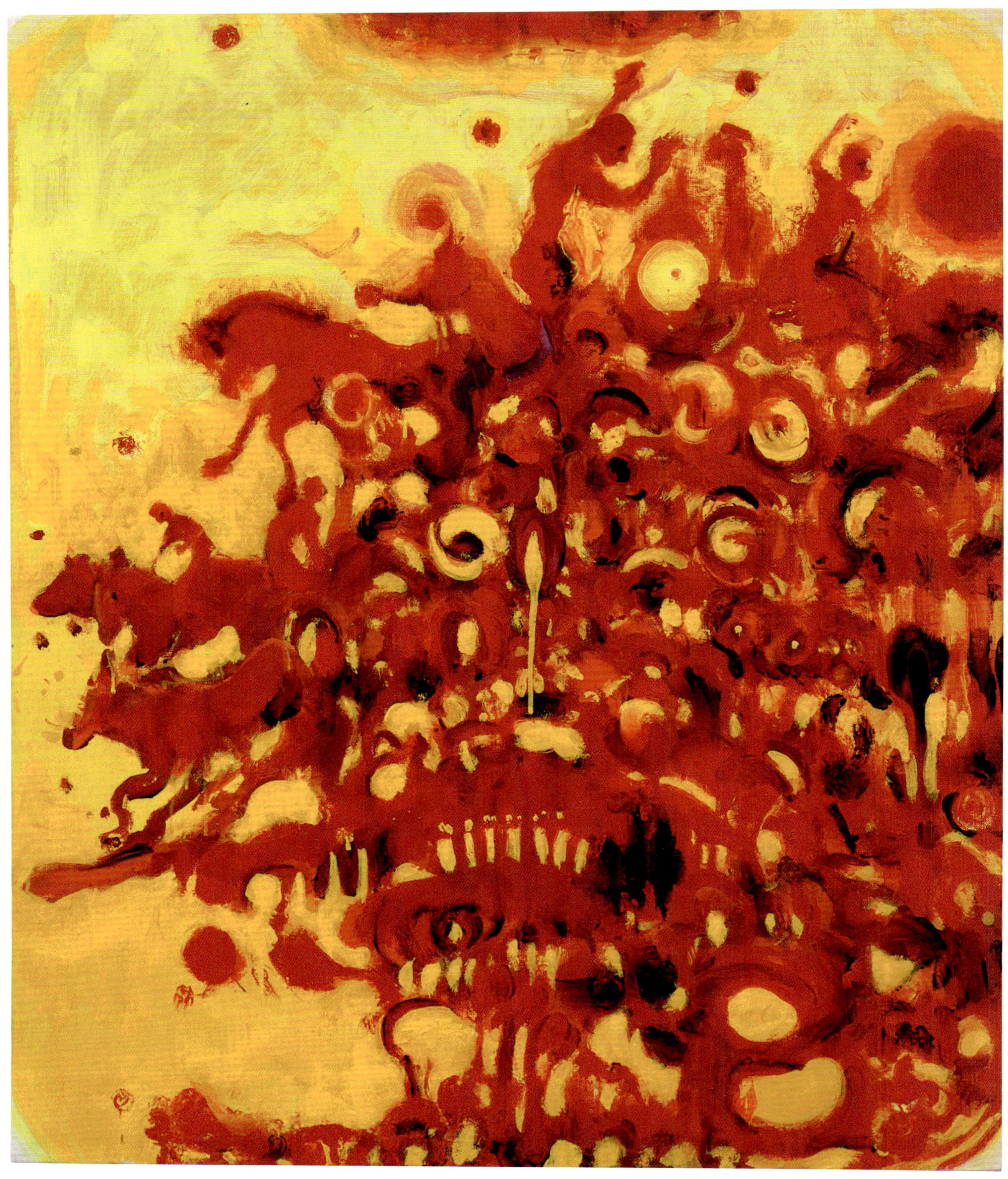

15. Sunday   2004

Oil on canvas
76.2 x 66 cm (30 x 26 in)
Lindemann Collection, Miami Beach

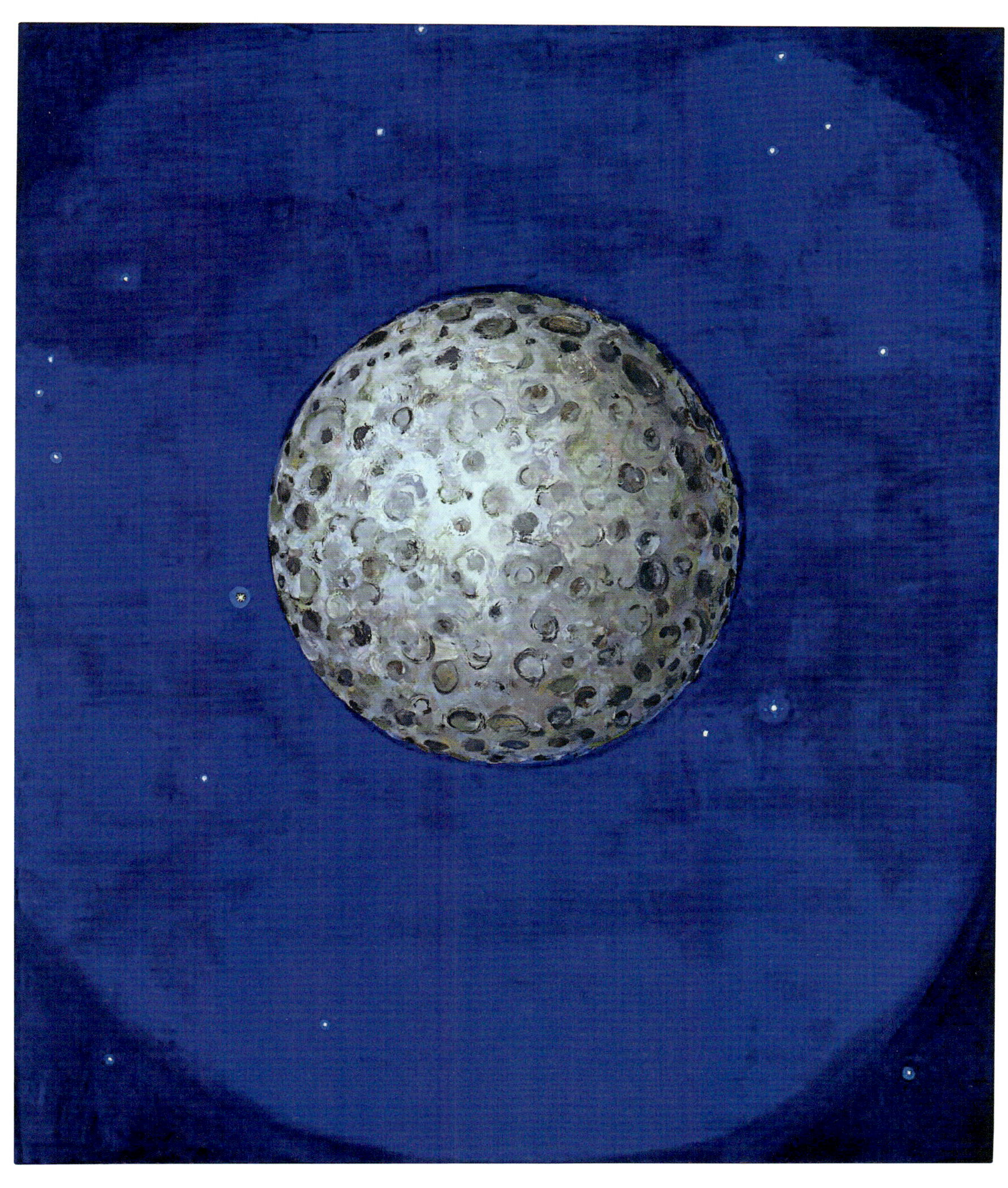

16. Wednesday   2004

Oil on canvas
76.2 x 66 cm (30 x 26 in)
Lindemann Collection, Miami Beach

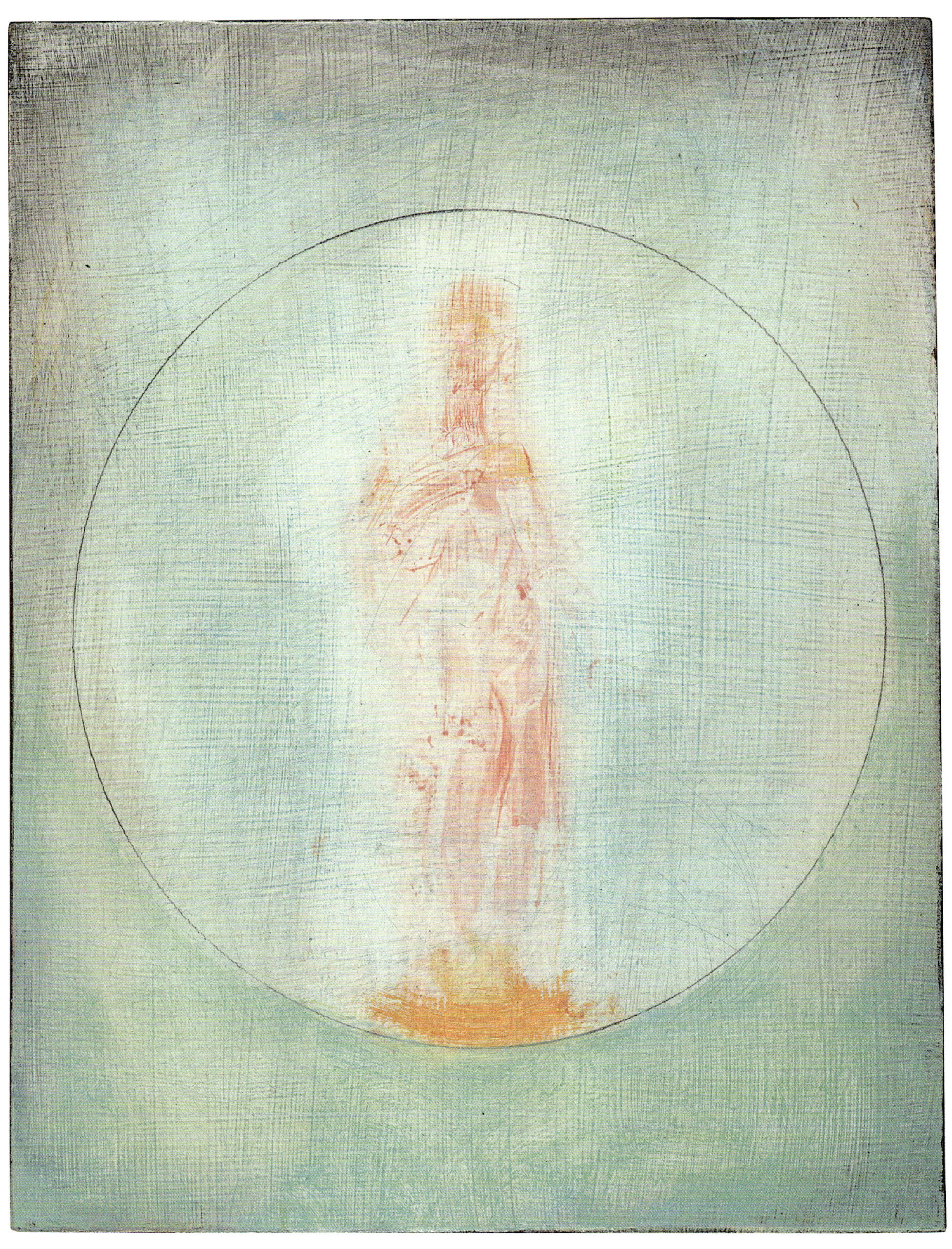

17. Sunday, Monday, Tuesday, Wednesday, Thursday, Friday, Saturday   2004

Oil on board
One of seven parts, each 25.4 x 20.3 cm (each 10 x 8 in)
Private collection

34

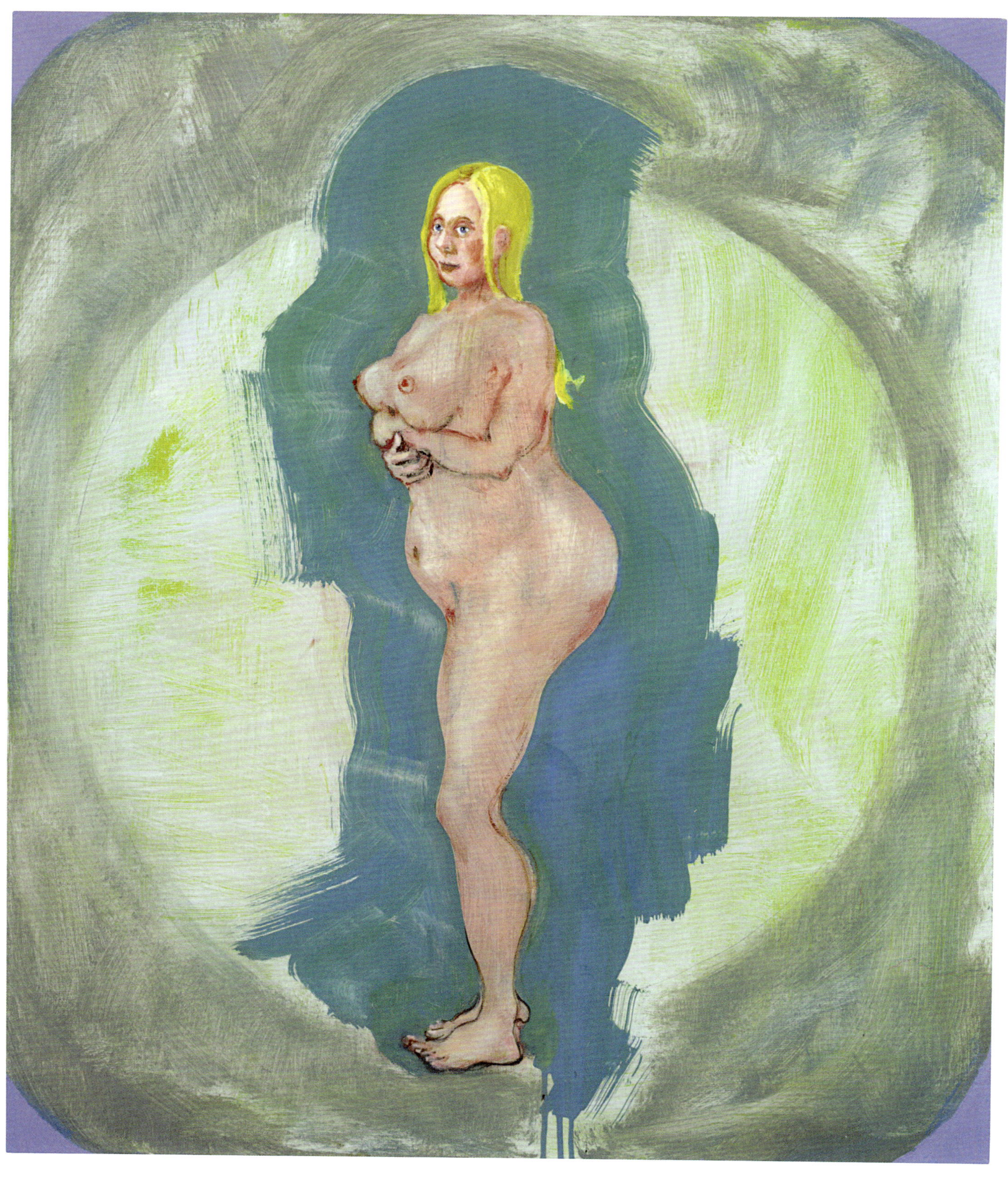

18. Friday   2004

Oil on canvas
76.2 x 66 cm (30 x 26 in)
Lindemann Collection, Miami Beach

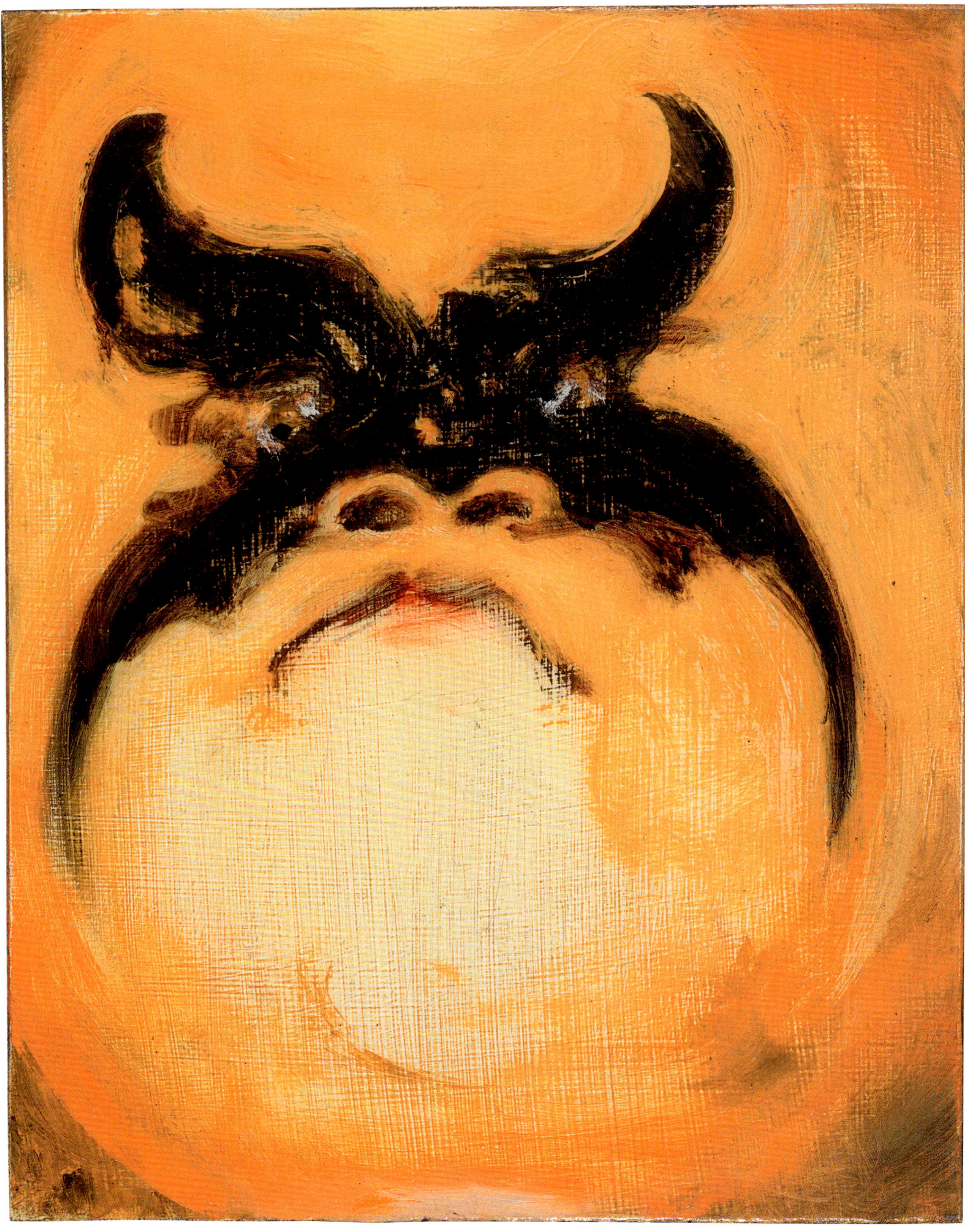

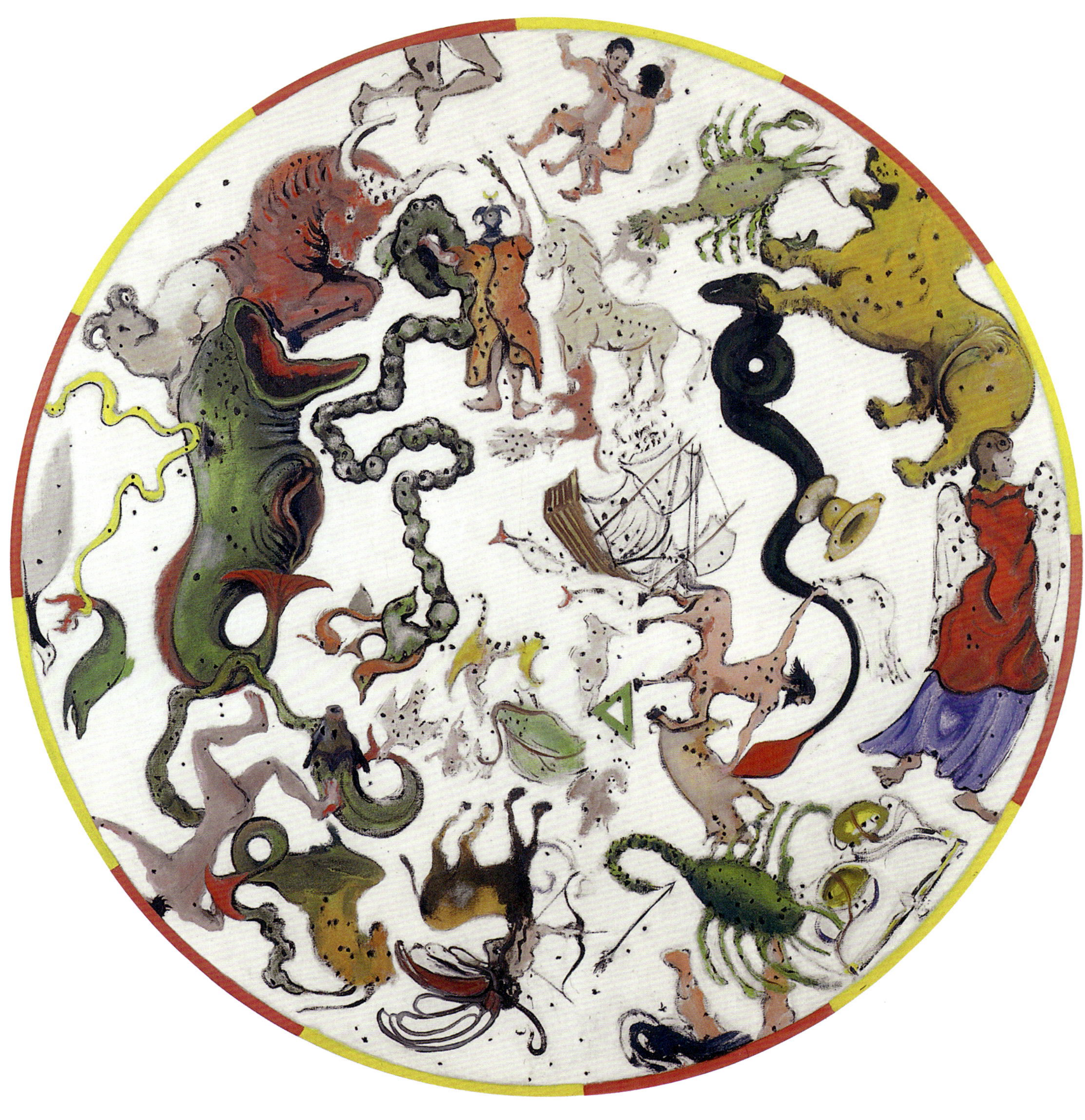

19. Sunday, Monday, Tuesday, Wednesday,
Thursday, Friday, Saturday   2004

Oil on board
One of seven parts, each 25.4 x 20.3 cm (each 10 x 8 in)
Private collection

20. Celestial Atlas (After 17th-Century
Illustrated Atlas)   2001

Oil on canvas
106.7 cm (42 in) diameter
Mima and César Reyes Collection, Puerto Rico

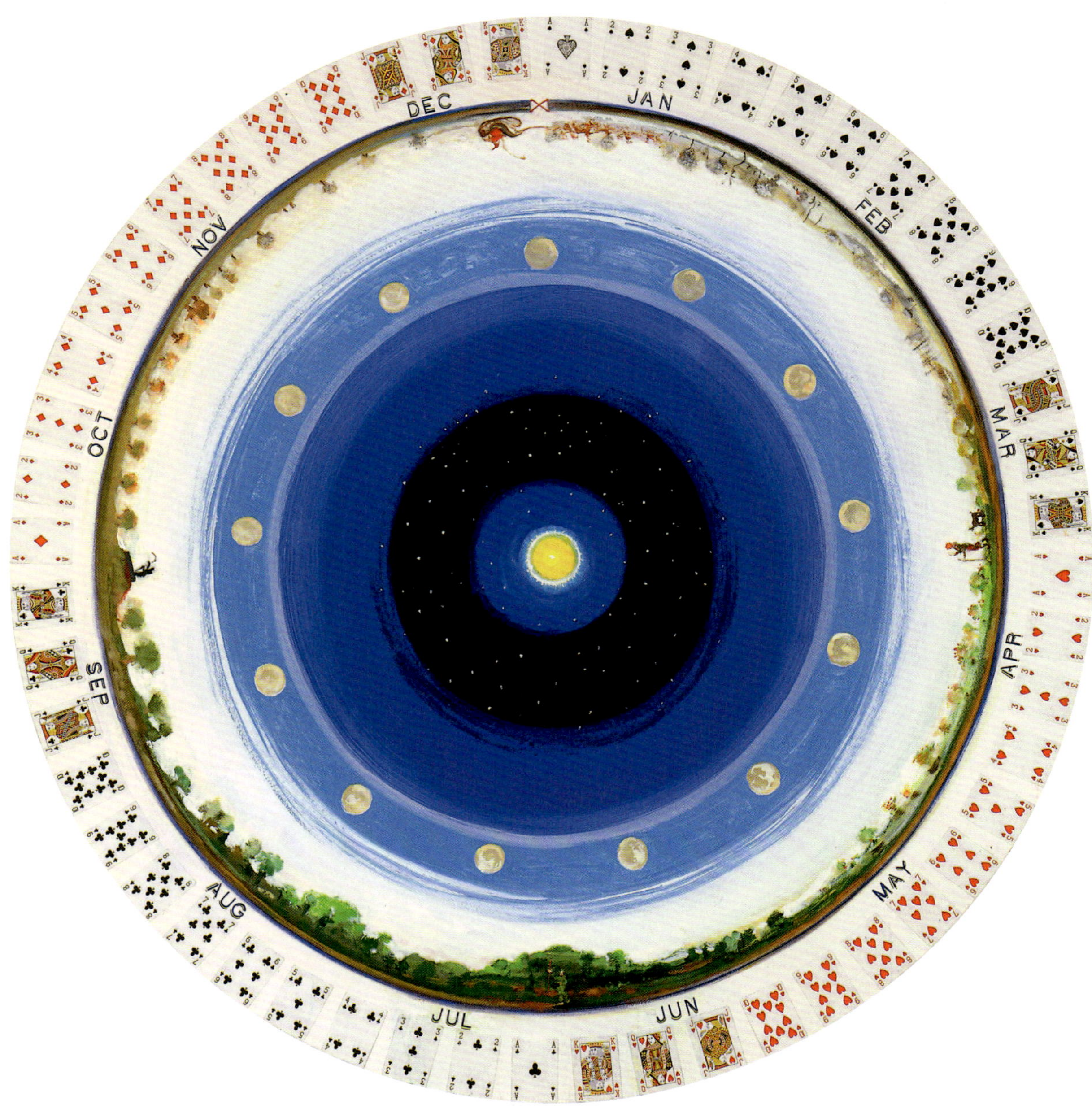

21. Calendar   2004

Oil on canvas
177.8 cm (70 in) diameter
Solomon R. Guggenheim Museum, New York,
purchased with funds contributed by the International
Directors Council

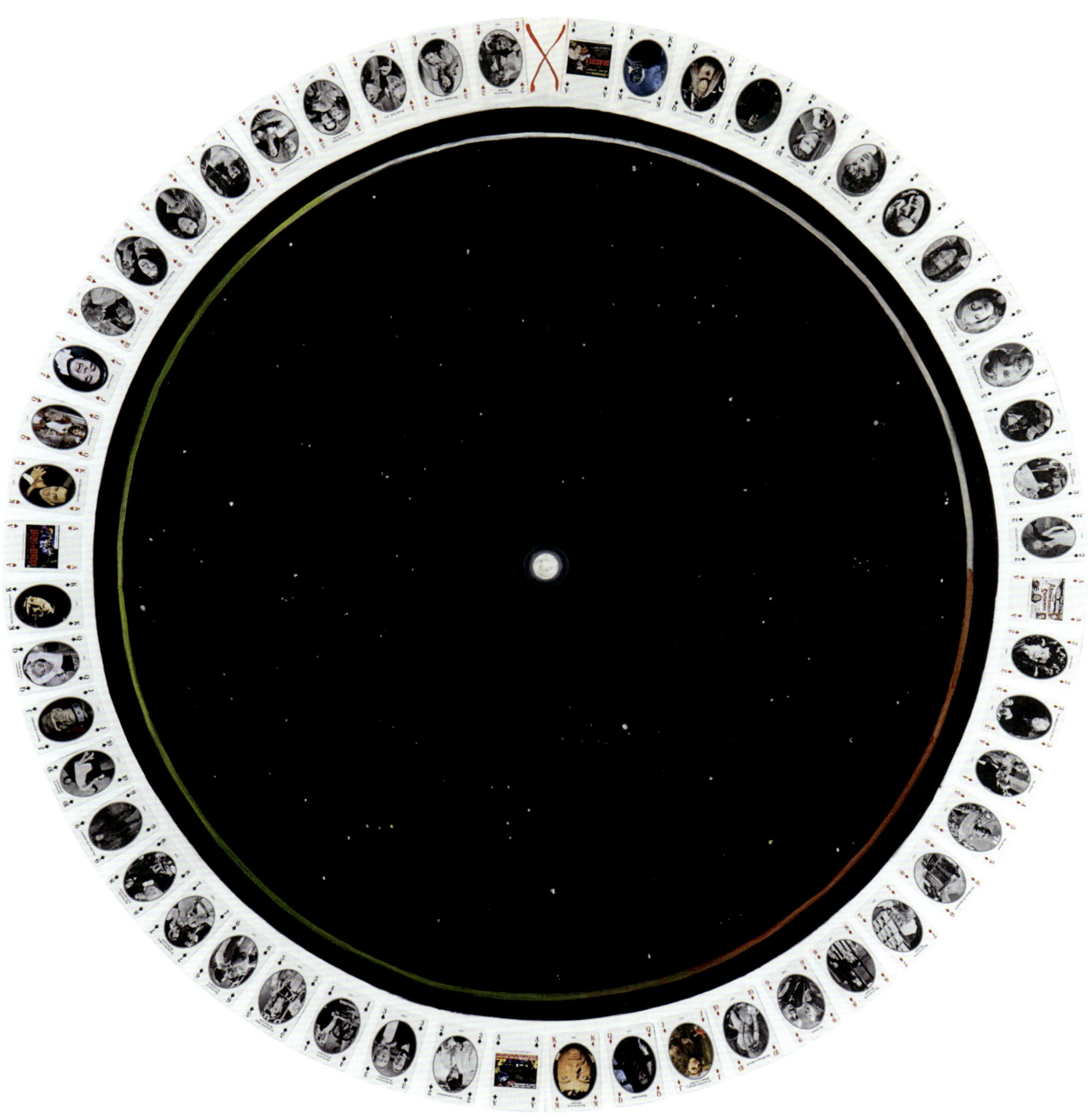

22. Calendar with the Hammer Deck   2006

Oil on canvas
123.2 cm (48½ in) diameter
Lindemann Collection, Miami Beach

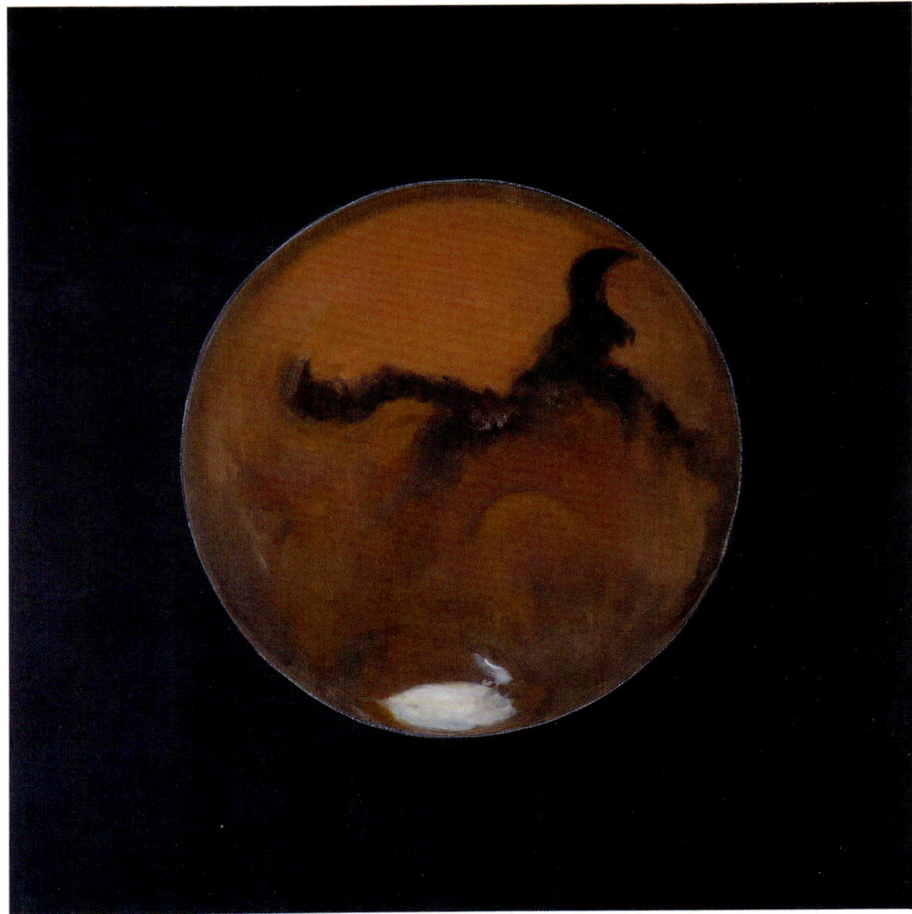

Atlas) (fig.20), a fanciful composition that shows a sinking ship surrounded by representations of constellations. Its source – albeit without the ship – was illustrated as a frontispiece in *Hamlet's Mill* by Giorgio de Santillana and Hertha von Dechend, a book (see below) that has had much influence on the artist.

Related to the calendars is the series 'The Days of the Week' (figs 26–31). Many of these imaginative images, which vary in size and style, are figurative and linked to the origins of their names; others are more literal, often painted in slightly odd colour combinations, with tweaked or asymmetric compositions.

There are also paintings of stars and planets, big and small. The most impressive is possibly *Big Bear* (fig.4), with its deep, dark blue sky, the Big Dipper (or Plough, as it is known in the UK) and the moon set within it, dawn rising on the horizon. In the foreground a bear is silhouetted. It appears to have been nuzzling a pan or 'dipper' but is now contemplating the sky. To its right is a pile of rubbish; on the left, perched on the side of the low valley, is a modern observatory. It is a painting full of implied narratives, oppositions and playful contrasts between the literal and symbolic.

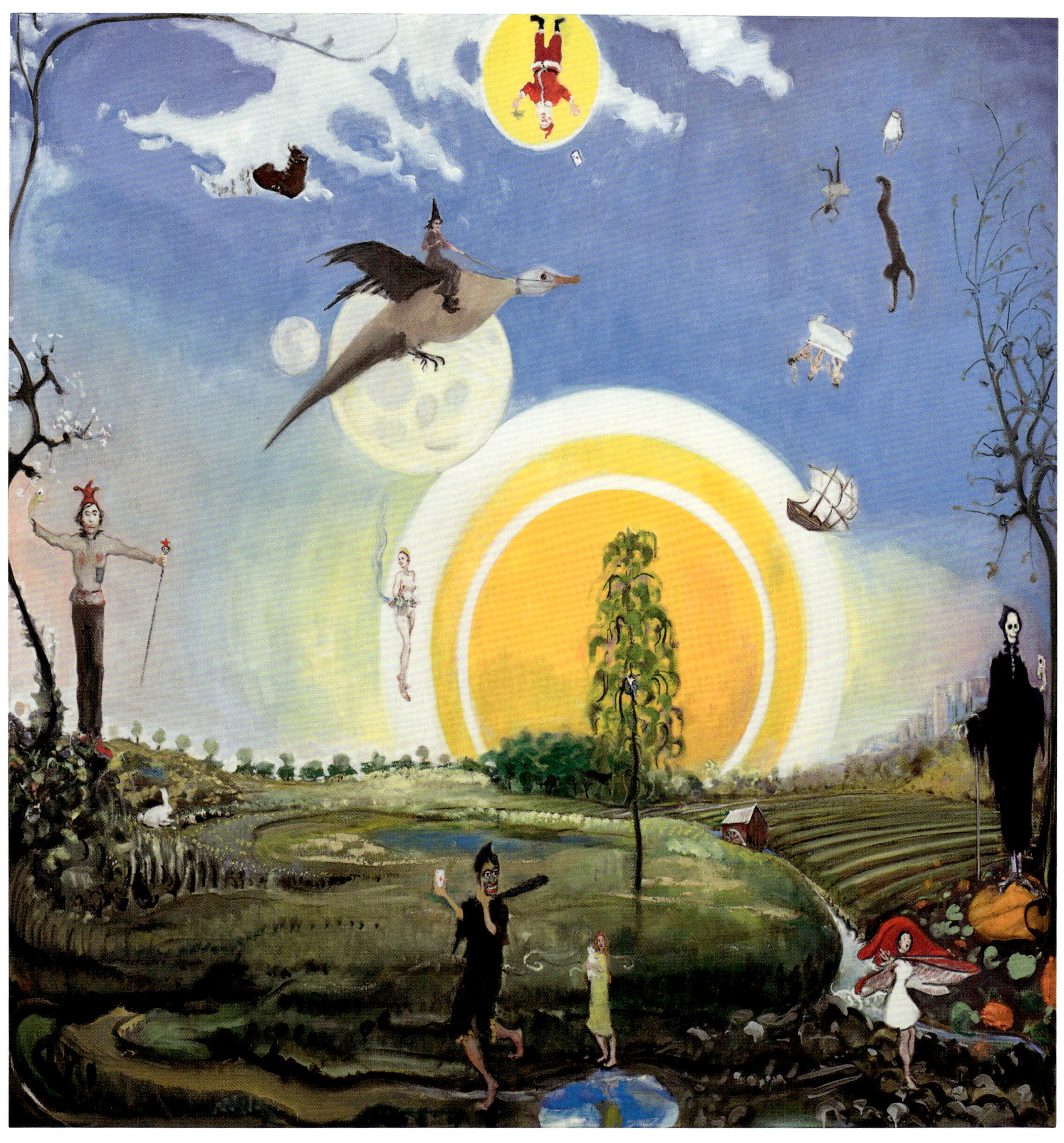

24. Pagans   2009–10

Oil on canvas
254 x 276.9 cm (100 x 109 in)
Private collection

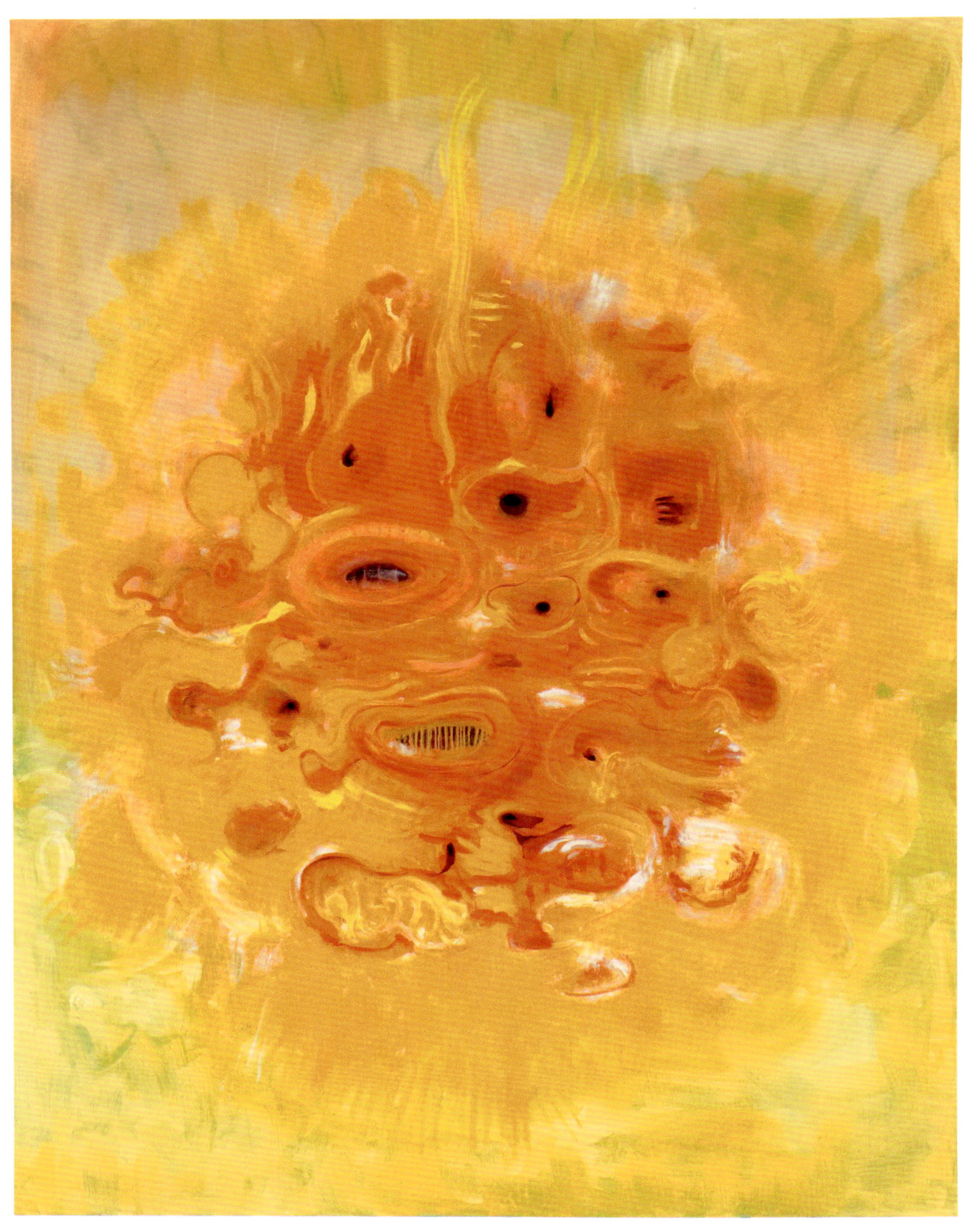

25. The Days of the Week (Sunday)   2005

Oil on linen
218.4 x 177.8 cm (86 x 70 in)
Private collection, London, UK

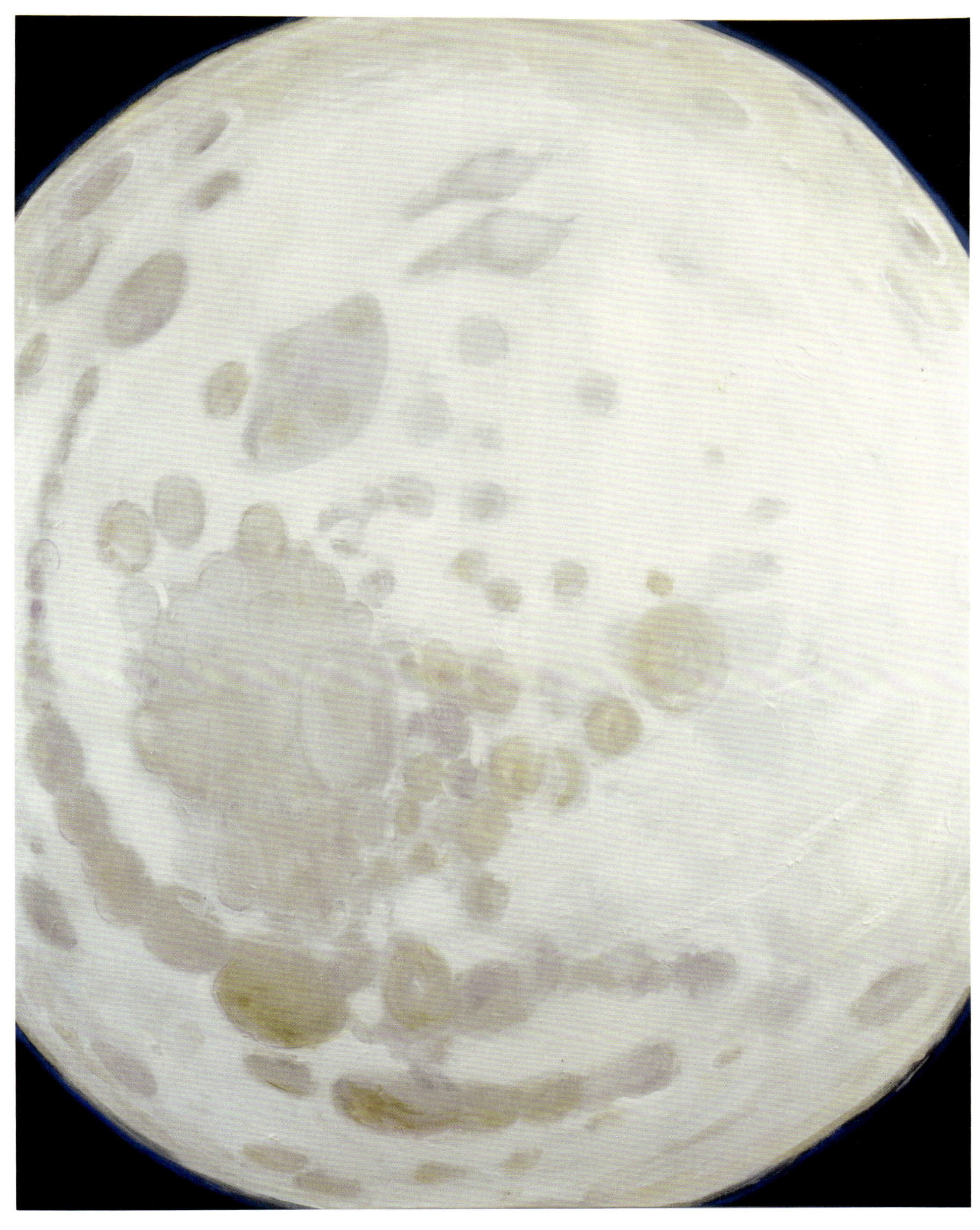

26. The Days of the Week (Monday)   2005

Oil on linen
218.4 x 177.8 cm (86 x 70 in)
Courtesy Victoria Miro, London/Venice

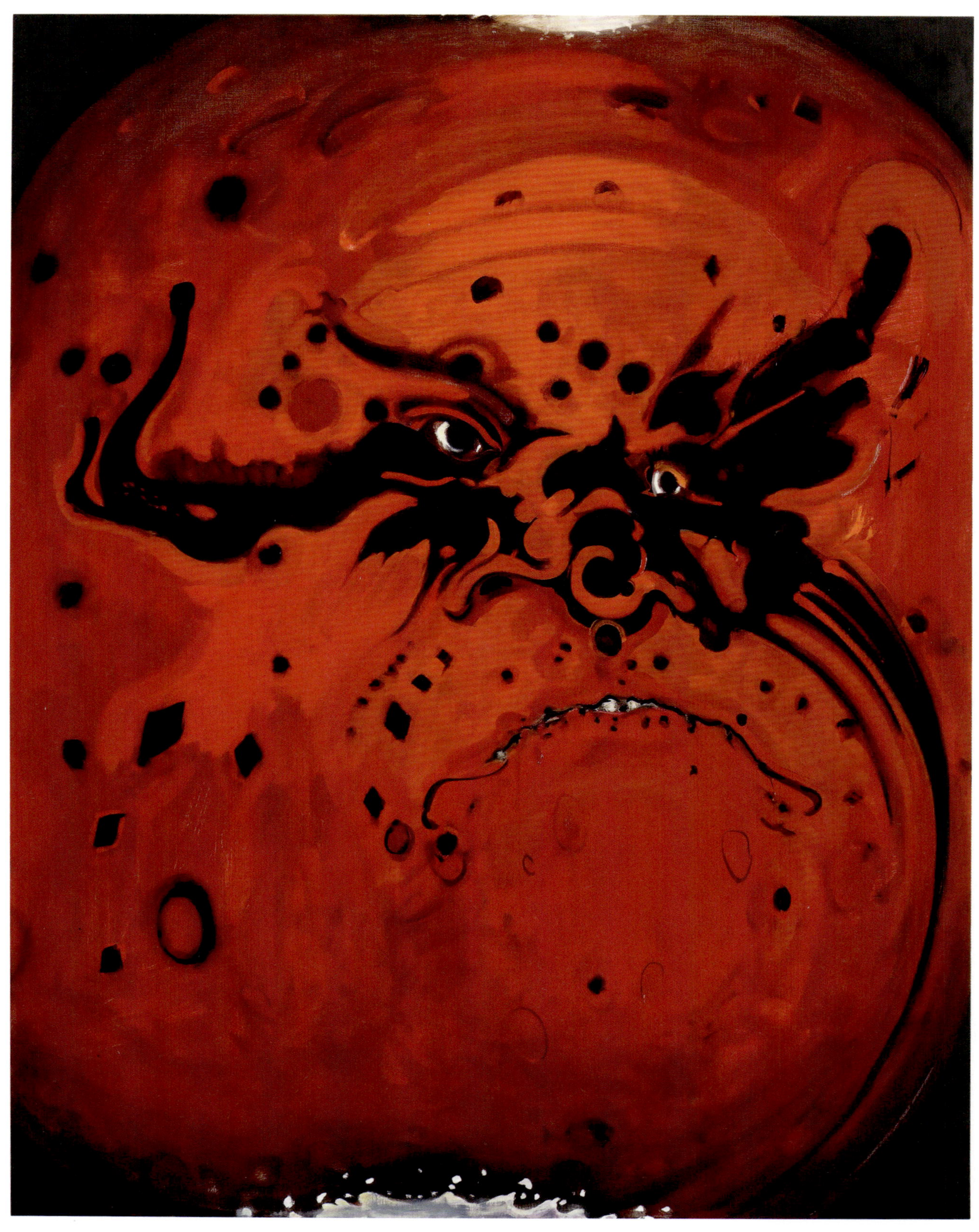

27. The Days of the Week (Tuesday)   2005

Oil on linen
218.4 x 177.8 cm (86 x 70 in)
Courtesy Victoria Miro, London/Venice

44

28. The Days of the Week (Wednesday)   2005

Oil on linen
218.4 x 177.8 cm (86 x 70 in)
Private collection

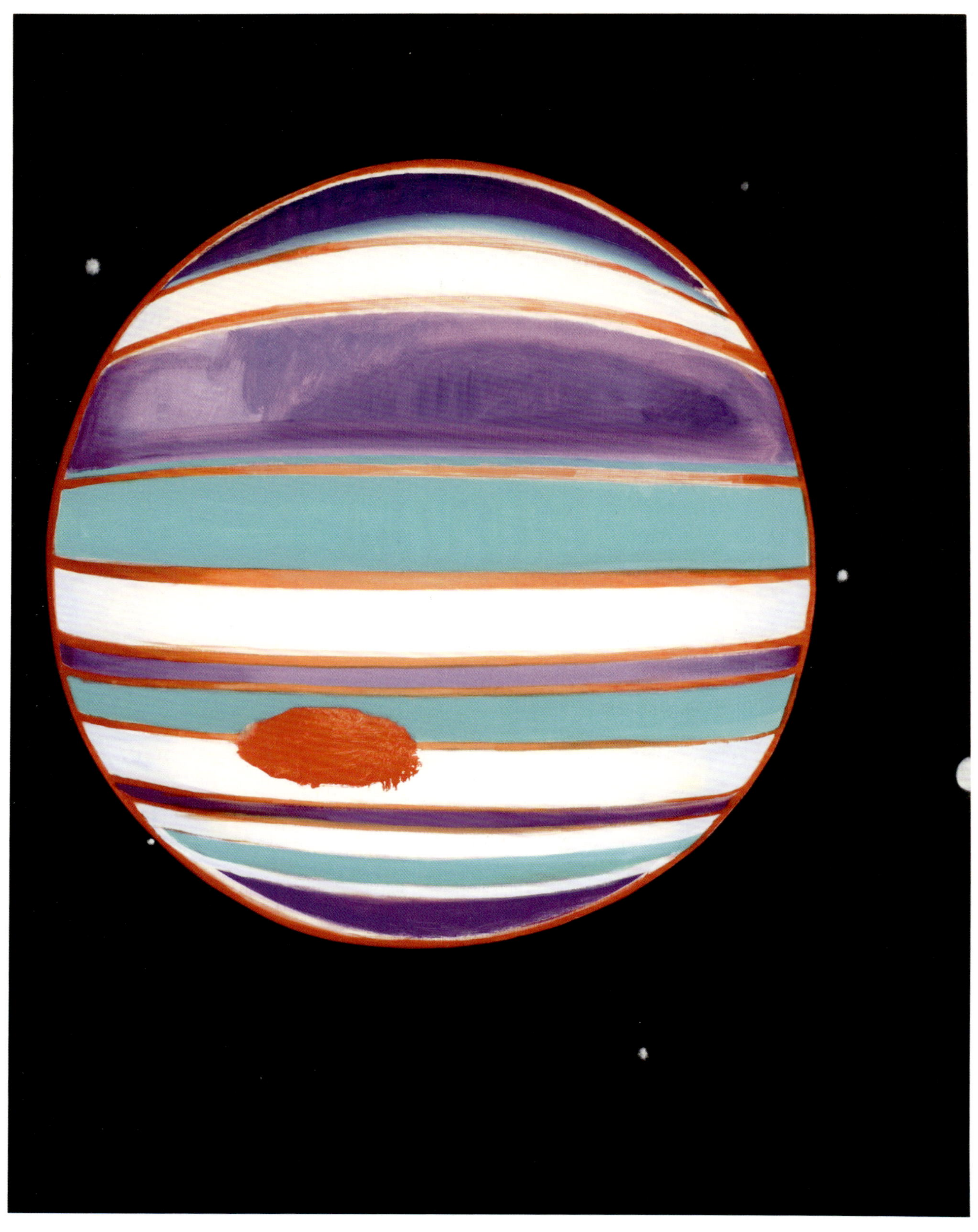

29. The Days of the Week (Thursday)   2005

Oil on linen
218.4 x 177.8 cm (86 x 70 in)
Courtesy Gavin Brown's enterprise, New York/Rome

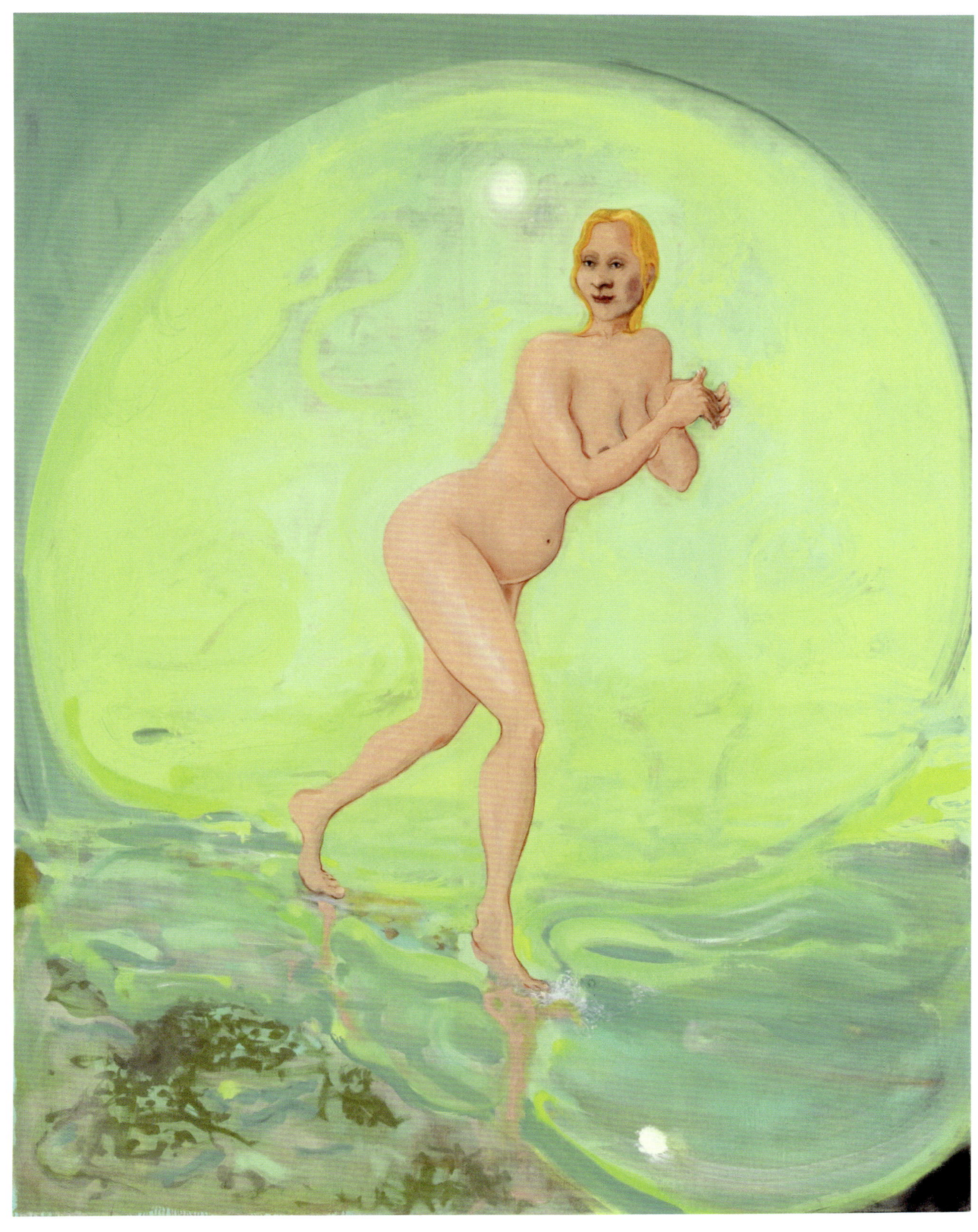

30. The Days of the Week (Friday)   2005

Oil on linen
218.4 x 177.8 cm (86 x 70 in)
Nunzia & Vittorio Gaddi Collection, Lucca, Italy

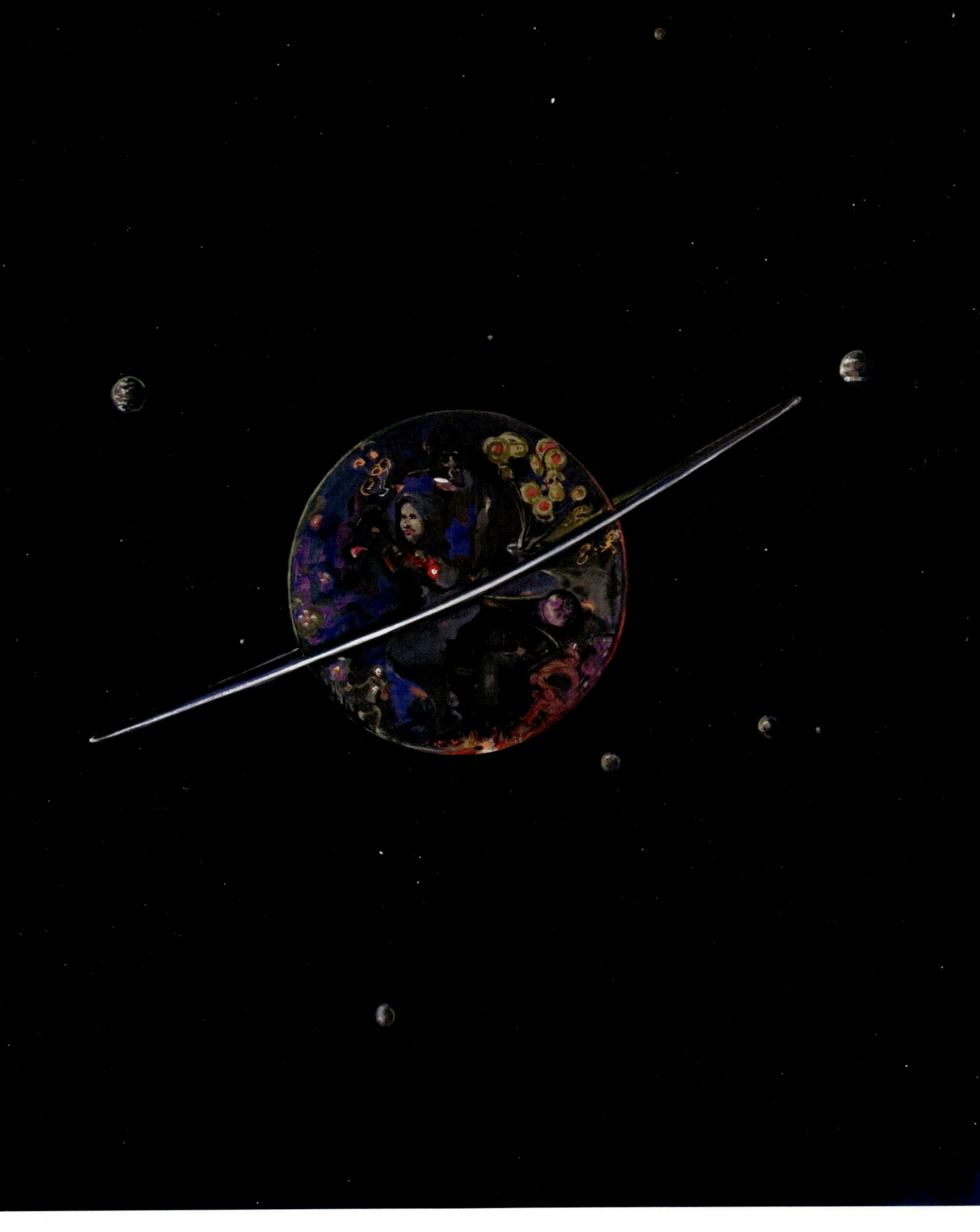

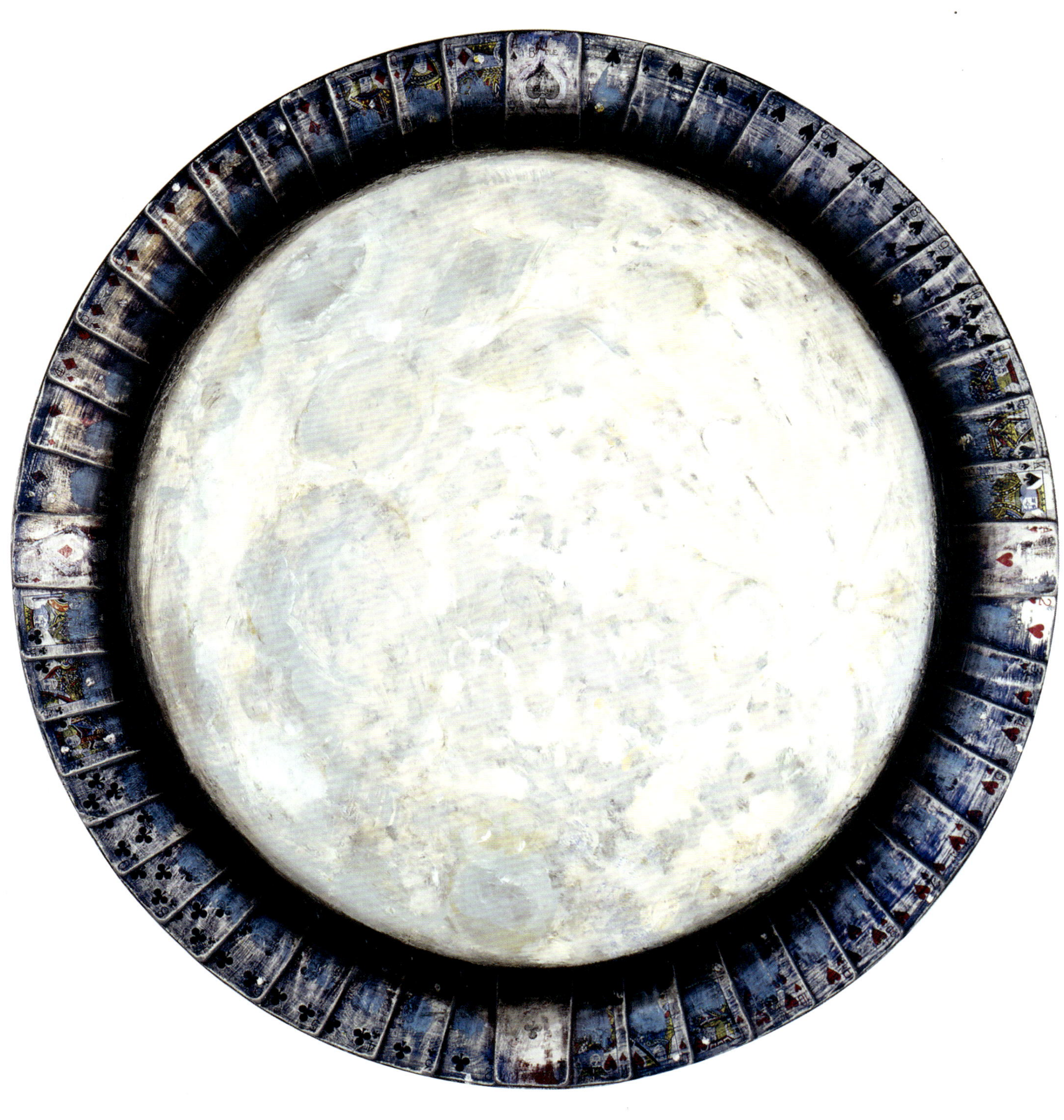

31. The Days of the Week (Saturday) 2005

Oil on linen
218.4 x 177.8 cm (86 x 70 in)
Private collection

32. Hare Deck 2008

Oil on canvas
61 cm (24 in) diameter
Lost or stolen

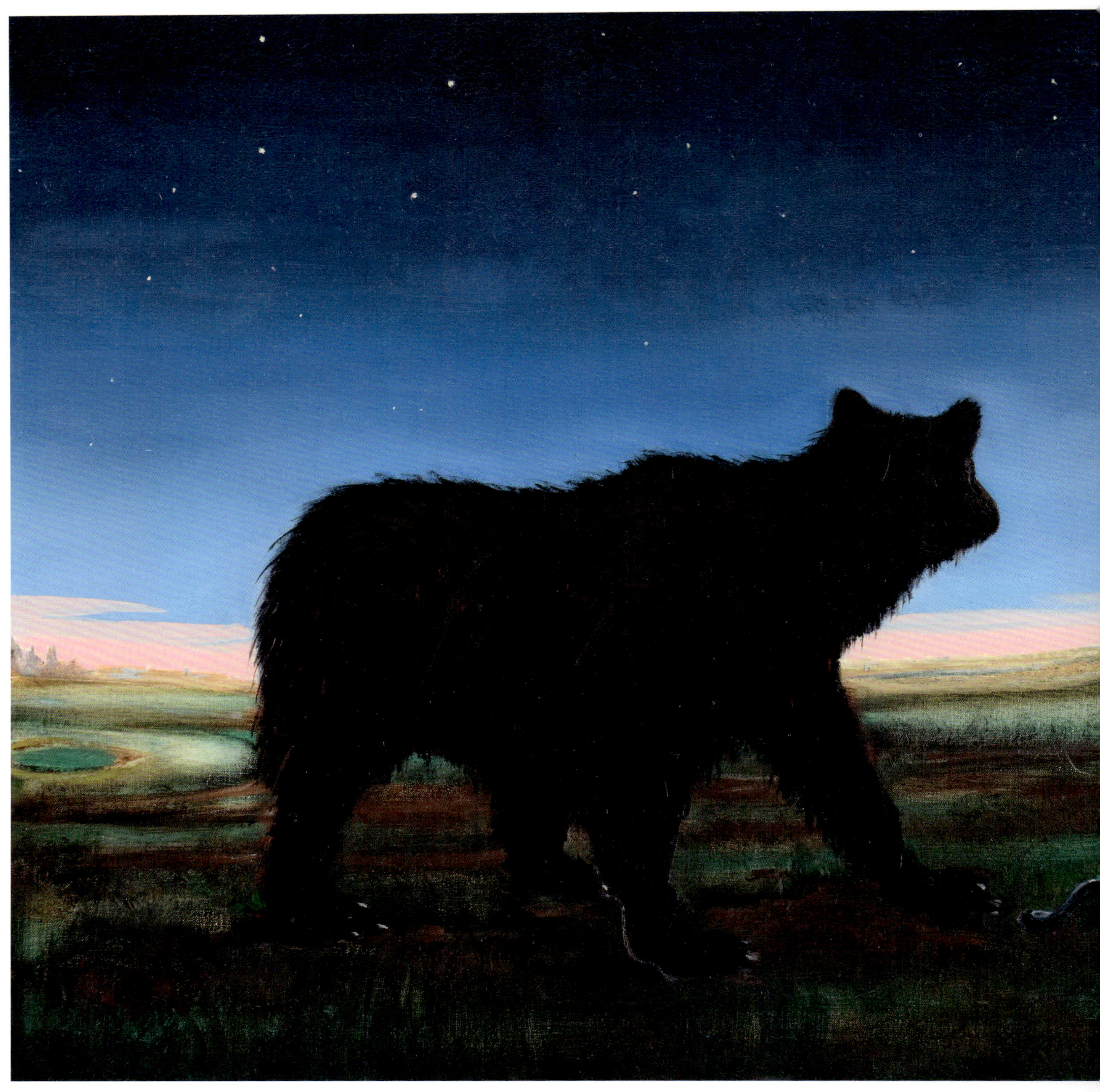

33. Big Bear   2000

Oil on canvas
40.6 x 55.9 cm (16 x 22 in)
Private collection

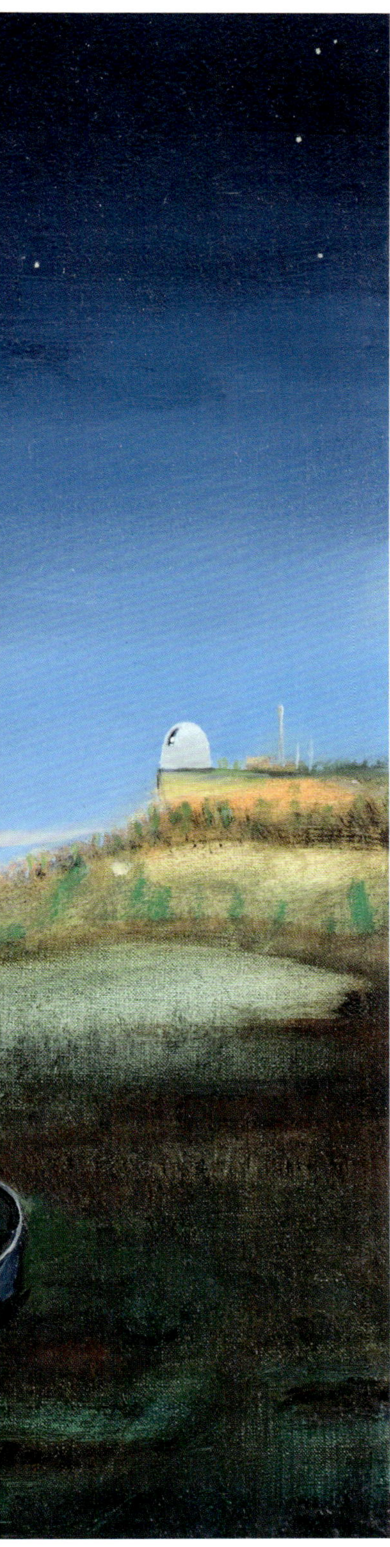

But it is *Pagans* (fig.24), an all-encompassing painting in which Dawson makes reference to a medley of the ideas that interest him, and *432*, an artist's book that was produced to accompany a 2004 exhibition at Dublin's Douglas Hyde Gallery (in which he lists examples of unexpected, curious and often scarcely believable facts that link contemporary life with the distant past), that give the most comprehensive reflection of the breadth of Dawson's knowledge of arcane and archaic culture, an interest that he has pursued since his schooldays. Much of it has roots in his contrarian interpretations of the early history of the world, ideas that were influenced by his Cooper Union teacher, Arthur Corwin, and also by a handful of unusual books.

One book that seems to have influenced Dawson's thinking is Arthur Koestler's *The Sleepwalkers*,[15] which focuses on four great figures in the history of modern cosmology: Copernicus, Kepler, Galileo and Newton. Koestler argues that there is much more to the creative act than can be accounted for rationally. Creative scientists, he proposes, do not really know what they are doing. As sleepwalkers, able to combine faith and science, they have an inner certainty that leads them onward, even though they may not be able to explain what it is they are looking for or why they are doing so. They often move towards their goal by means of extraordinary and logically questionable methods, and, when they arrive, they may not realize that they have got there.

The work of Alexander Marshack,[16] another of Dawson's inspirations, consistently asks questions of archaeologists that have challenged usual ways of thinking. For example, Marshack observed intriguing details in the marks of some bone objects from the European Paleolithic period, suggesting that they might have been notations of lunar phases. Although no one has dismissed his basic proposition that there is something interesting in the bone markings, his conclusions have not been widely accepted, and many of the marks that Marshack analysed are popularly thought to be tally counts of some kind, related to hunting or perhaps connected with fertility rites. Few archaeologists accept that they represent arithmetical or astronomical concepts, or that they are what Marshack calls 'storied events'.[17]

Similarly, the arguments in another of Dawson's early guiding texts, Giorgio de Santillana and Hertha von Dechend's *Hamlet's Mill*,[18] are not generally accepted, even though their erudition is admired. The book's core idea is that there was a Paleolithic discovery of the 'precession' of the equinoxes and that an associated Megalithic civilization of 'unsuspected sophistication' became deeply involved with astronomical and astrological observation. This knowledge, according to the authors, was encoded in mythology around the world, which is therefore to be interpreted primarily in terms of 'archaeoastronomy'. The dense and lengthy *Hamlet's Mill* considers world mythology, especially the mill myths alluded to in its title, with reference to the cosmographic relics and fragments, rituals and behaviours that have survived the attrition of time.

Whether or not these unconventional views are academically or scientifically sound seems to have mattered less to Dawson than their potential to stimulate his

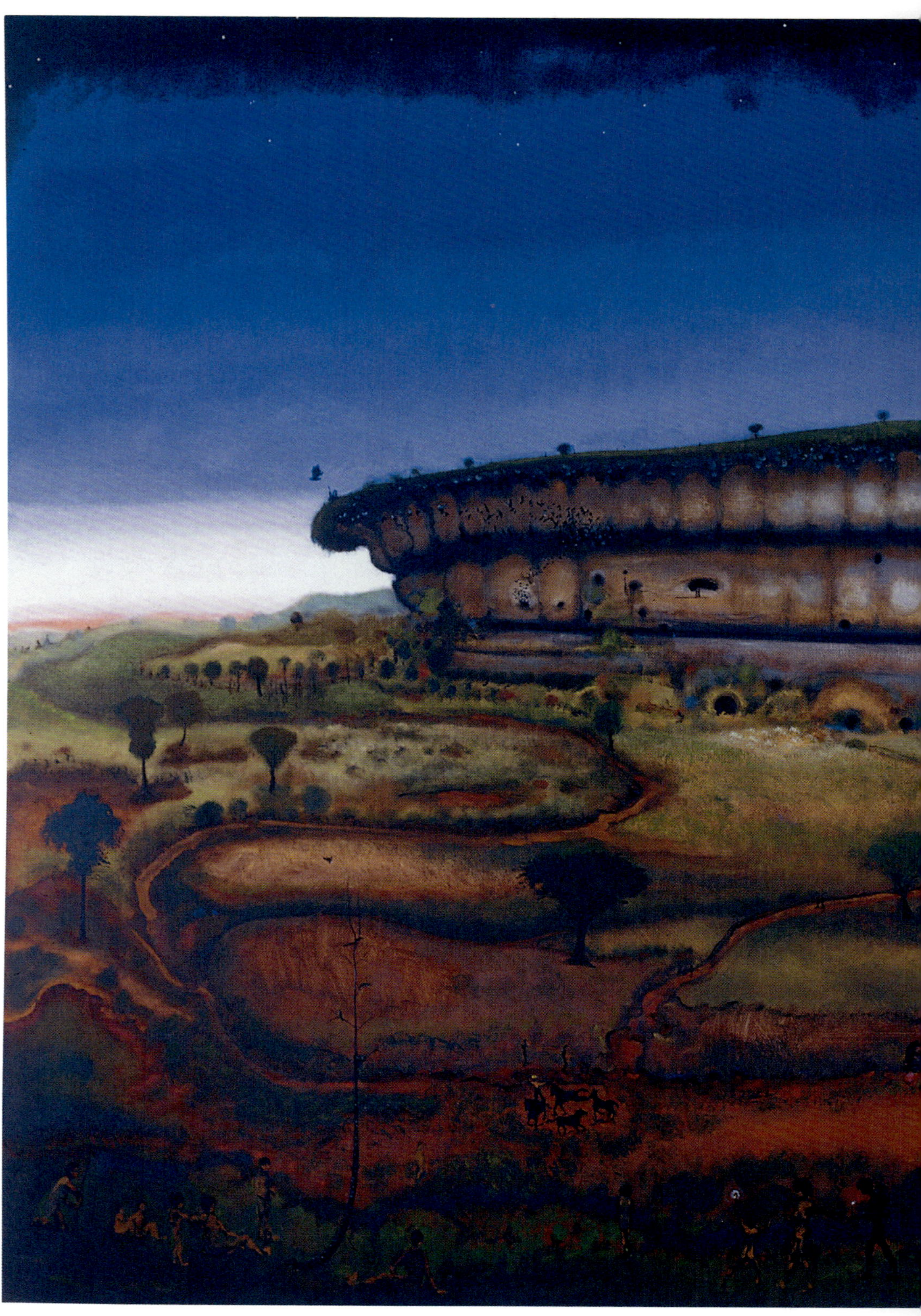

34. The Circus 2001

Oil on canvas
208.3 x 365.8 cm (82 x 144 in)
Ringier Collection, Switzerland

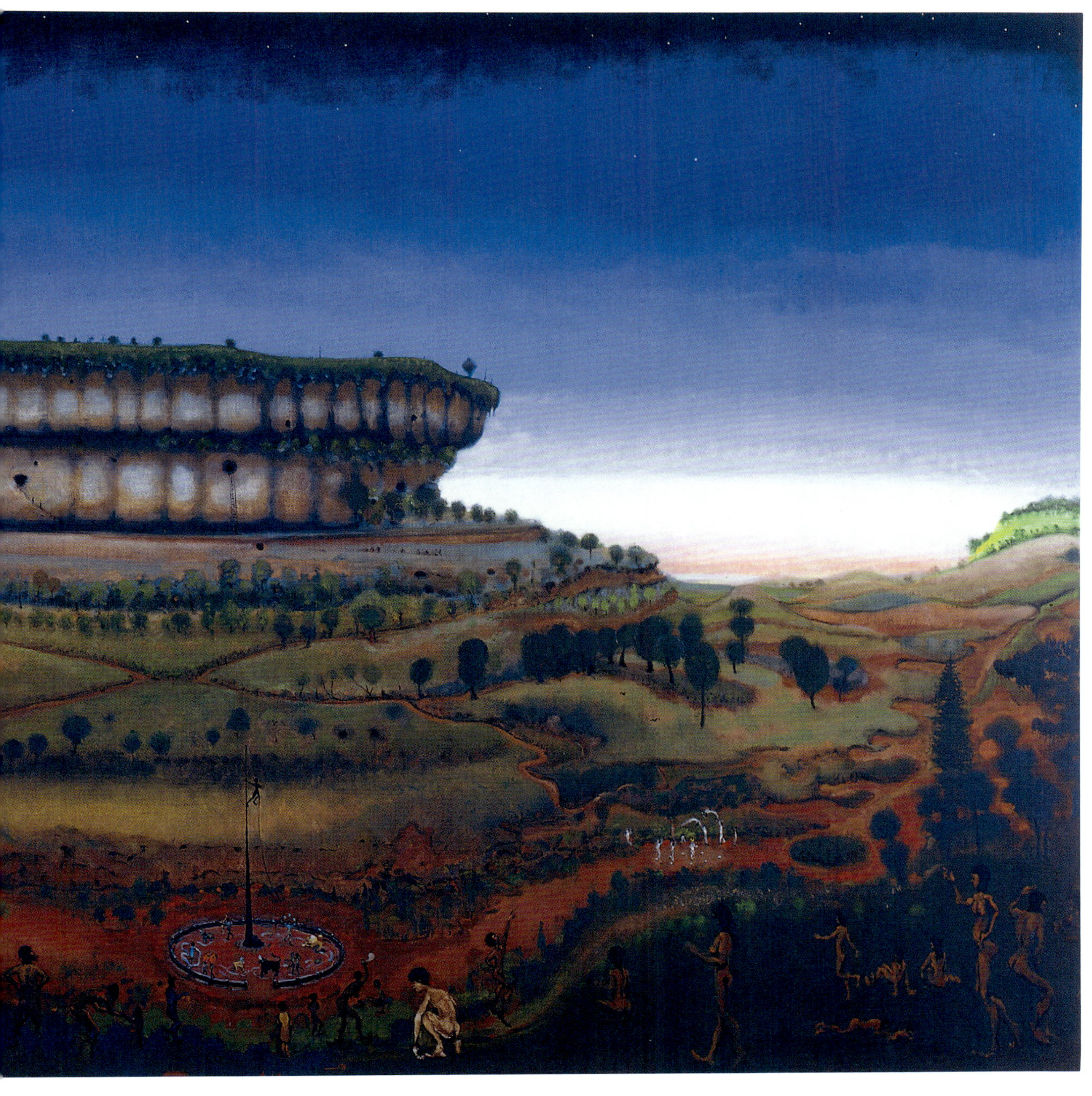

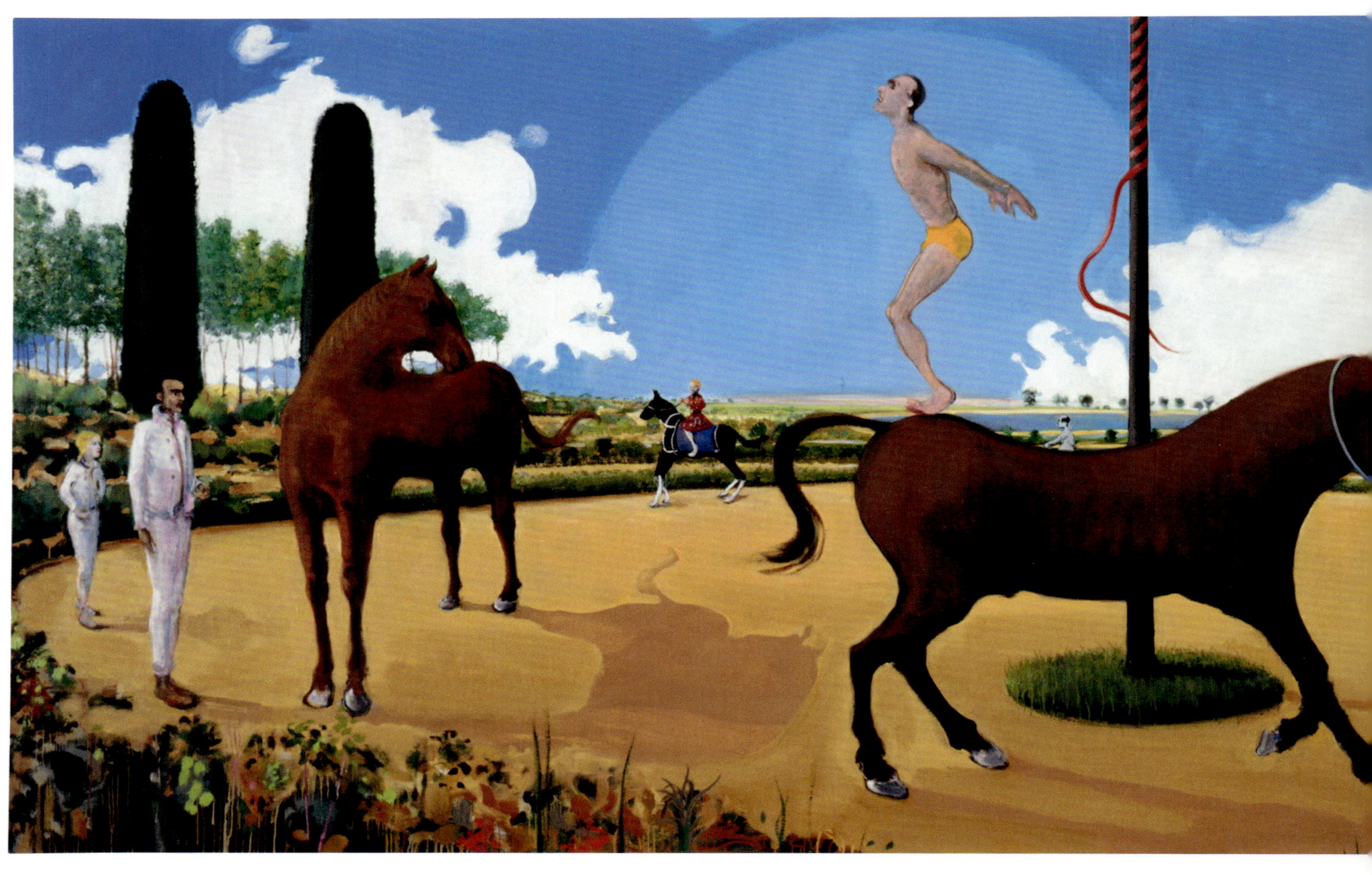

35. Ring   2007

Oil on canvas
182.9 x 426.7 cm (72 x 168 in)
Private collection

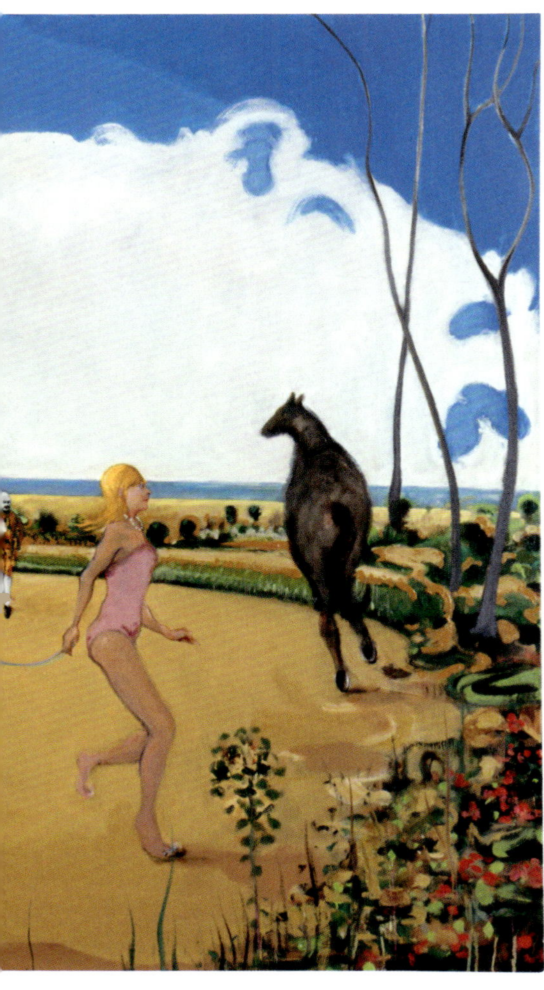

imagination. His images of circuses, central to his work, bring many of these ideas into play. They range from the magnificent early *The Circus* (fig.34), with its stylized references to the supposed cradle of civilization, Olduvai Gorge in Tanzania, with a tiny ring in the valley, complete with pole and animals, to the more modernist *Ring* (fig.35), with its distant echo of Pablo Picasso's Saltimbanques (itinerant circus performers) series. Circuses are 'the most intact manifestation of Paleolithic life', Dawson explains. 'There is a pole holding up the Big Top and you have a ring. Within that ring, animals come in and circle around: it's a model of the heavens and the Zodiac. In a three-ring circus, you have another pole for the moon, and another one for Venus. So it's basically a model of Stone Age astronomy, being done as a ballet.'[19] Elsewhere, he adds:

> A circus, like the sky, is in motion. It rolls into town and puts up its big tent, a model of the universe. Up goes the big centre pole just like the axis of the earth. Everything rotates above and below it. Then down below you have your ring with the opening right in the middle – like in Stonehenge and like the zodiac. You have all these animals coming into the ring and going round this big circle.[20]

Related to the circus pictures are those of acrobats and aerialists, some of them depicted in tents, others set against plain, usually blue, coloured backgrounds. One, *Circus*, painted in 2002, is an intimate small oval with a landscape, sky and moon in the background (fig.38); its mood is lyrical and remote. Later versions are larger, more ambitious and based on photographs, for example, *Aerialists (Blue)* (fig.36). They have a sense of stretched and tenuous balance, their awkward figuration occasionally evocative of French painter Francis Picabia (1879–1953). Once again founded on the notion of stars and constellations moving in the sky, the rhythms of the flying figures suspended in the air between ropes and cables also suggest a longing for connection and trust. However, the contrary is also true, as in the huge *Aerialists (Red & White)* (fig.37), which seems to embody rigidity and risk.

Over the decades, Dawson has painted numerous representations of classic fairy tales, all of them quite faithful to the well-known stories, but also focused on their astronomical implications. *Jack and the Beanstalk* (fig.39) depicts the eponymous hero scaling an impossibly thick and verdant stalk. It is at once a careful illustration of a story as well as an allegory of solstices, processes of nature and when to plant seeds. Dawson's 'Jack and Jill' pictures (figs 40 and 41), which would not be out of place in a children's book, make reference to the waxing and waning of the moon.

Most dramatic of all his fairy-tale works are the two threatening versions of 'Little Red Riding Hood' (figs 3 and 42), both set in wintry landscapes with red moons, leafless trees and a bold wolf standing on two feet. Some folklorists have interpreted the tale of Little Red Riding Hood as a tale that weaves a narrative around the cycle of the sun; the red hood representing the sun that is ultimately swallowed by the

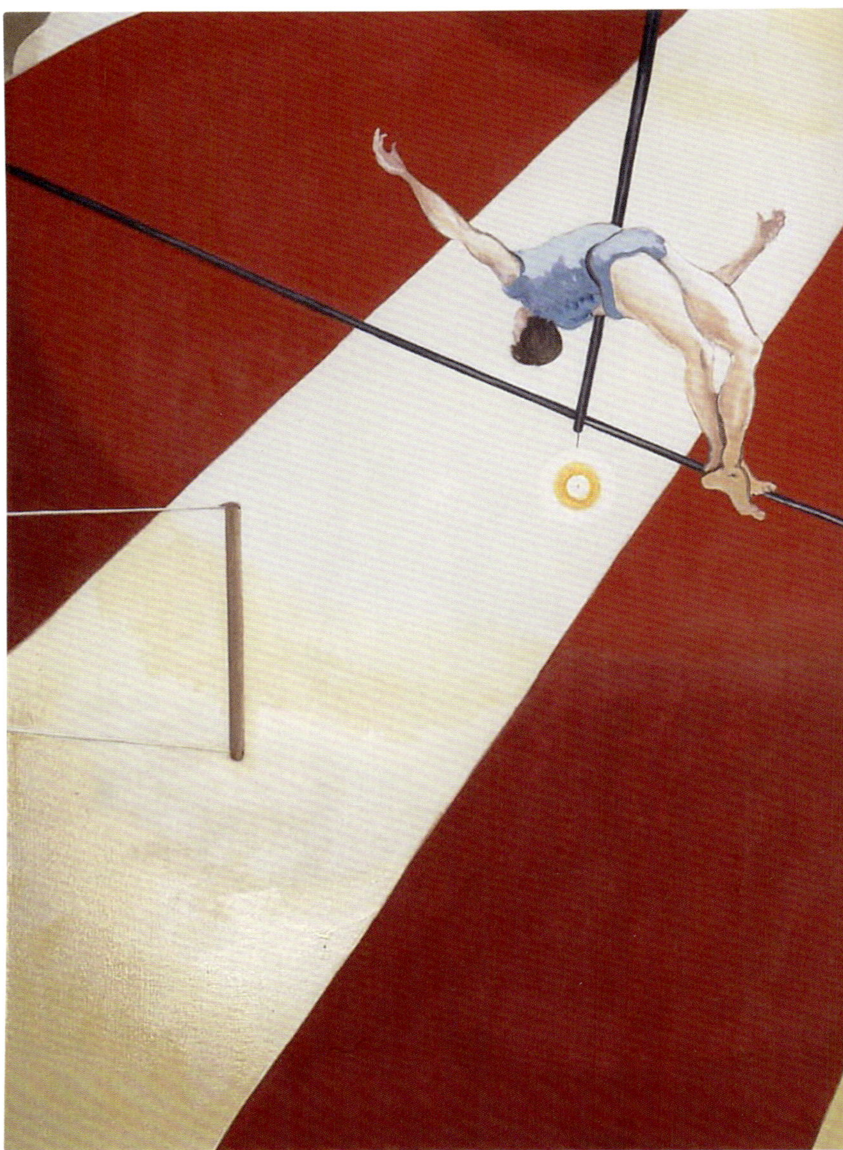

36. Aerialists (Blue)   2003

Oil on canvas
182.9 x 426.7 cm (72 x 168 in)
Collection of Maja Hoffmann

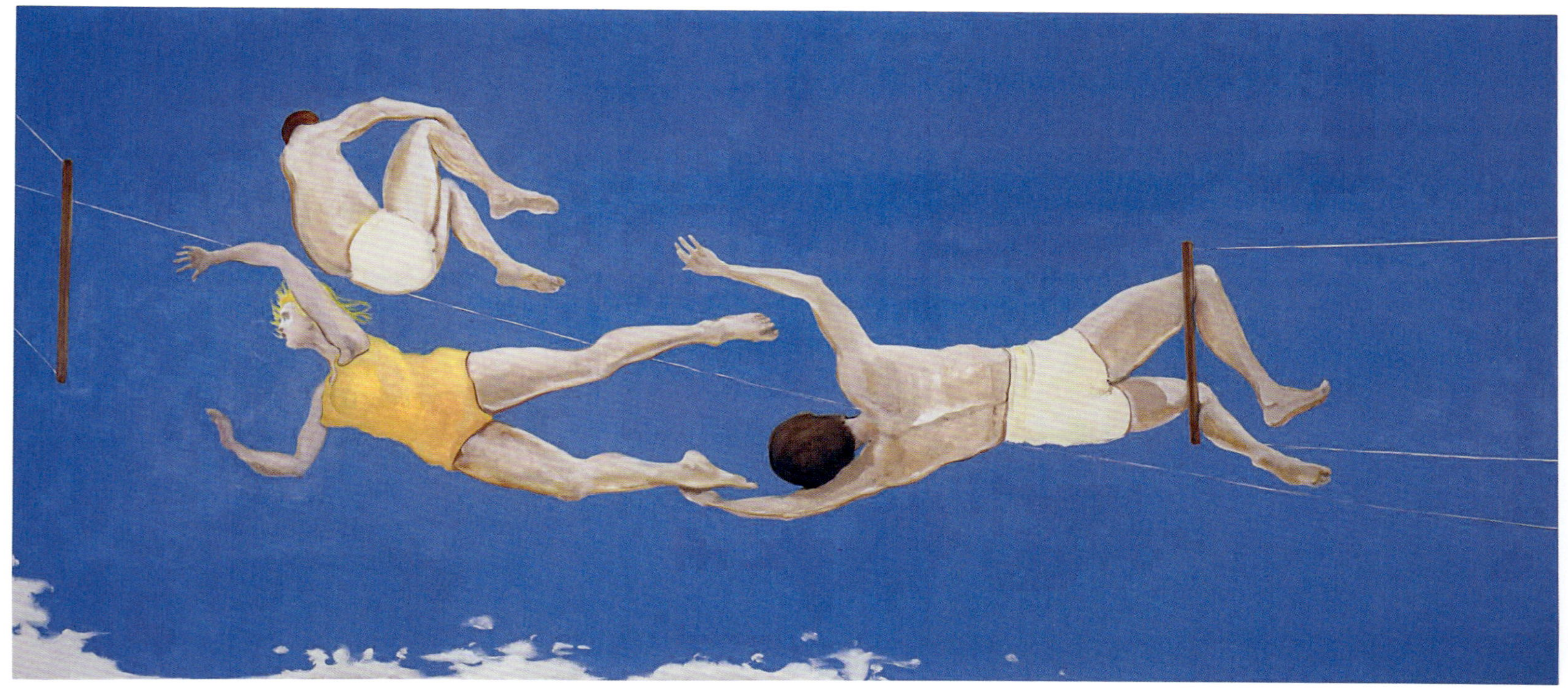

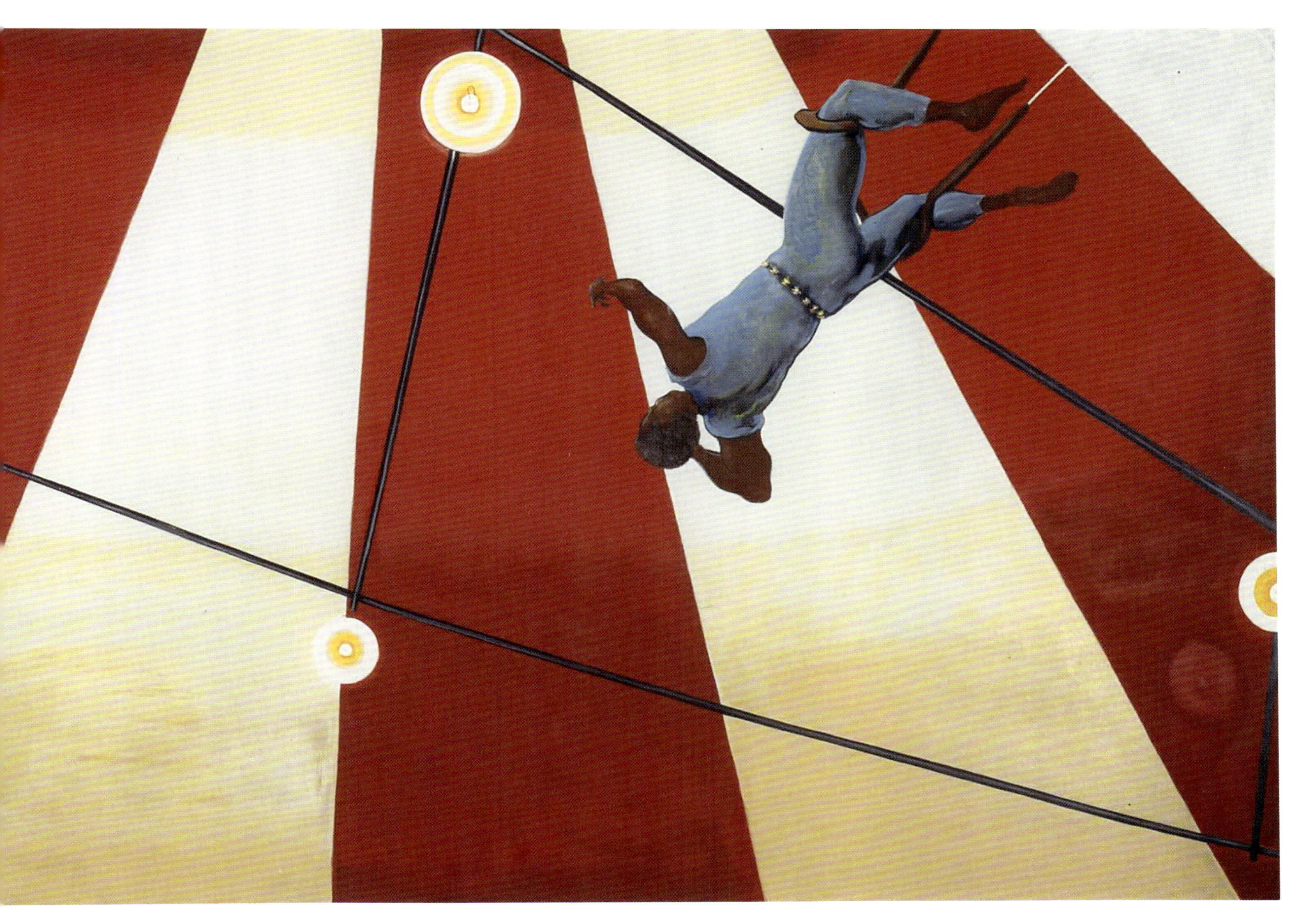

37. Aerialists (Red & White)   2003

Oil on canvas
182.9 x 426.7 cm (72 x 168 in)
Friedrich Christian Flick Collection

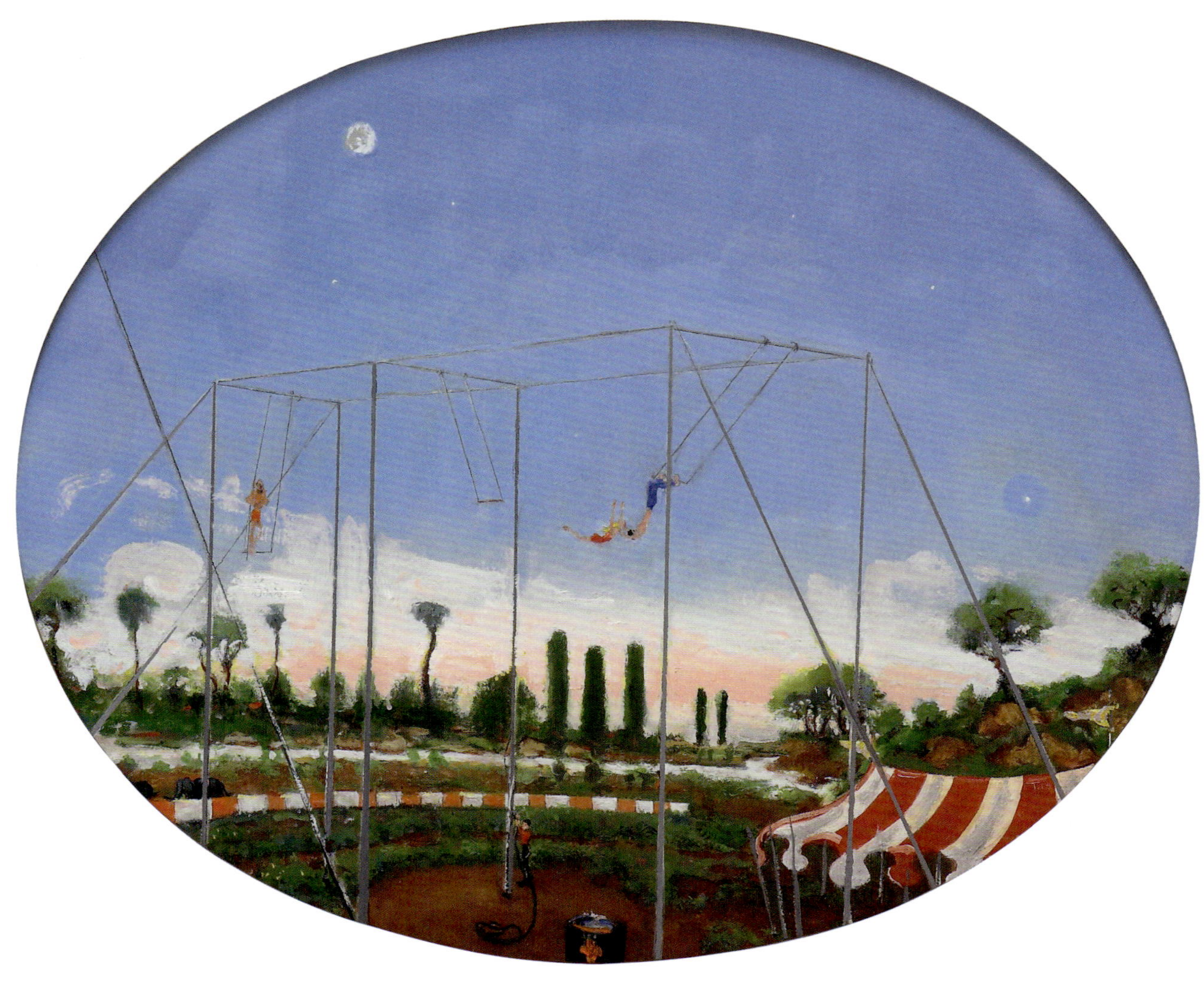

38. Circus   2002/2003

Oil on canvas
61 x 76.2 cm (24 x 30 in)
Dianne Wallace, New York

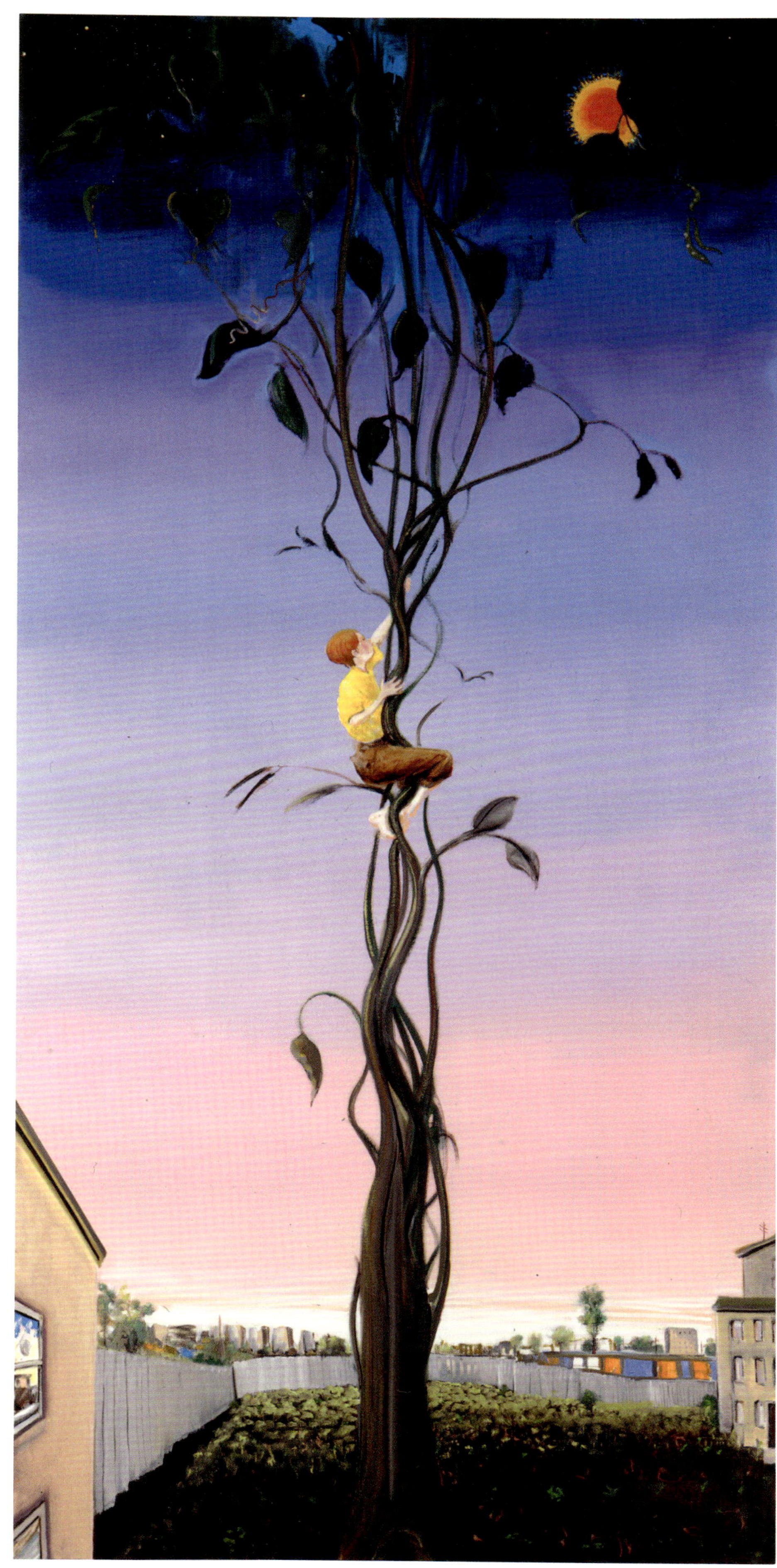

39. Jack and the Beanstalk   2006

Oil on canvas
365.8 x 182.9 cm (144 x 72 in)
Collection of Victoria and Warren Miro,
London, UK

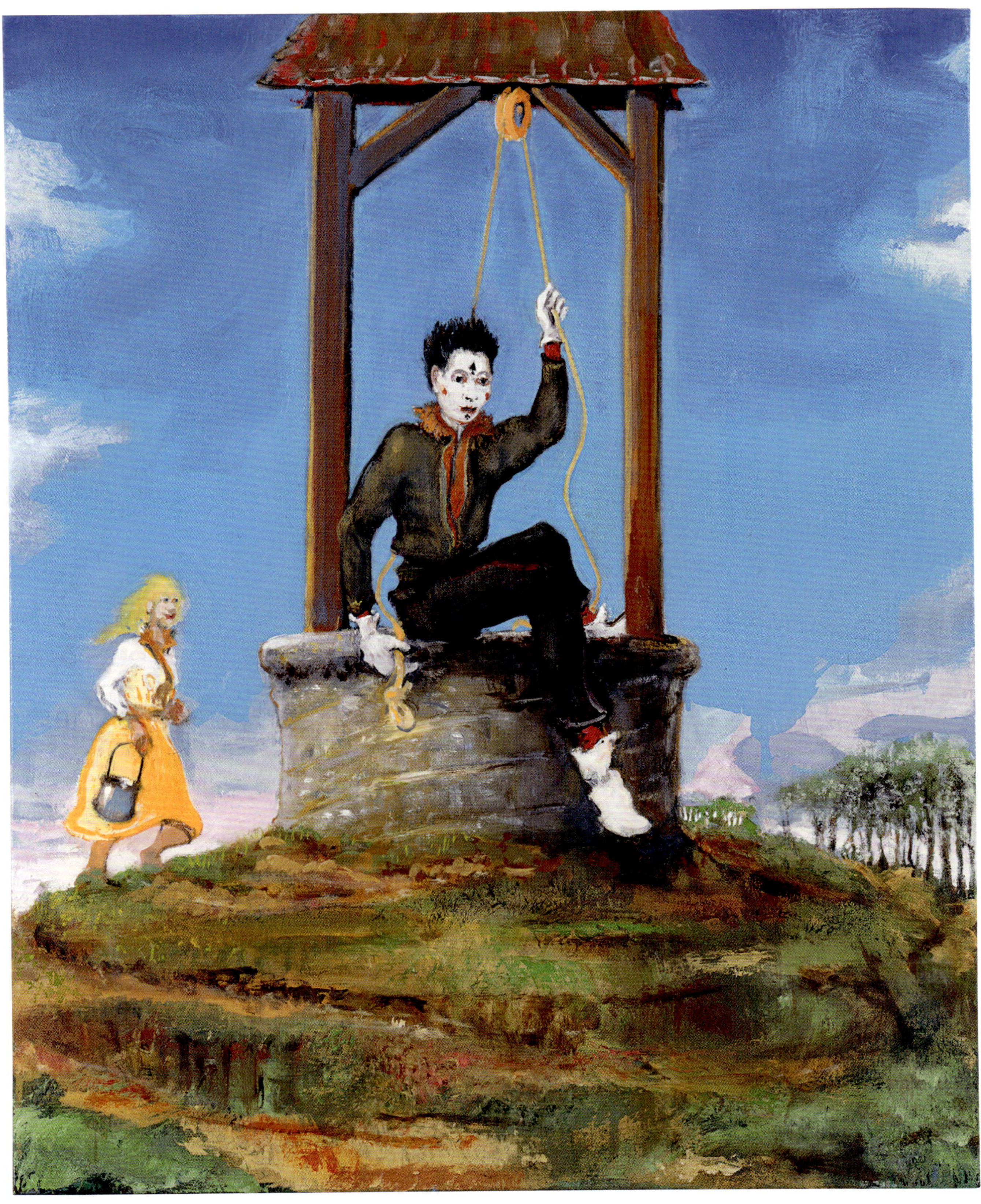

40. Jack and Jill   2007

Oil on canvas
73.7 x 61 cm (29 x 24 in)
Burger Collection, Hong Kong

60

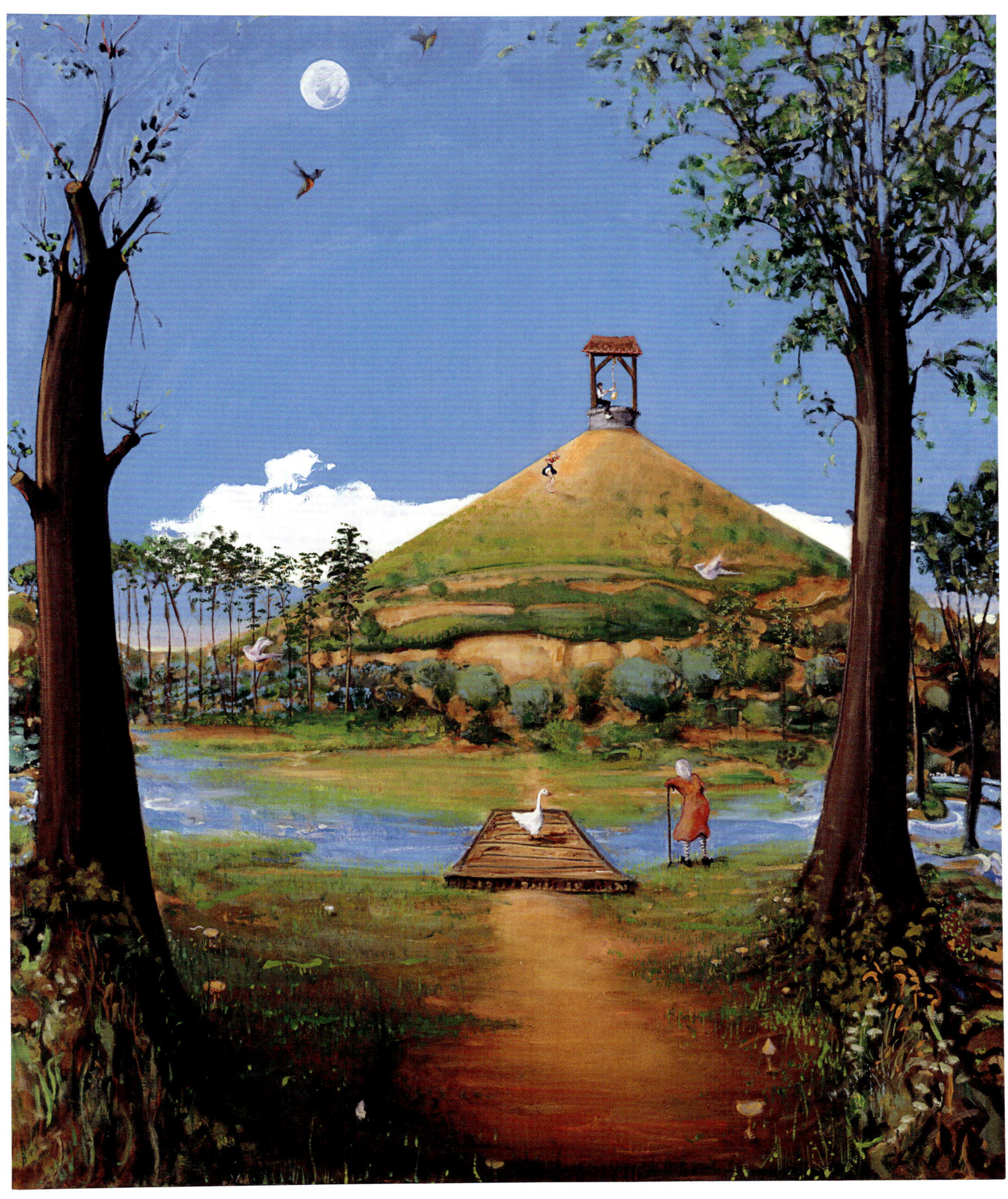

41. Jack and Jill *2007*

Oil on canvas
213.4 x 180.3 cm (84 x 71 in)
Private collection

night, personified by the wolf. In Dawson's preferred interpretation, the story is about a lunar eclipse, in which the 'wolf moon' turns red. There are other different and plausible readings of the story, many of them sexual or psychological, and Bruno Bettelheim, in *The Uses of Enchantment: The Meaning and Importance of Fairy Tales*, devotes much space to their exploration.

Although it is not always obvious, many of Dawson's paintings have a distinct psychological charge. One of his major series, three large canvases that tell the biblical story of Jonah and the Whale (figs 43 and 44), while nominally founded on astronomical concepts, is also full of personal references, both literal and metaphorical. In the first painting, Jonah has fallen overboard into a stormy sea, while his ship, flying the American flag and facing a dark sky, is tossed by great waves. In the second, he is inside the whale, which is seen from his point of view; the cavernous interior is overwhelming and has distinct sexual overtones. In the third of the paintings, the exhausted seafarer is beached beside the dead whale. Jonah's story, Dawson once explained, is fundamentally a solar or lunar tale: the whale is Cetus, a constellation that is most often seen from the southern hemisphere but is briefly visible on the horizon in the northern hemisphere at the time of the winter solstice. He continued:

> Like Jesus, the 'Sun' of God, things go very badly for Jonah for a period, just as for us in the north our tribulations mount in the winter with the decline of the arc of the sun's travels. Jonah is a burden on ship, a real 'Jonah' as they say, a bummer. Was he pushed or did he fall? The sun drops lower and lower in winter, dropping to its apogee during the moon's monthly disappearance. It reappears three days later, like Jesus, and the dying of light is reversed, as the sun returns.
>
> The personal in these paintings is indulgent and even embarrassing, but it is also part of them. Firstly, I was a sailor for eleven months, a Jonah. I made the trip from Virginia to Iceland on a frigate, on the North Atlantic in mid-winter. I was discharged from the Navy shortly after that ordeal because I was sleepwalking. The paintings were made twenty-five years later during the winter while Laura, my wife, was frequently away, and while I was recovering my health. Our house was in the North, in the Pennsylvania countryside, and I was quite alone, isolated, in pain, with relentless blizzards and ice all around me. Let's just call it a bad passage; we all have them.[21]

★

In the early 19th century, American artists idealized the landscape, mourning what they saw as the gradual disappearance of its grandeur and beauty. Their attitude to nature was Arcadian, 'Arcadia' being an ancient myth about a place of bountiful natural harmony and beauty, inhabited by shepherds and other rural people who lived

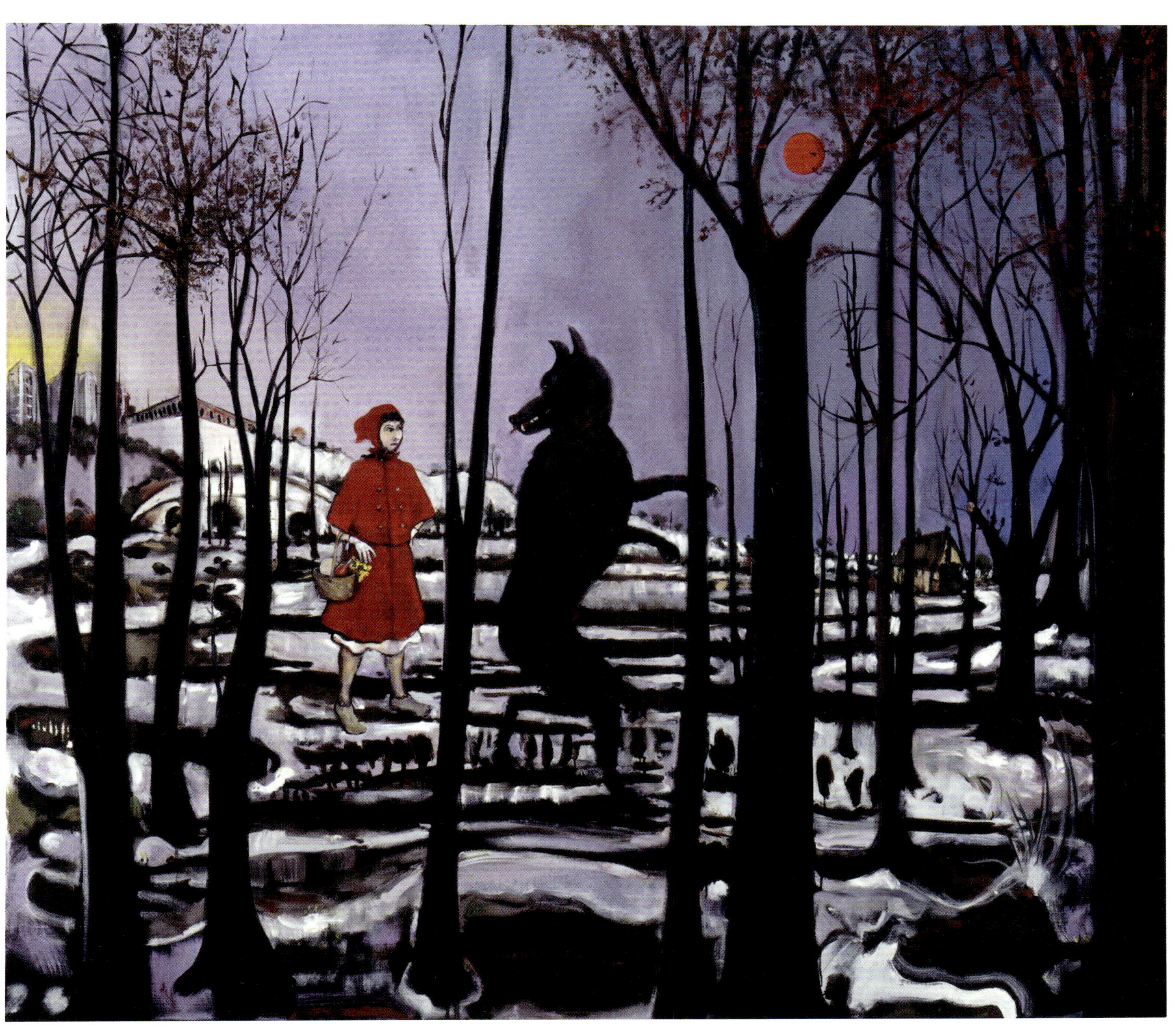

42. Red Riding Hood   2006

Oil on canvas
182.9 x 213.4 cm (72 x 84 in)
Private collection, Switzerland

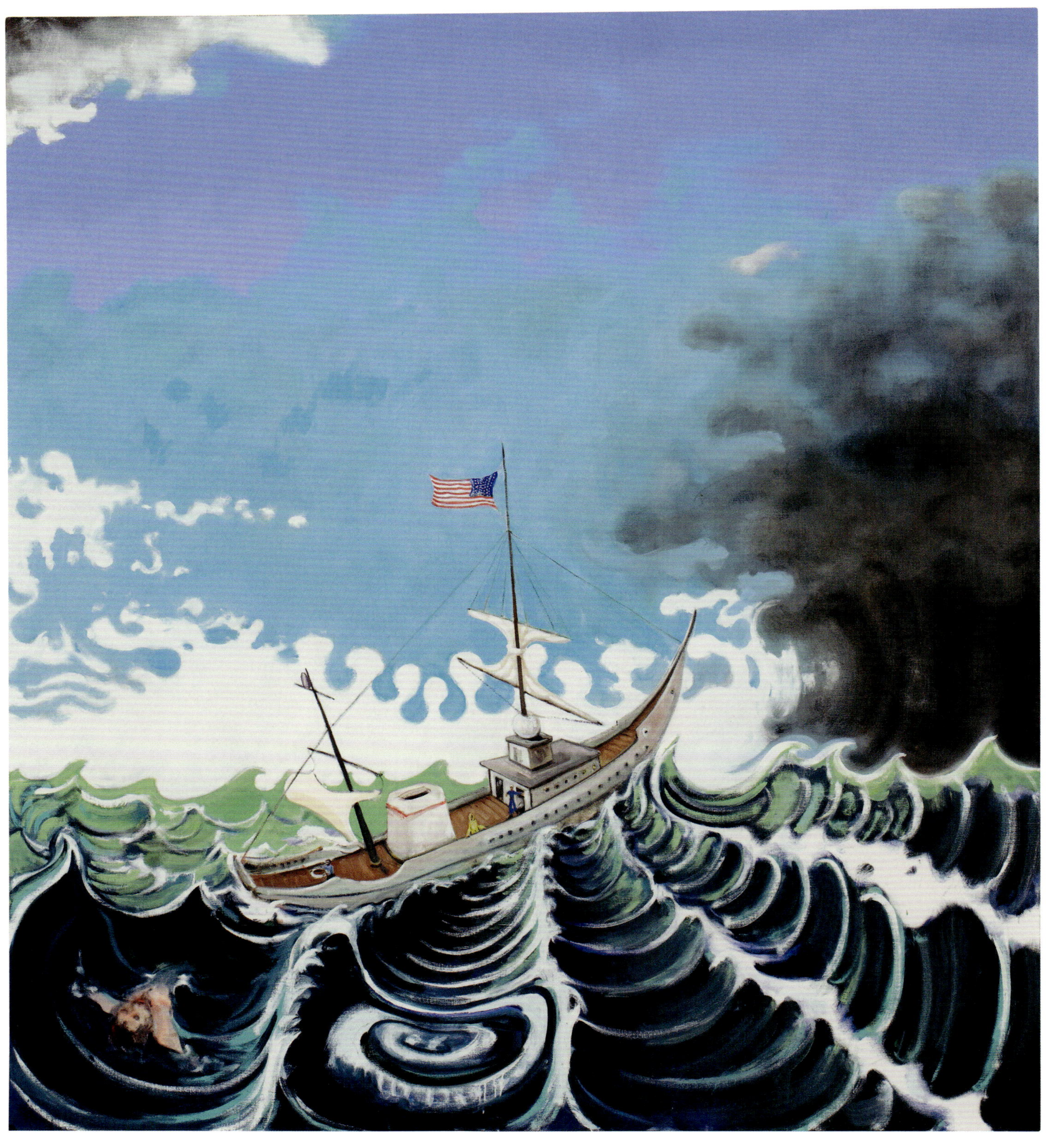

43. Jonah and the Whale (Overboard)   2009

Oil on canvas
274.3 x 254 cm (108 x 100 in)
Ringier Collection, Switzerland

64

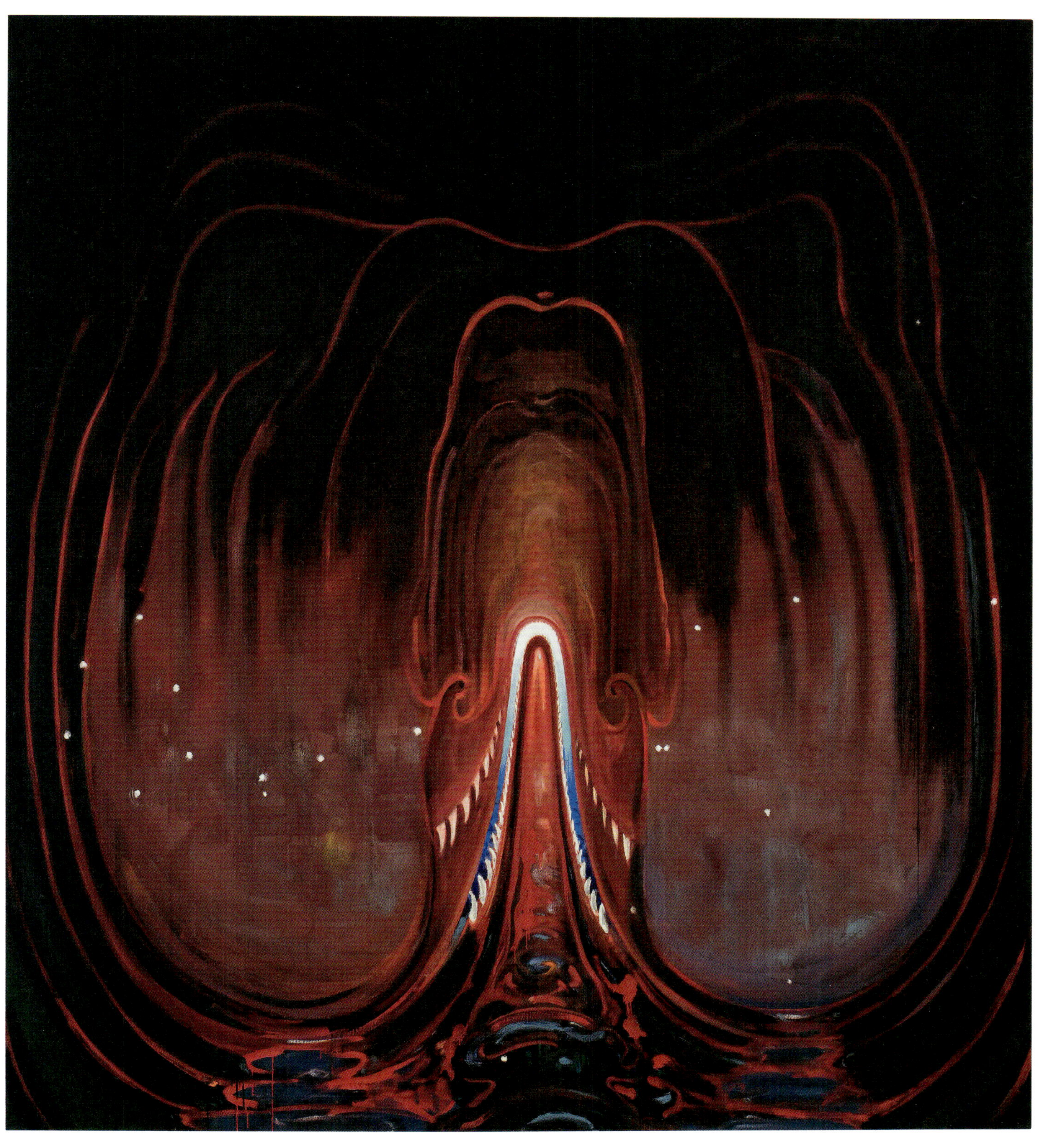

44. Jonah and the Whale (in the Whale)   2009

Oil on canvas
274.3 x 254 cm (108 x 100 in)
Ringier Collection, Switzerland

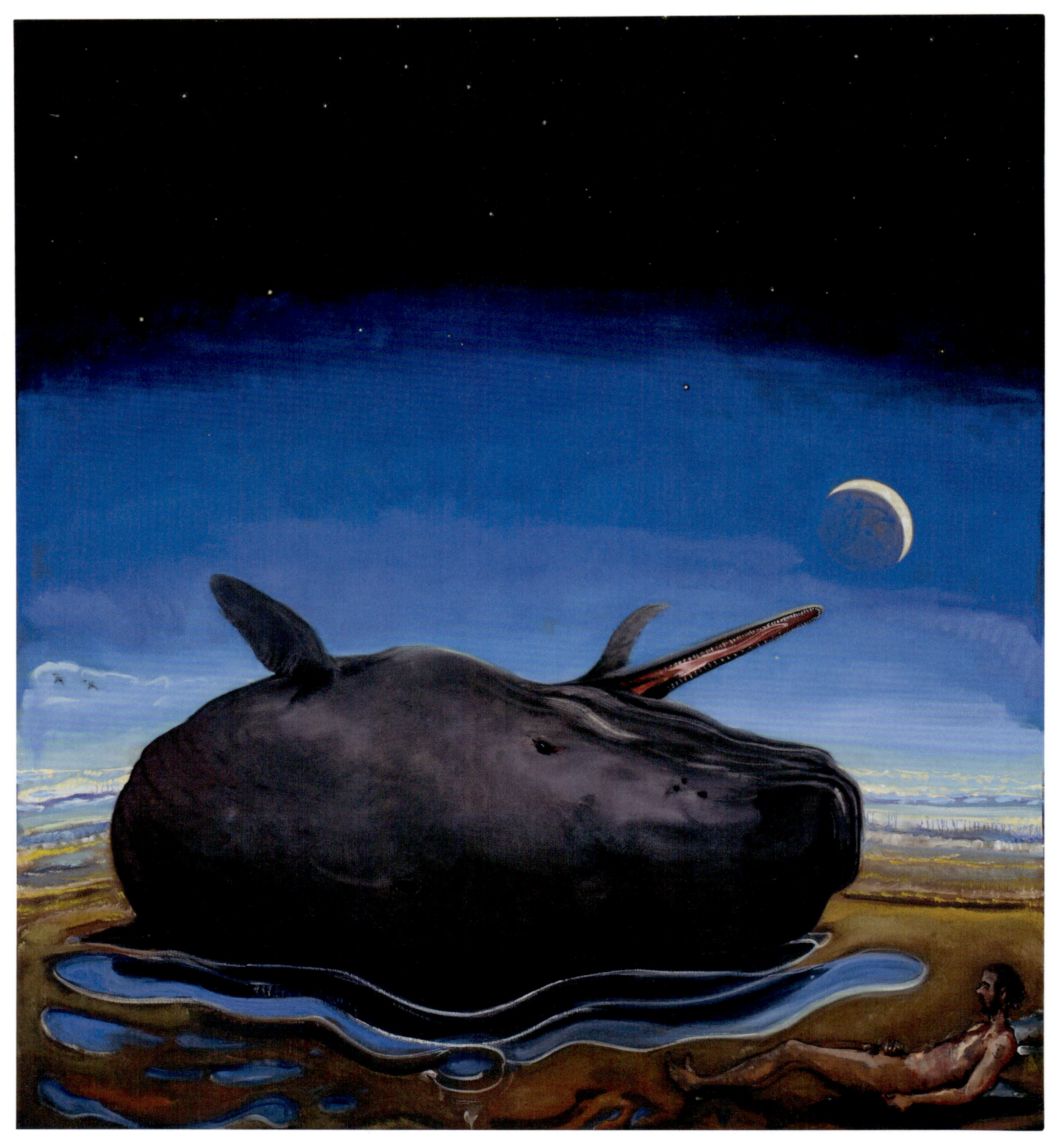

45. Jonah and the Whale (Beached and Spit Out) 2009

Oil on canvas
274.3 x 254 cm (108 x 100 in)
Ringier Collection, Switzerland

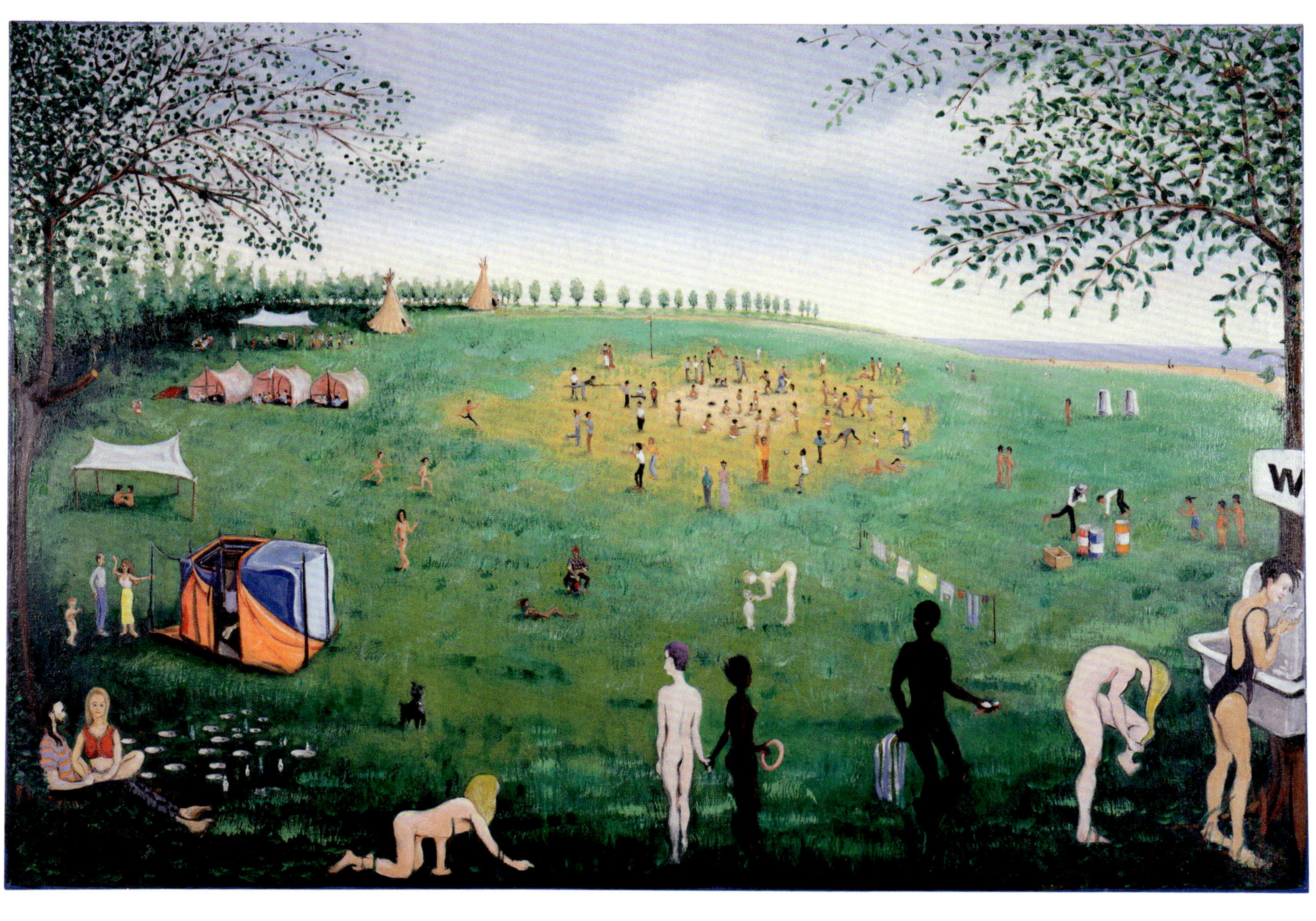

46. Rainbow Gathering   1998

Oil on canvas
124.5 x 184.8 cm (49 x 72¾ in)
Mima & César Reyes Collection, Puerto Rico

there without the pride and greed that corrupted other regions. As a trope, Arcadia refers to a lost and ideal way of life, differing from Utopia in its emphasis on the past, as opposed to the future. The inhabitants of Arcadia have something in common with the 'noble savage': they live close to nature, uncontaminated by civilization, as did the Native Americans who were depicted, although often only as token figures, in many American landscapes of the time.

Verne Dawson has painted individual Arcadian scenes, as well as a short series on the topic. In images such as *Rainbow Gathering* (fig.46) people live freely, happily and uninhibitedly in tune with the natural world. More often than not, however, his vision of the ancient world is darker and ambivalent. There are at least three series of paintings (figs 52–54) of the four seasons, collectively called 'Cycle of Quarter-Day Observances, circa 23,800BC', in which he depicts scenes that might have taken place one precession ago, more or less at the time of the Lascaux cave paintings. In them, ordinary people engage in simple work and communal life. Expanses of blue sky dominate the upper part of these paintings, and that emptiness renders the humans below small and insignificant in comparison. In *Solstice Procession in the Magdalenian Era* (fig.55), the vastness of nature is suggested by an immense mound, topped by a glowing sun, which is directly inspired by the Olduvai Gorge in Tanzania, believed to be the earliest known site of human habitation.

It is not, perhaps, by chance that Dawson's style of painting also alludes to the past. He deliberately adheres to traditional techniques: he employs lead white ground on fine linen, oil and pigments, a variety of brushes and, frequently, as if to echo ancient painting, he uses his fingers. His style is pragmatic, with only moderate effort spent on finesse: details are relatively coarse, his palette is light and modern and generally there are few glazes. And although Dawson declares that he wishes his paintings to be as beautiful as possible, they are not conventionally aesthetic. Their vision and stories are of primary importance, and the paint surface of most of his canvases is, as was once remarked about the 19th-century American landscapes of Thomas Cole, 'manifestly functional – it strives neither to efface itself nor to create an expressive network of meaning on its own account'.[22] And yet, in contrast, there is sometimes an almost rococo decorativeness in Dawson's landscapes, which can be seen in the curves of the clouds, in landscape contours, in the trees, and even in the configuration of figures (fig.68).

The connection to Thomas Cole (1801–48), one of the group of American artists that has become known as the Hudson River School, may not be entirely fortuitous, as Dawson is an admirer of his landscapes. Cole's dramatic images, particularly of upstate New York, were hugely celebrated and influential in his own day and were understood to refer, even then, in the middle years of the 19th century, to the careless erosion of nature by civilization. Occasionally he combined them both harmoniously; in one of his most famous paintings, *View from Mount Holyoke, Northampton, Massachusetts, after a Thunderstorm – The Oxbow*, 1836 (fig.47), Cole depicts the

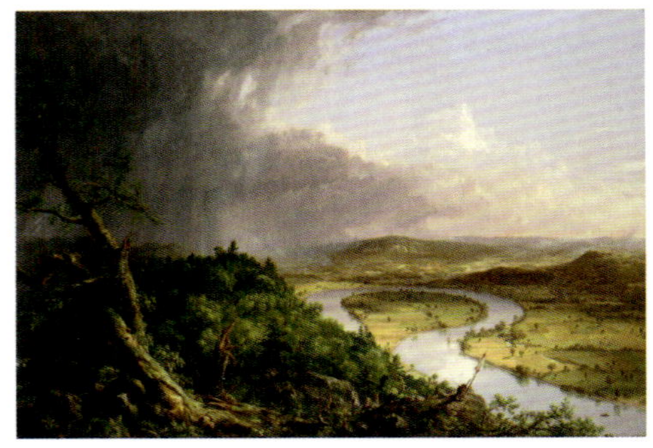

47. Thomas Cole
The Oxbow 1836

Oil on canvas
130.8 x 193 cm (51½ x 76 in)
The Metropolitan Museum of Art, New York

wilderness, complete with 'blasted tree', a traditional Romantic landscape motif, on the left, while on the right he paints a valley, agreeable and cultivated, replete with a meandering oxbow river – a device that Dawson uses, often to the point of parody, in many of his own landscapes (figs 55 and 56).

Frederic Church (1826–1900), another artist of the Hudson River School and admired by Dawson, extended Cole's heroic landscape ambitions by adding to his literary and historical allusions. Church made grand pictures infused with national and religious meanings, with specific reference to the abundance and fertility of God's creation. Establishing his reputation with immense paintings of American scenic wonders such as Niagara Falls, Church was also deeply impressed by the travel stories and scientific tracts of German naturalist Alexander von Humboldt (1769–1859). These inspired him to travel to South America, where he painted large landscapes of the equatorial Andean regions. In an interesting echo of Church's enthusiasm for exotic travel, Dawson made a series of paintings, perhaps more fanciful than factual, in which he depicts Hernando de Soto's 16th-century expedition through the American Southeast at the head of a motley band of Spanish conquistadors on a quest for the fabled fountain of youth (fig.57).

Best known for his Western landscapes, Thomas Moran (1837–1926), yet another painter of the Hudson River School, was unusual in that he occasionally inserted modern references into his classical compositions. In *Lower Manhattan from Communipaw, New Jersey*, painted in 1880, Moran depicted new variations on the traditional 'Sublime'. Although his foreground is a bucolic portrait of rural New Jersey, smokestacks and even skyscrapers are visible in the distance. Dawson has painted an intriguing variant on this theme in *Newark International Airport* (fig.51), in which, far away, a passenger jet takes off, while other planes are in the sky waiting to land. In the foreground, however, naked figures – upon close inspection, native peoples – wade through chest-high grass in a primeval landscape, recognizable as what is now the Meadowlands. A companion piece, *Manhattan* (fig.50), shows a broad river and scrubby land with a thin covering of trees. Smoke from a tiny fire curls into the vast sky in this barren, barely inhabited landscape.

★

Images such as *May Day, Les Eyzies* and *When Santa was a Shaman* (fig.52), both part of the large 'Cycle of Quarter-Day Observances, circa 23,800BC' series, and *Rainbow Gathering* (fig.46) include groups of people that evoke a communitarian spirit and the ethos of 1960s countercultural or hippie festivals. These events, in turn, had their roots in cultural currents that had flourished decades beforehand. Utopian ideals in 19th-century America were at least as influential and widespread as they were a hundred years later – not only were they just as radical, but also a far broader range of people adopted them. Unlike the 1960s, when the counterculture

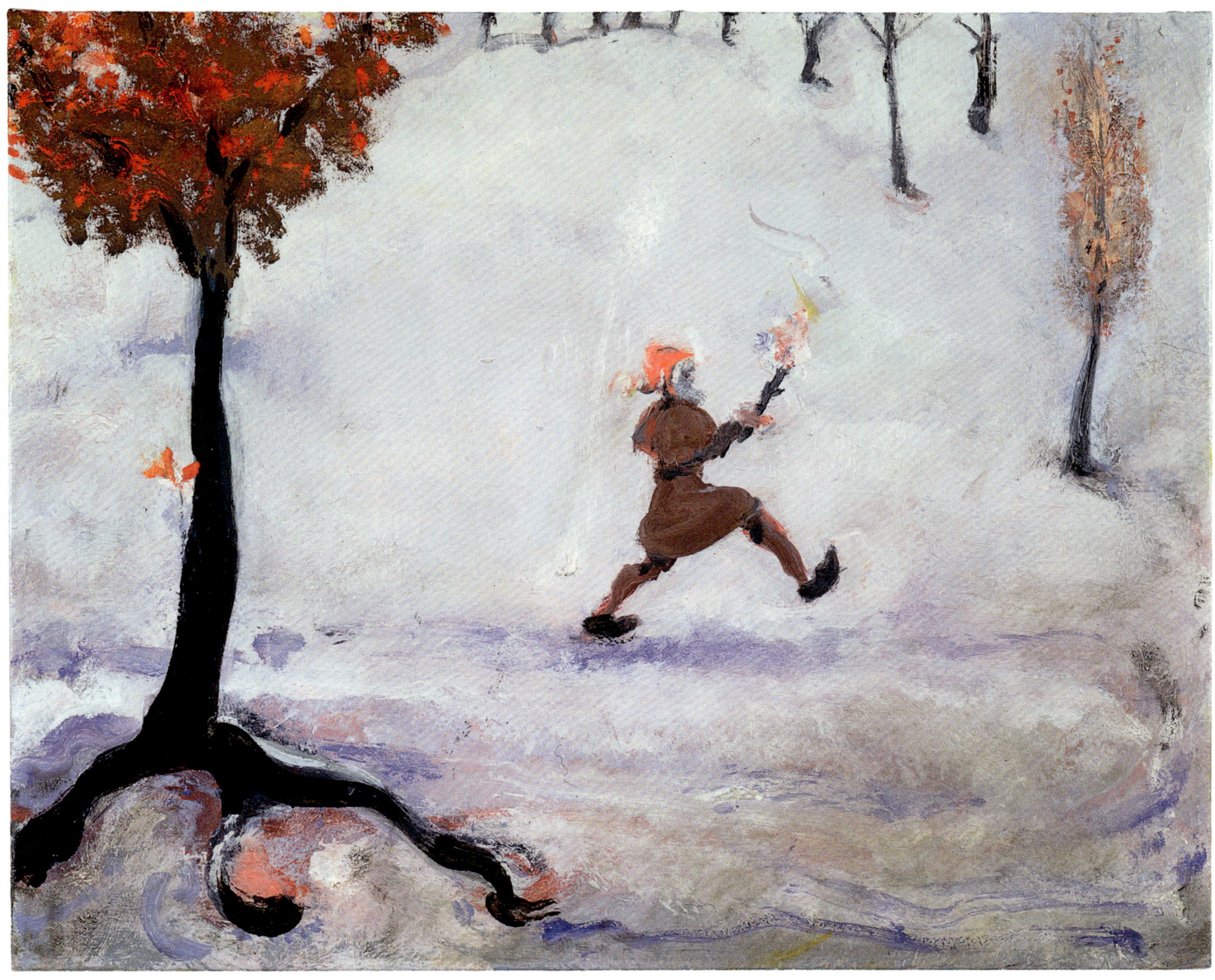

48. Study for Winter   2001

Oil on canvas
40.6 x 50.8 cm (16 x 20 in)
Ringier Collection, Switzerland

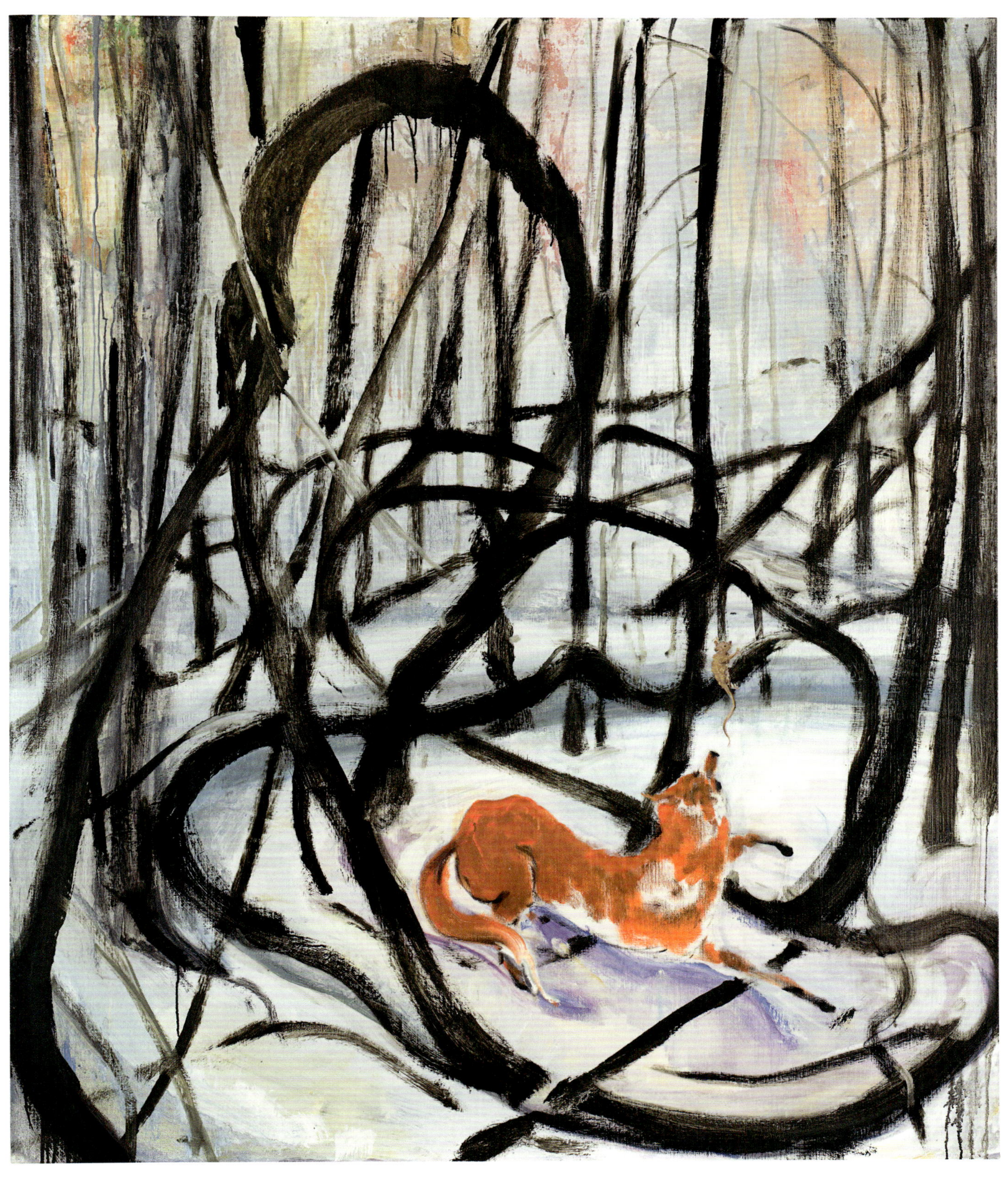

49. Fox in the Snow (Bonjour M. Courbet)   2008

Oil on canvas
160 x 137.2 cm (63 x 54 in)
Dallas Museum of Art, gift of the Rachofsley Collection

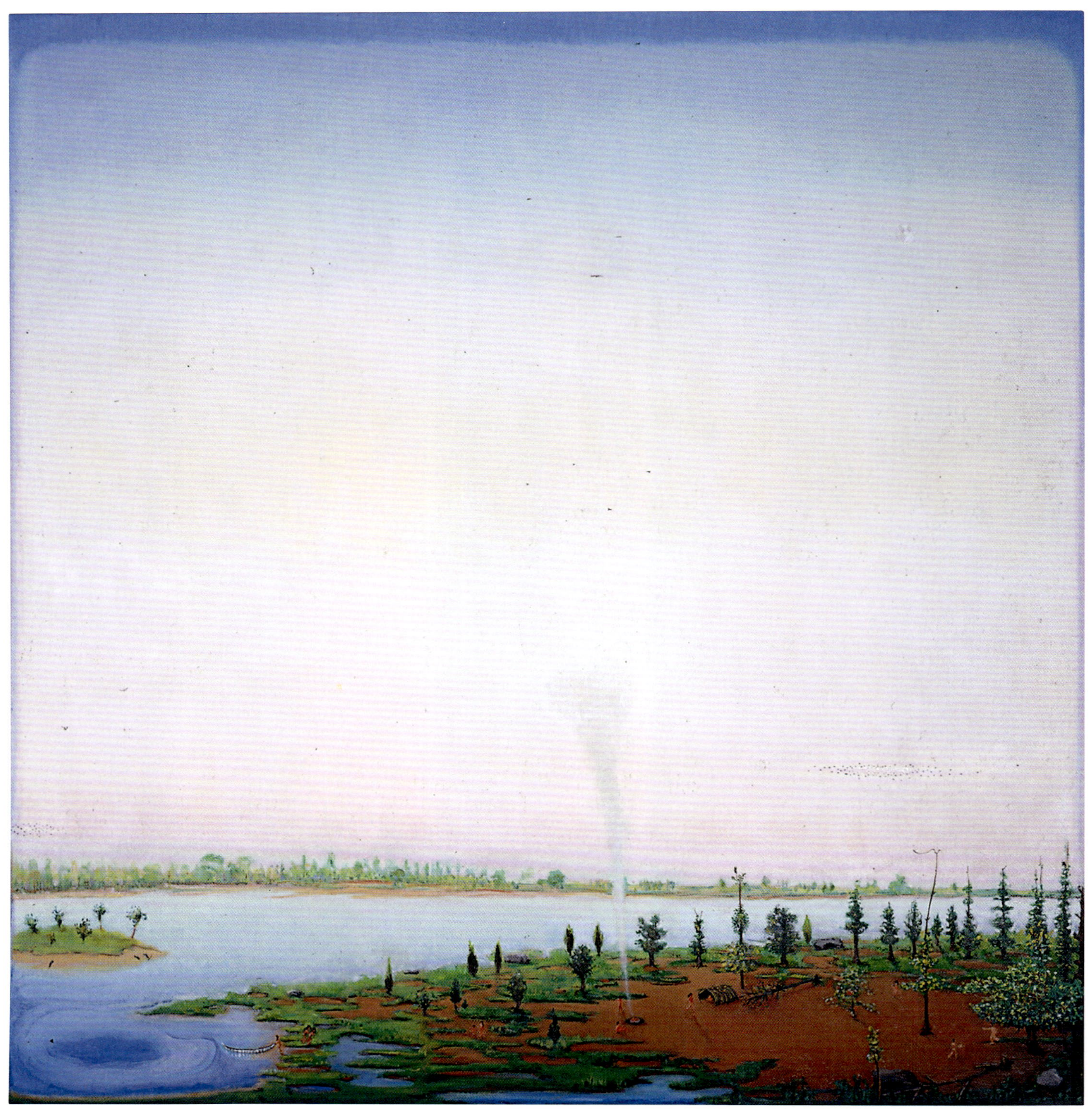

50. Manhattan   1998

Oil on canvas
182.9 x 182.9 cm (72 x 72 in)
Ringier Collection, Switzerland

51. Newark International Airport   1998

Oil on canvas
102.2 x 92.1 cm (40¼ x 36¼ in)
Private collection

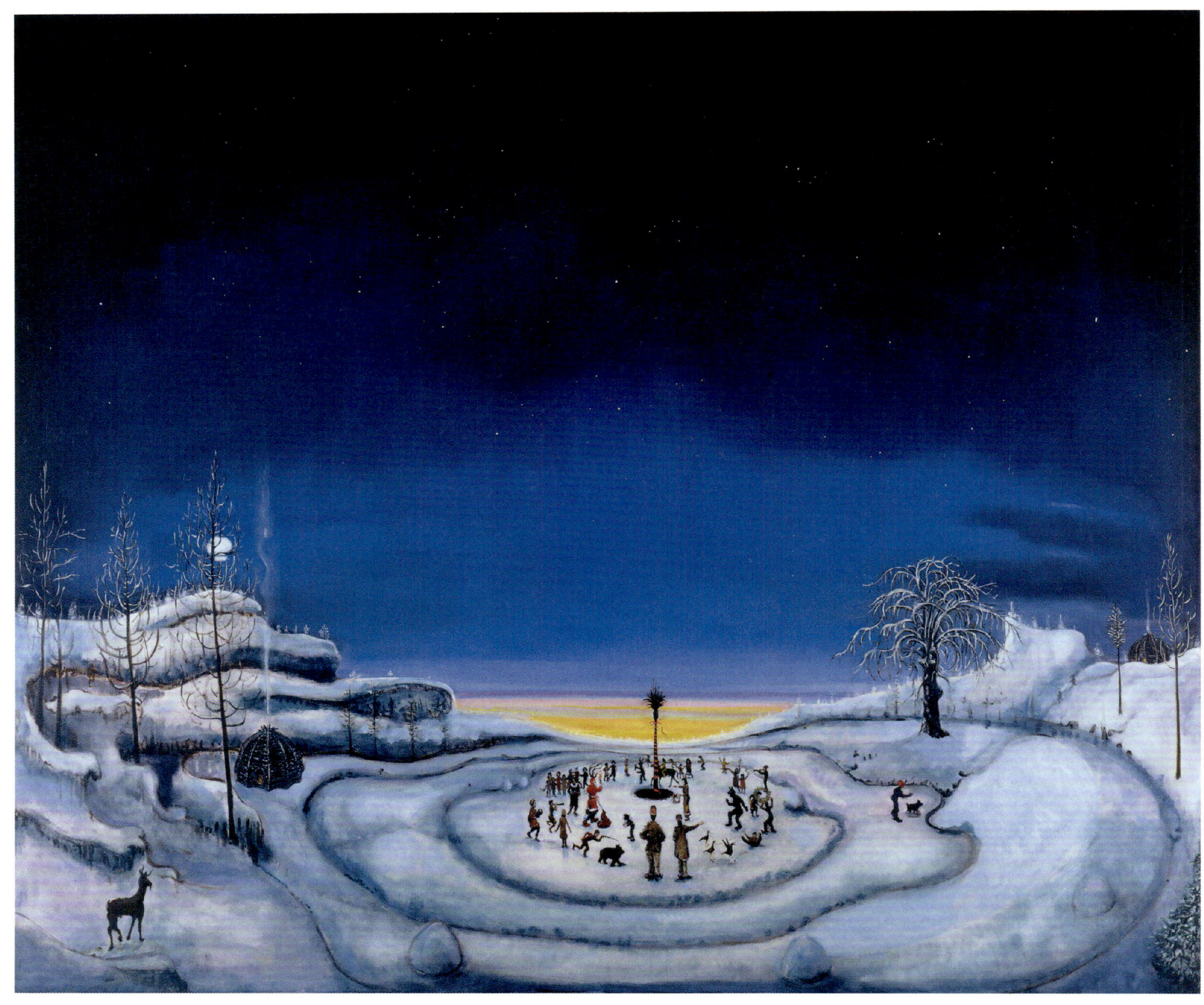

52. Cycle of Quarter-Day Observances, circa
23,800BC When Santa was a Shaman   1999

Oil on canvas
208.3 x 254 cm (82 x 100 in)
Mima & César Reyes Collection, Puerto Rico

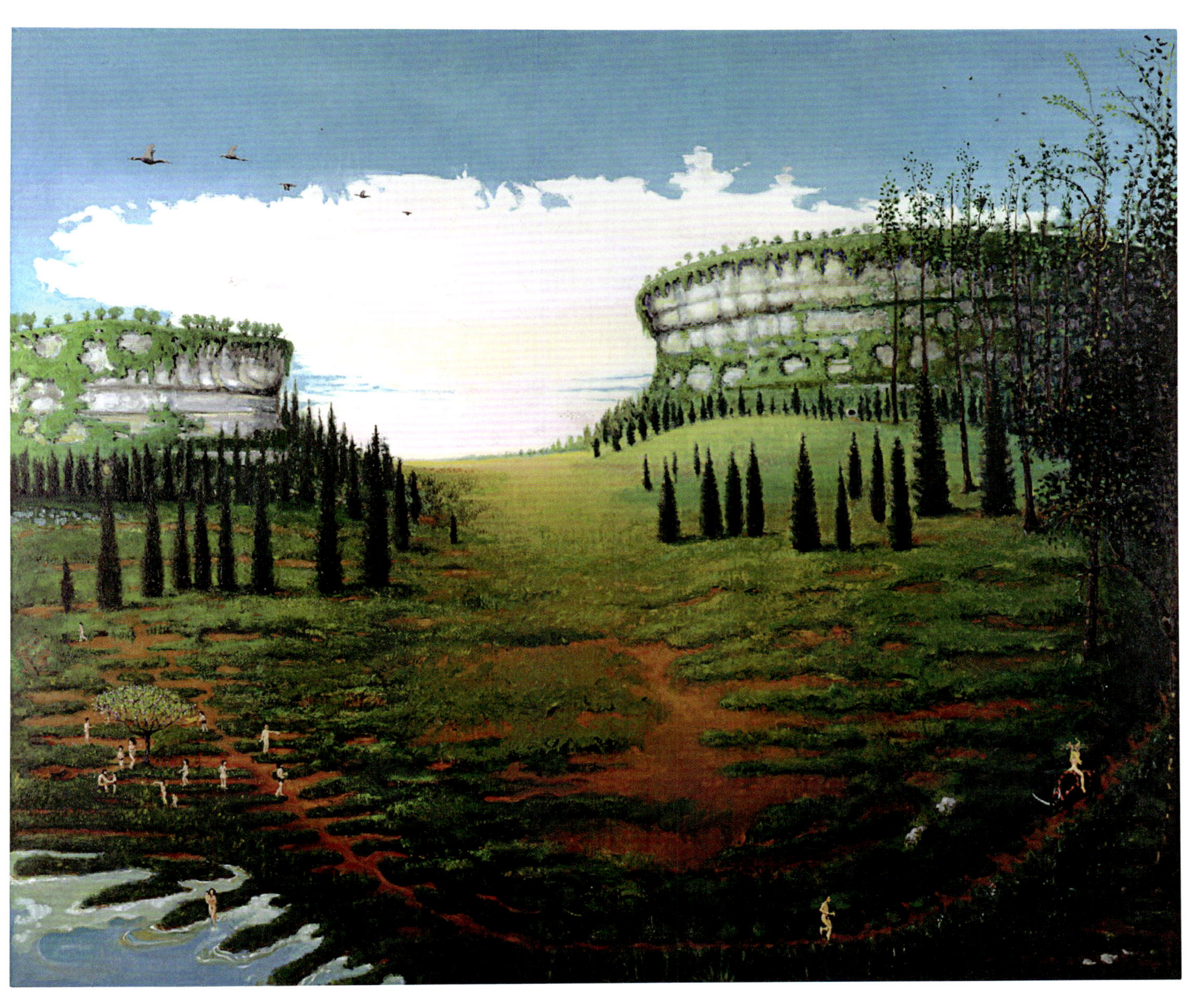

53. Cycle of Quarter-Day Observances, circa 23,800BC May Day, Les Eyzies   1999

Oil on canvas
208.3 x 254 cm (82 x 100 in)
Nancy Delman Portnoy, New York

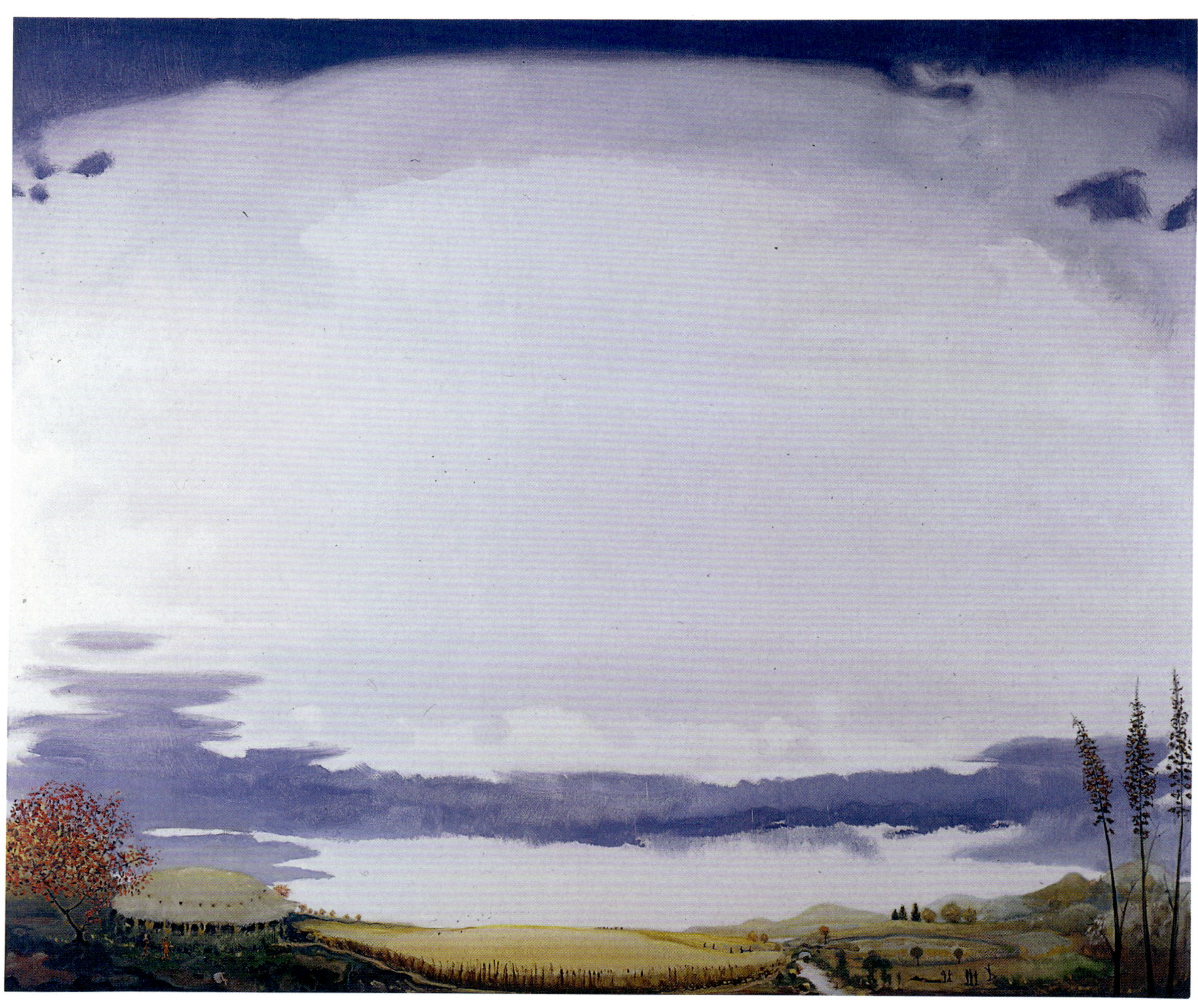

54. Cycle of Quarter-Day Observances, circa
23,800BC Burial in Autumn   2001

Oil on canvas
208.3 x 254 cm (82 x 100 in)
Private collection, New York

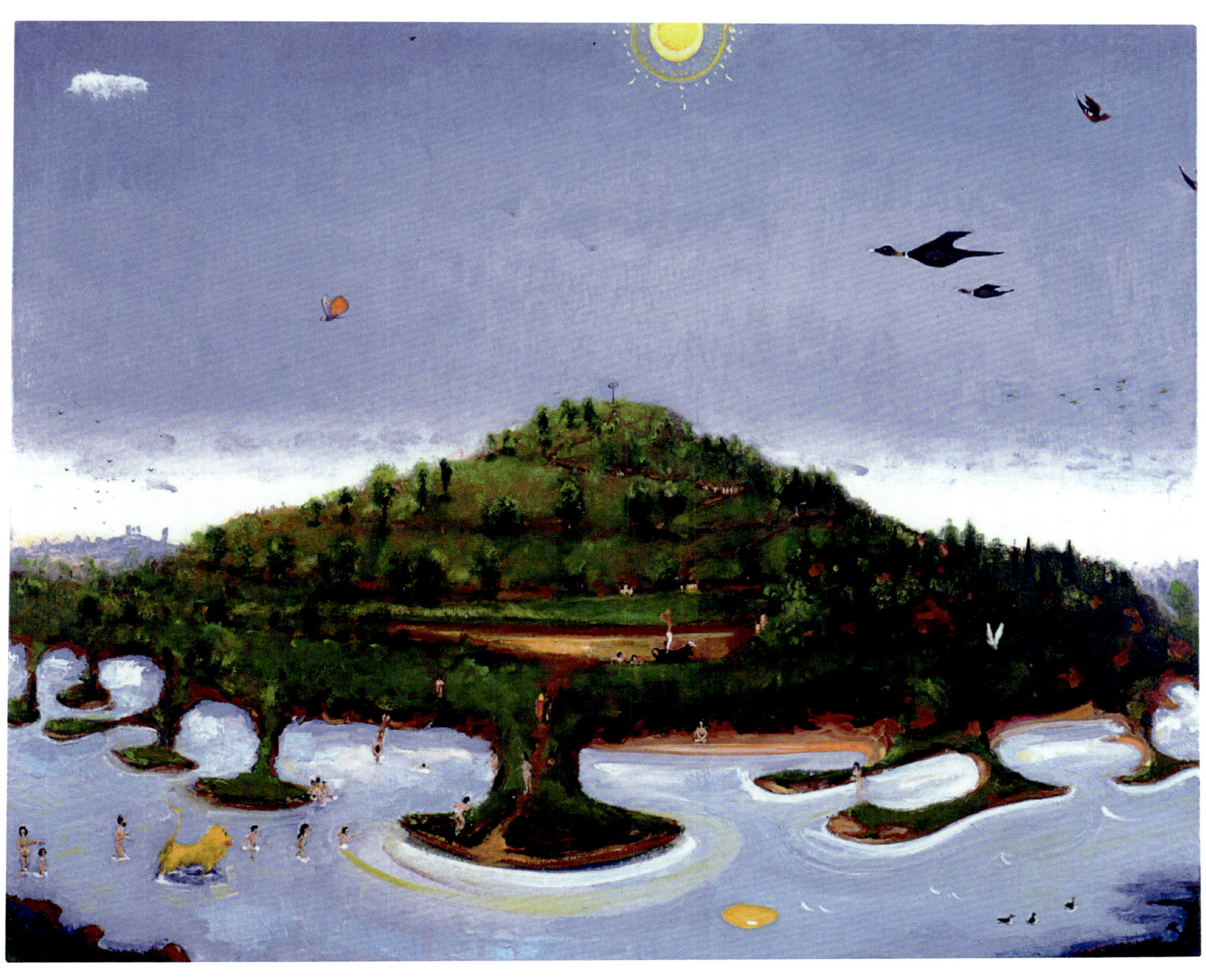

55. Solstice Procession in the
Magdalenian Era   2000

Oil on canvas
One of four parts, each 76.2 x 96.5 cm (each 30 x 38 in)
Speyer Family Collection, New York

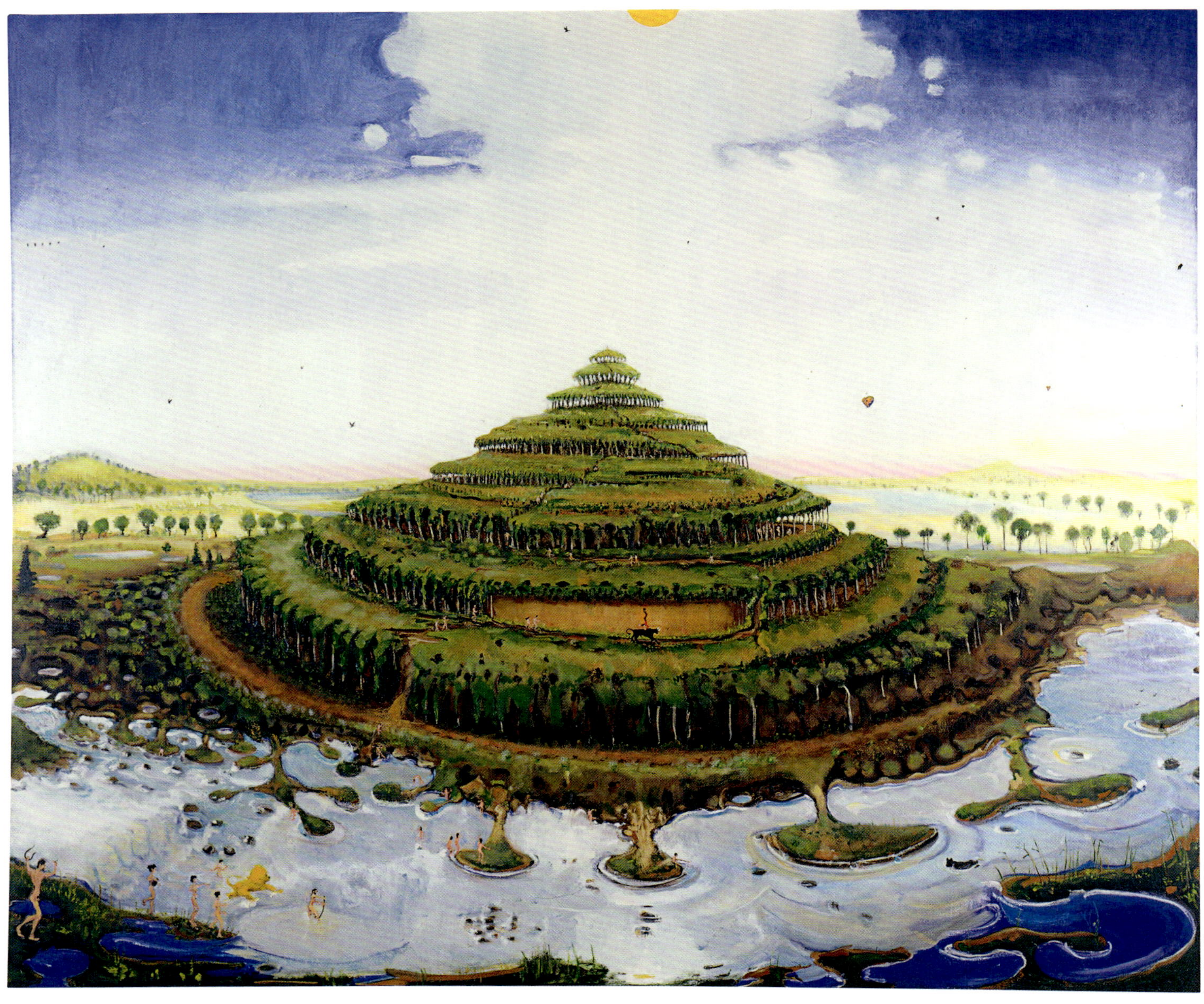

56. Cycle of Quarter-Day Observances, circa 23,800BC
Solstice Procession in the Magdalenian Era   2001

Oil on canvas
208.3 x 254 cm (82 x 100 in)
Courtesy Gavin Brown Collection, New York

57. Apalachicola   2011

Oil on canvas
40.6 x 30.5 cm (16 x 12 in)
Private collection

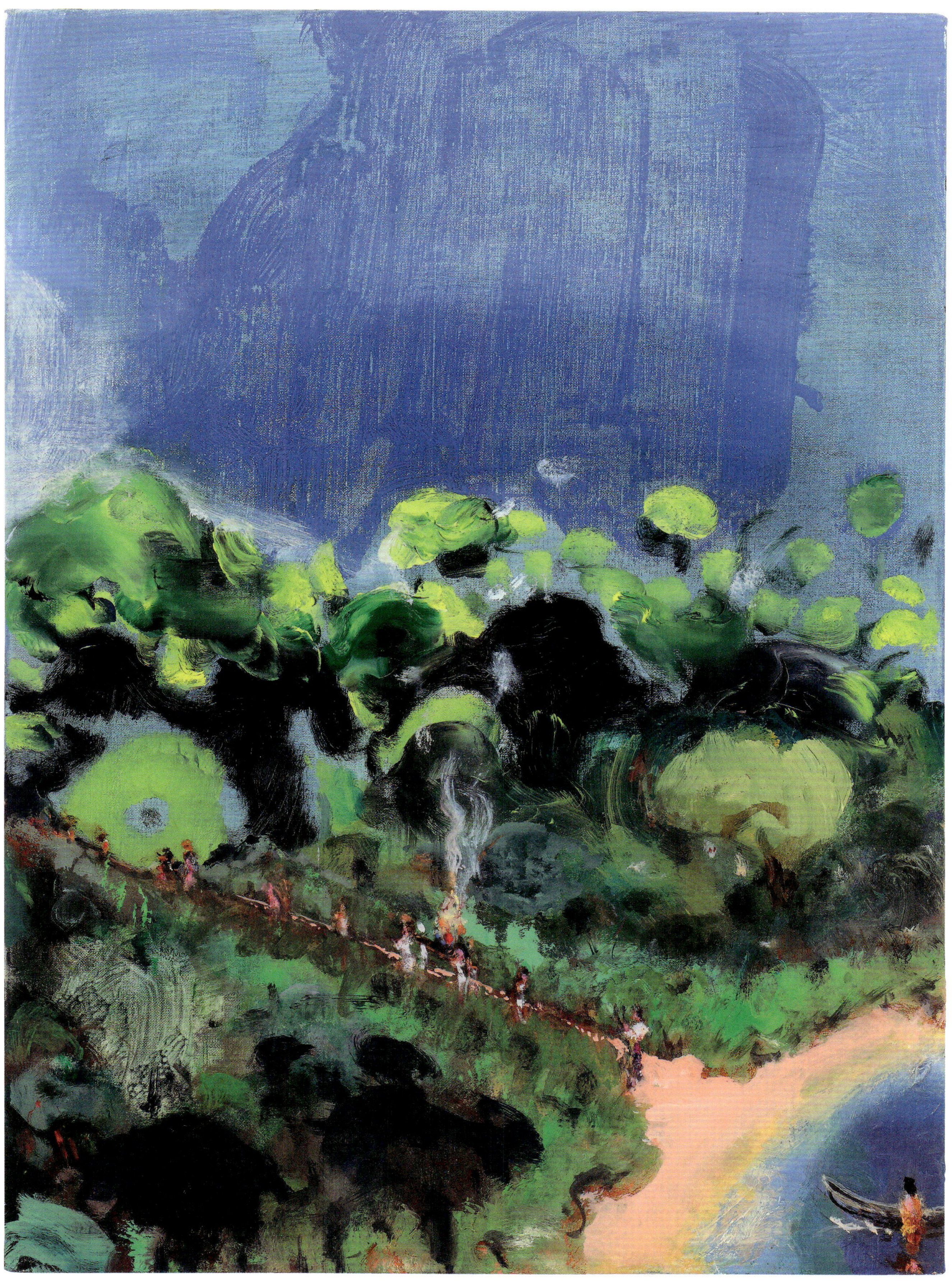

was mainly composed of 'dropouts' and students, 19th-century Utopians included farmers, preachers, writers and bankers. They were all attracted to progressive ideas and often joined communities, based on the belief that the earth could become something of a paradise in which these notions could be expressed and lived. Most of these communities were short-lived, in part due to the Civil War, which destroyed or eroded cultural optimism. Nonetheless, in the economic boom that followed the war, the Utopian spirit came to life again. German-American painter Alfred Bierstadt, with his sweeping views of the Sierra Nevada and Yosemite, reflected that new sense of optimism. As in the decades after World War II, the American economy flourished, bringing with it dramatic expansion into the West, and especially into California, which became the place in which people could invest their dreams and fantasies.

Connections between 19th- and 20th-century Utopianism in California, and a faint German influence on their expression, are intriguing. In the 1940s, Nat 'King' Cole sang a song to live audiences about a boy who wanders the earth in search of his dream 'to love and be loved in return'. When he later decided to record the song, called 'Nature Boy', it became an international hit. Its composer, Eden Ahbez, however, could not be found. Eventually he was traced to a campsite under the first 'L' of the HOLLYWOOD sign in the hills behind Los Angeles. Ahbez, who spent his early years in the Brooklyn Hebrew Orphan Asylum of New York, and then, after adoption, in Kansas, also slept in the backyard orchard of John and Vera Richter, raw-food enthusiasts who lived in Silver Lake and owned several health-food restaurants in Los Angeles. Ahbez, long before the hippies of the 1960s, wore shoulder-length hair, a beard, sandals and flowing white clothes.

In their natural lifestyle, the Richters were influenced by the late-19th-century German *Naturmensch* and *Wandervogel* movements, and their younger friends and followers, including Ahbez, eventually became known as 'Nature Boys'. Although in the vanguard of postwar countercultural life, they were not actually innovators – in 1916, a German immigrant and *Naturmensch* called William Pester (1885–1963) arrived in Palm Springs when it was a small village populated by a handful of settlers and Native Americans. He and his friends, who have been described as the original hippies, lived the simple life well into the 1940s and 1950s, in caves and canyons, almost oblivious to mainstream cultural concerns. In a period when most of America was recovering from the effects of World War II, this group of German and American young people, some of them Jewish, were living together in almost Neolithic fashion, subsisting on fruit and nuts, swimming in pools under waterfalls in the desert canyons, hiking through the mountains, practising yoga and composing music.[23] None of this, it must be said, has had a direct influence on Dawson, but American Utopianism is undoubtedly an ideological context in which his work resonates strongly.

The 1960s American counterculture was predominantly idealistic, but it also had a negative aspect, not only because it was in part defined by resistance to the Vietnam War, but also because it suffered from waves of irrational malevolence, as reflected by

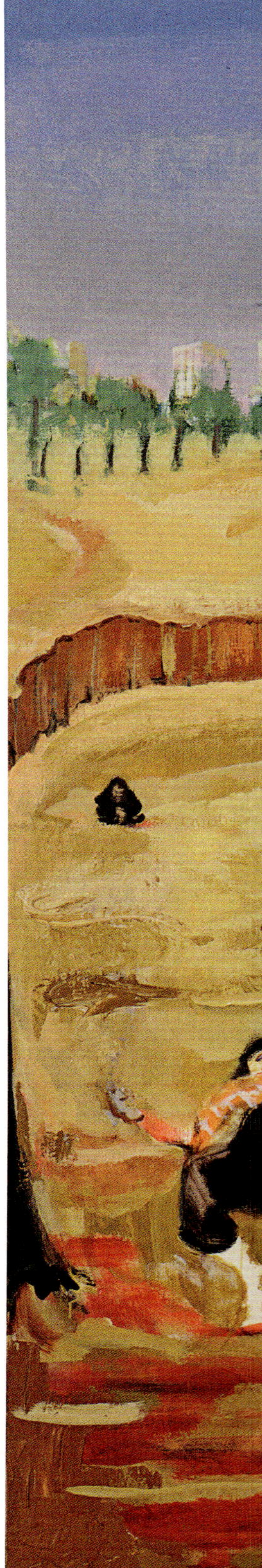

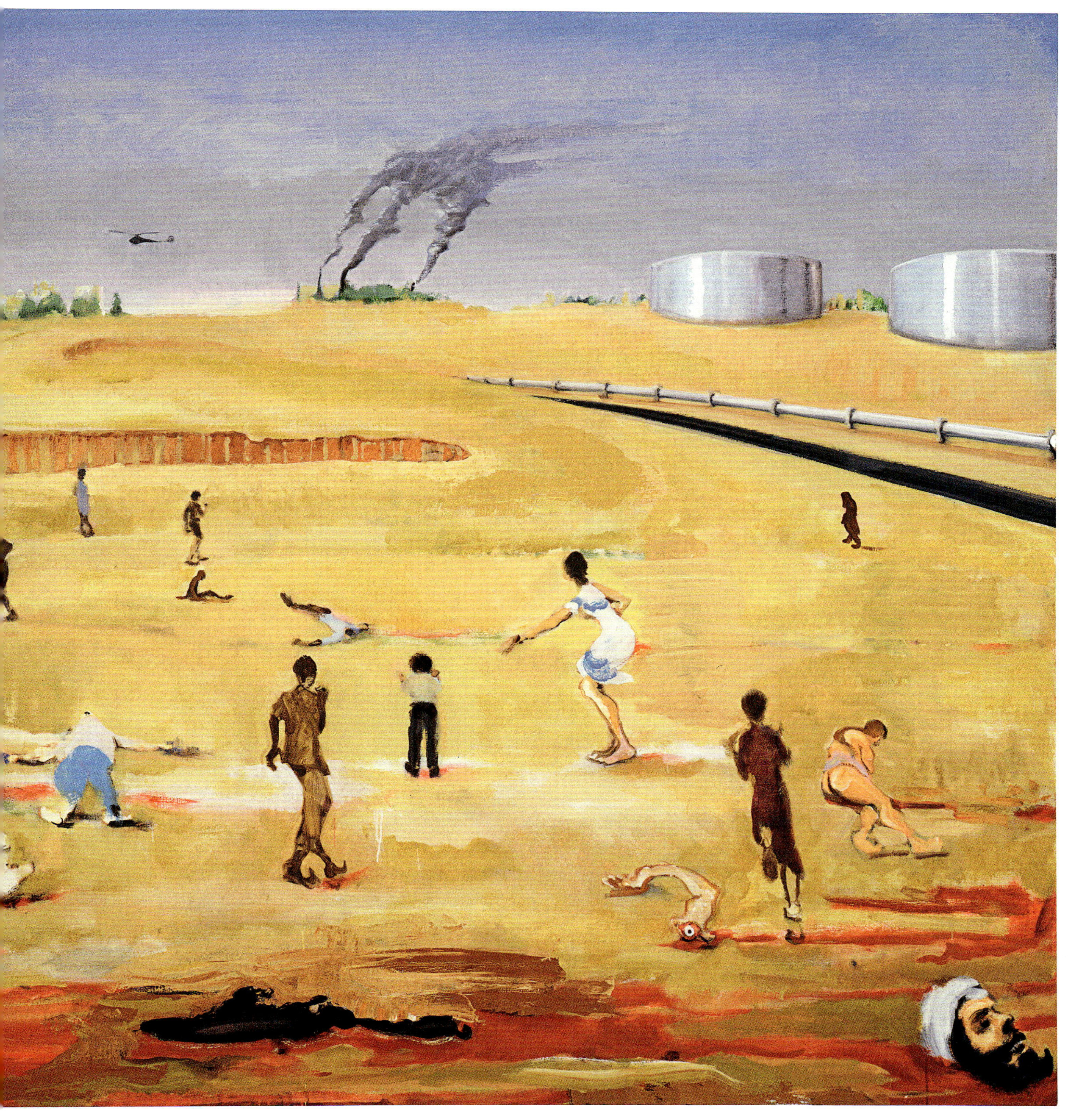

58. Massacre   2004

Oil on canvas
177.8 x 218.4 cm (70 x 86 in)
Ringier Collection, Switzerland

the violence at the Altamont music festival in 1969, the Charles Manson murders and, fictionally, in the film *Easy Rider* (Dennis Hopper, 1969). By the same token, Verne Dawson has painted several gruesome images that counter his own prelapsarian idylls. There are the two hard-hitting *Massacre* scenes (fig.58) that recall the spirit of Francisco Goya's gloomy series 'The Disasters of War' (1810–20), but refer to more contemporary conflicts in the Middle East. There is also a pair of more far-fetched and slyly humorous earlier images called *Massacre of the Little People by the Big People* (figs 59 and 60), which tells the story of the massacre of diminutive tribes of people in Britain by the Saxons, Franks and Vikings. It is said, Dawson explains, that when these little people were threatened they went deep into the woods and forests to hide from the slaughter. After their disappearance, they became increasingly smaller in the imagination of their assailants and were thus the possible source of tales about leprechauns and fairies.[24]

There is precedence for epic violence in contemporary Southern tales, most famously perhaps in the 1972 film *Deliverance* (John Boorman). Shot in the countryside not far from Dawson's home, and featuring the famous 'Dueling Banjos' as its theme tune, the film is a catastrophic nightmare of brutal machismo and tells of a clash between urban and wilderness cultures in rural Georgia. Although he has seen it several times, Dawson does not cite the film as a direct influence; he does, however, credit the more recent and more uplifting film set in the South, *Beasts of the Southern Wild* (Benh Zeitlin, 2012). Some echoes of the film, about a devastating flood in a bayou community in Louisiana, appear in Dawson's paintings *Flood on the Delaware* (fig.61) and the lyrical *Infant with Alligator* (fig.62). In the film, a community of misfit survivors live on a strip of land called 'the Bathtub', situated on the vulnerable side of a levee somewhere on the coast of Louisiana. Their shacks are rough, dirty and broken; dogs, chickens and pigs live with the humans in relaxed and easy squalor. No one is concerned with cleanliness, proper behaviour, material wealth or social status, but the values of loyalty, caring and affection come to the fore when the Bathtub is struck by crisis. Seen through the eyes of its protagonist, a young girl called Hushpuppy, the film has an almost hallucinatory quality. As the story slowly unfolds it begins to echo a countercultural myth: the people of the Bathtub, anarchically independent, have no wish to do anything but enjoy their unconventional and archaic existence in untrammelled freedom.

★

Jacques Vallée (b.1939), a French scientist and expert in ufology, suggested that encounters with aliens, whether real or imaginary, might be of the same order as those with fairies in the past, and that they are part of a phenomenon that is variously interpreted but essentially constant.[25] In a book called *Passport to Magonia: From Folklore to Flying Saucers*, published in 1969, at the height of the counterculture, Vallée further proposed that it might be more reasonable to suppose that we may be

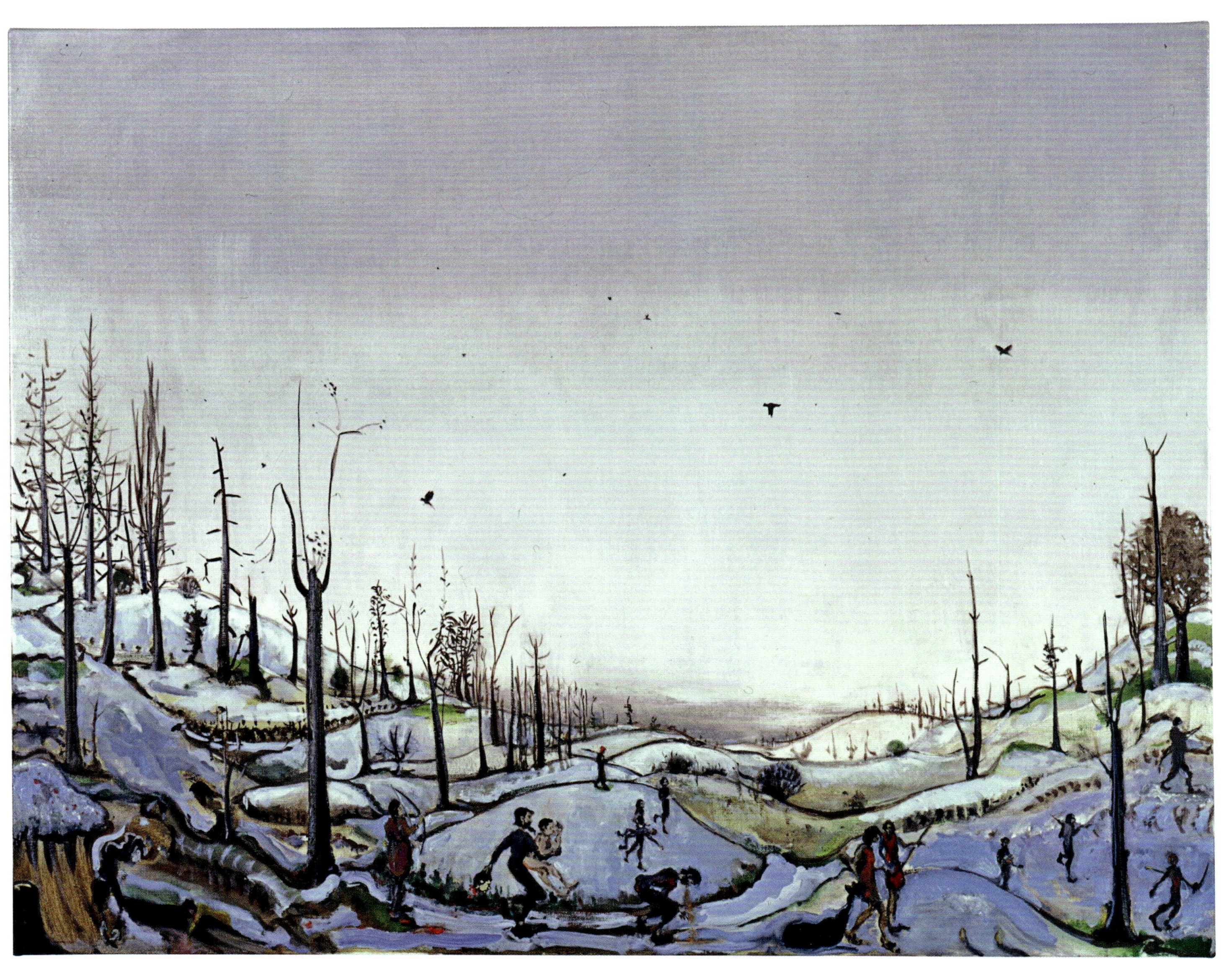

59. Massacre of the Little People by the
Big People   2002

Oil on canvas
91.4 x 116.8 cm (36 x 46 in)
Collection of James Keith Brown and Eric Diefenback

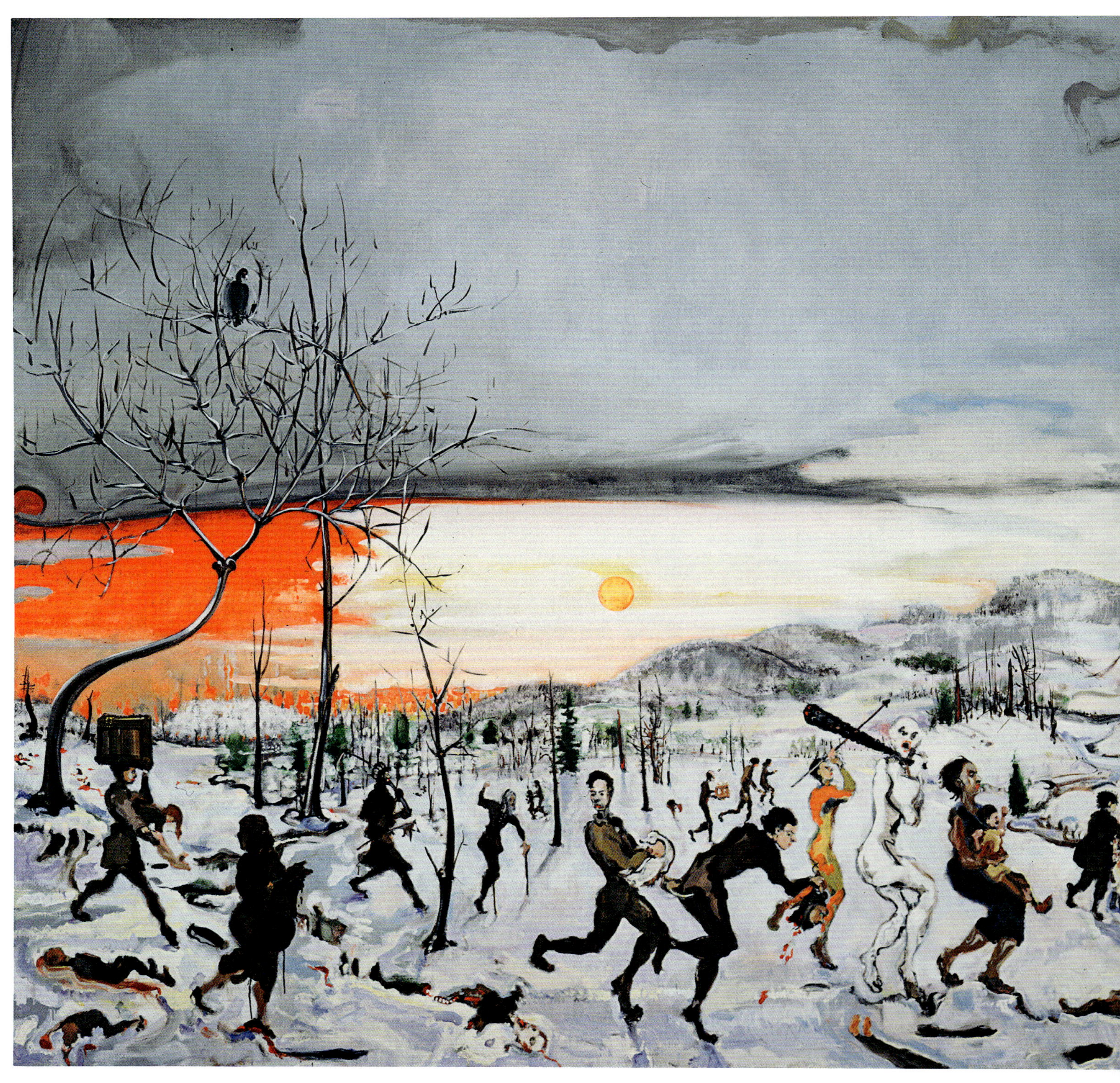

60. Massacre of the Little People by the Big People   2002/2003

Oil on canvas
208.3 x 254 cm (82 x 100 in)
Private collection

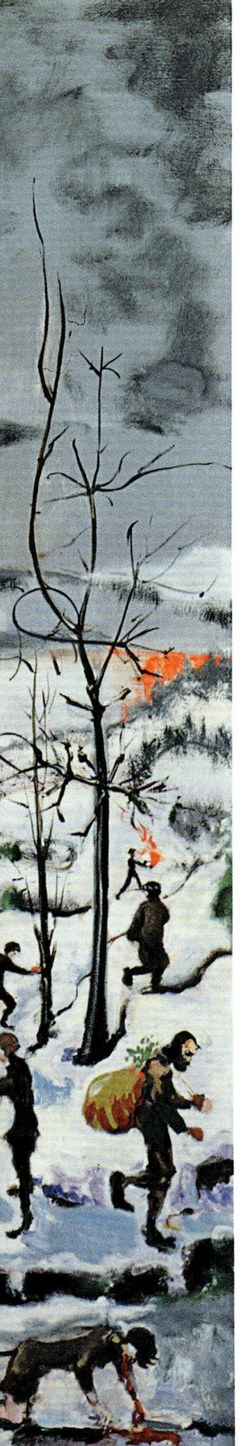

61. Flood on the Delaware   2007

Oil on canvas
160 x 137.2 cm (63 x 54 in)
Burger Collection, Hong Kong

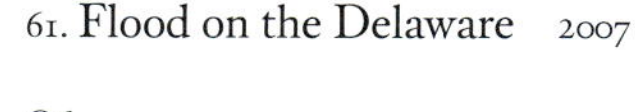

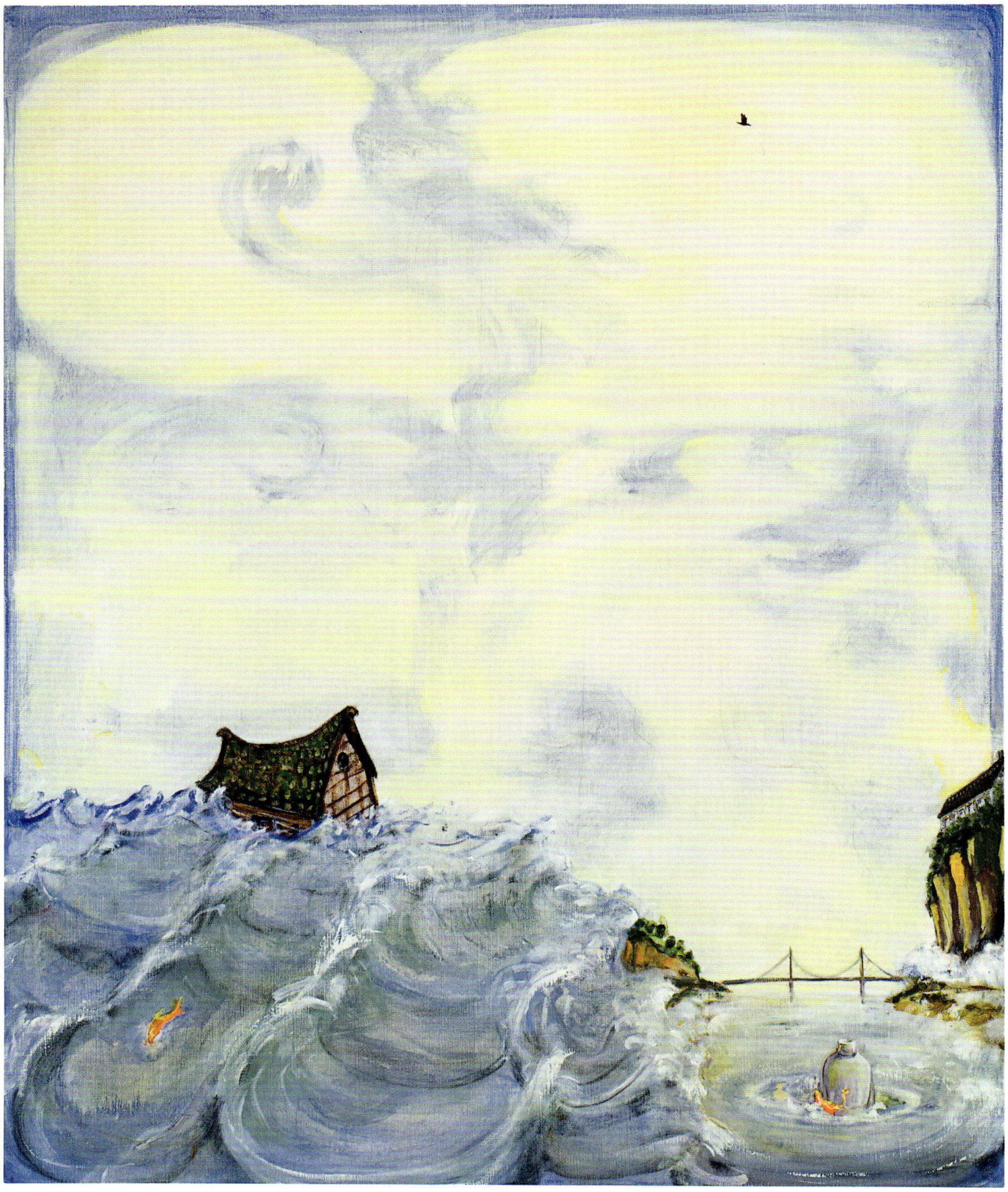

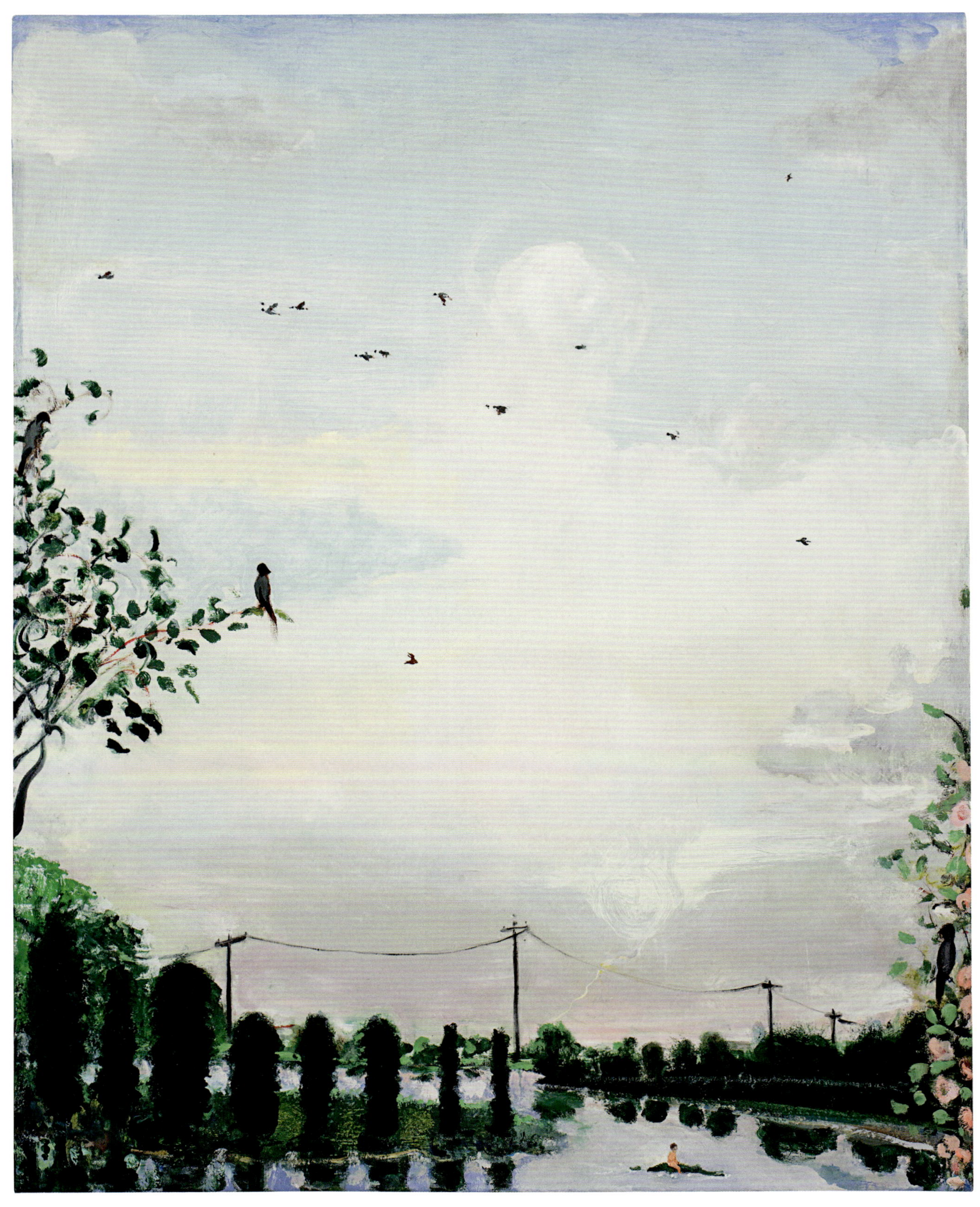

62. Infant with Alligator   2009

Oil on canvas
111.8 x 91.4 cm (44 x 36 in)
Private collection

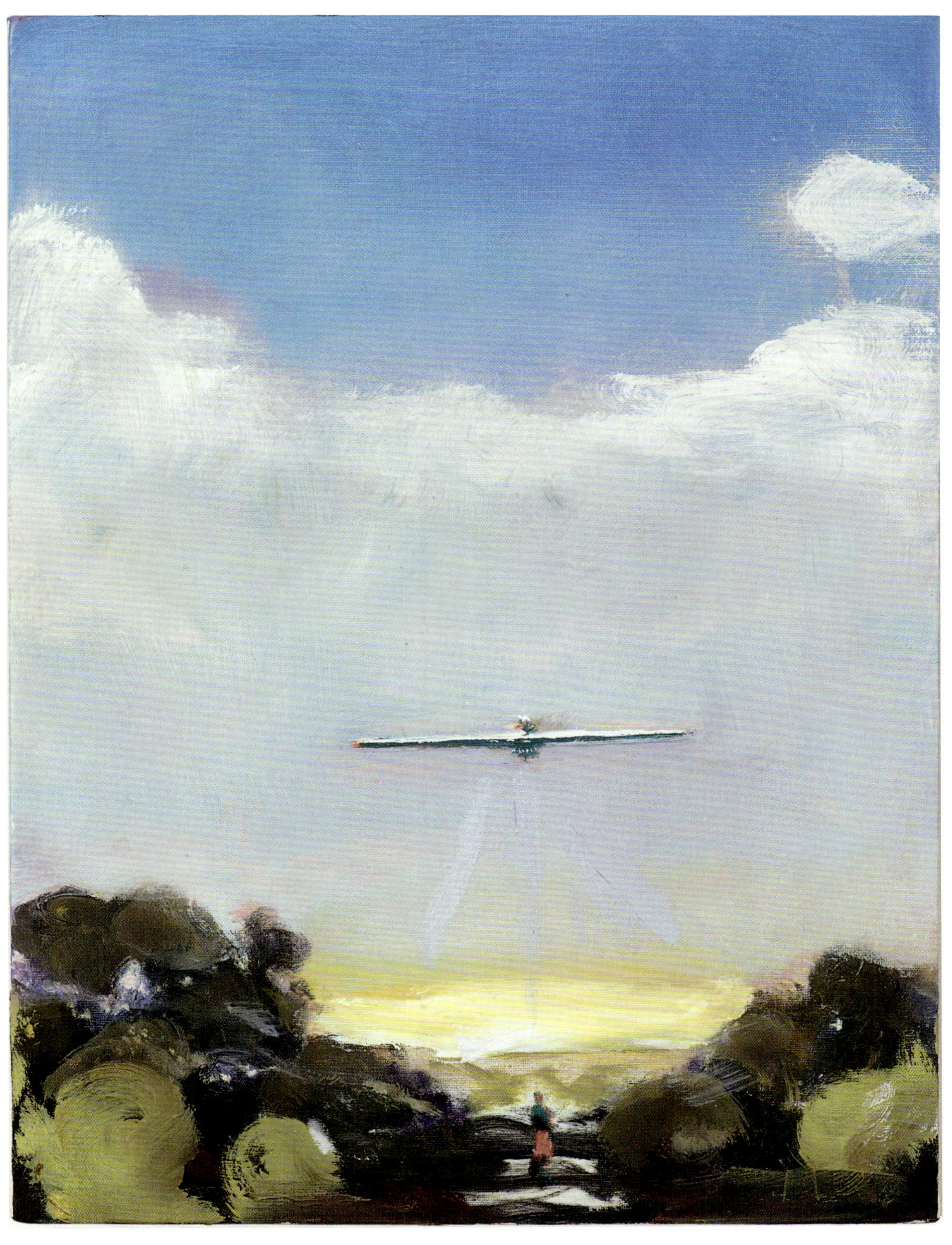

63. UFO (2)   2015

Oil on canvas
45.7 x 35.6 cm (18 x 14 in
Collection Keller, Switzerland

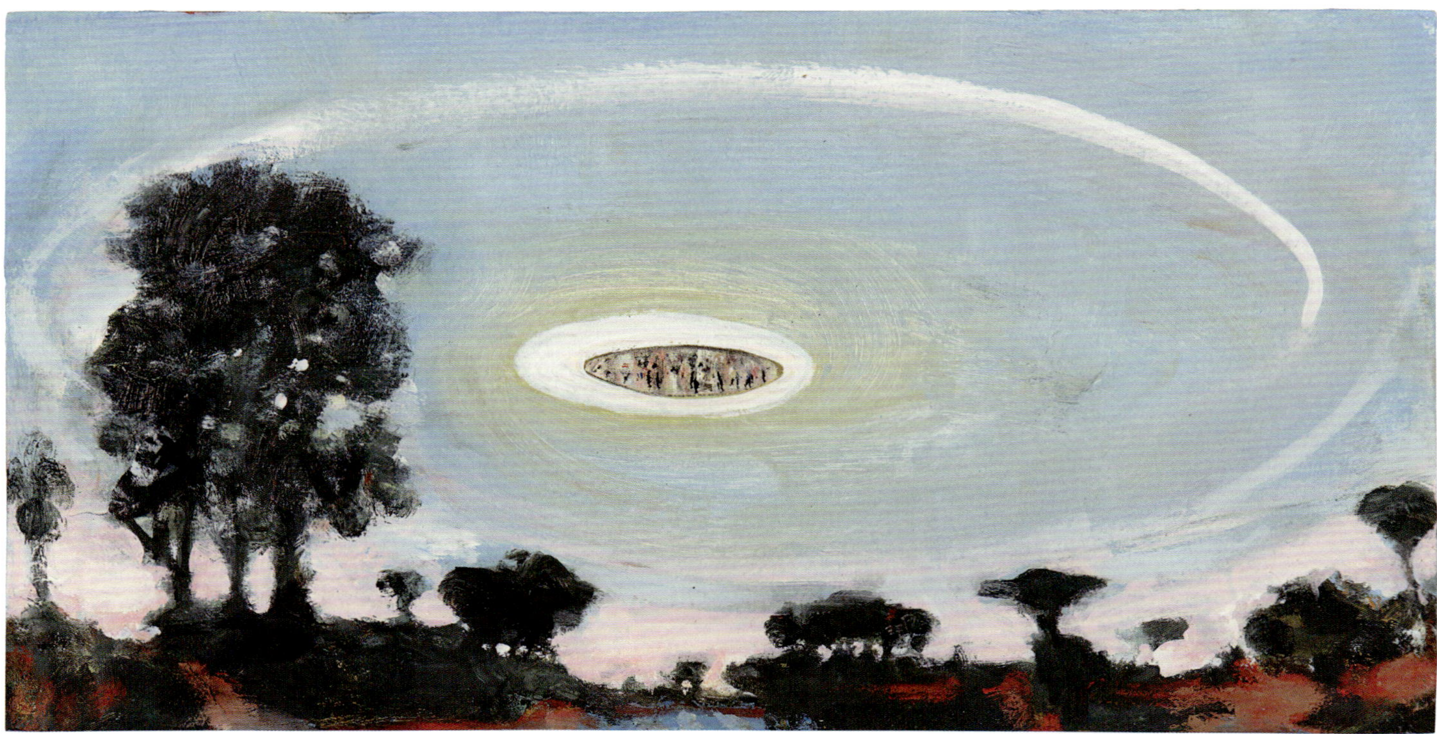

64. UFO   2017

Oil on wood panel
30.5 x 61 x 1.9 cm (12 x 24 x ¾ in)
Courtesy Gavin Brown's enterprise, New York/Rome

projecting space-age notions on to a timeless and persistent experience than to believe in visitations by aliens from other worlds. Vallée called himself a 'heretic among heretics' — a believer in UFOs who also rejected the UFO community's hope that their research might one day become part of mainstream science.

Verne Dawson, who has painted several pictures of UFOs (figs 63 and 64), has some sympathy with Vallée's ideas, just as he has an abiding interest in other places, or convergences, where science, imagination and chance intersect. He also enjoys collapsing differences and inverting expectations: he depicts decorative images of exploding atom bombs as well as a precise rendering of psilocybin mushrooms (figs 65 and 66); he juxtaposes a portrait of Santa Claus as a shaman with one of terrorist Theodore Kaczynski, the Unabomber (fig.67), suggesting a degree of commonality in their characterization as psychological 'wild men'.

He has also been influenced by Terence McKenna (1946–2000), an American botanist, ethnographer, lecturer, author and general 'psychonaut', who advocated the responsible use of drugs derived from plants. McKenna wrote about a broad variety of subjects, including psychedelia, drugs and intoxicants, shamanism, metaphysics, alchemy, philosophy, technology, environmentalism and the origins of human consciousness.[26]

In 1971, McKenna, his brother Dennis and three friends travelled to the Colombian Amazon in search of *ookoohé*, a mysterious plant preparation containing dimethyltryptamine (commonly known as DMT), but they abandoned the quest

when they found fields full of large *Psilocybe cubensis* mushrooms, which then became
the focus of their attention. Nearby, in La Chorrera, McKenna and his brother
became the subjects of an outlandish psychedelic experiment in which they attempted
to bond harmine (a psychedelic compound they used in combination with the
mushrooms) with their own neural DNA, through the use of special vocal techniques.
Their aspiration was access to the collective memory of the human species and to a
union of spirit and matter.

In the early 1980s, drawn to the idea that psychedelics might be a form of trans-
dimensional travel, McKenna began to lecture on plant-based psychedelics such as
psilocybin mushrooms, ayahuasca, cannabis and the plant derivative DMT. Using
earlier experiments as proof, he proposed that DMT opened up a parallel dimension,
and that psychedelics enable us to encounter 'higher dimensional entities' who might
be ancestors or spirits of the earth. He went even further, speculating that psilocybin
mushrooms may be a species of high intelligence that arrived on earth as spores
travelling through space in order to establish a symbiotic relationship with human
beings.

Only slightly less bizarrely, in his 1992 book *Food of the Gods*, McKenna suggested
that the transformation of humans' early ancestor *Homo erectus* into the species *Homo
sapiens* was in large part due to the presence of the mushroom *Psilocybe cubensis* in its
diet, an occurrence that was related to the desertification of the African continent.
He claimed that the forerunners of *Homo sapiens* were forced out of the disappearing
tropical forest in search of new sources of food, probably following herds of wild cattle
whose dung nurtured the insects that would have formed part of their diet, just as
it harboured the *Psilocybe cubensis* mushroom. According to McKenna, access to and
ingestion of psychedelic mushrooms was an evolutionary advantage to our hunter-
gatherer ancestors, and also provided their first religious or spiritual experiences. As
if making a cognate point, Dawson's painting *Olduvai Gorge* (fig.68), the cradle of
Homo sapiens civilisation, depicts early human beings, circuses and a single image of a
psilocybin mushroom.

A more significant convergence between McKenna's ideas and Dawson's artwork
is found in one of McKenna's main concepts, namely the idea that Western civilization
is currently undergoing what he called an 'archaic revival' (also the title of one of his
best-known books[27]). McKenna believed that Western society had fallen ill and was
undergoing a healing process – in much the same way that human beings produce
antibodies when they feel unwell, humanity as a whole was trying to cure itself
through what he called 'a reversion to archaic values'.

Terence McKenna, as befitted his empathy with shamanic traditions, could
be a trickster, and it is not always easy to tell whether or not he was being serious,
especially as he had a sense of humour. Nonetheless, subsequent research on DMT
has provided even more peculiar food for thought. In the 1990s, a doctor called Rick
Strassman (b.1952) began to administer DMT to volunteers as part of a medical

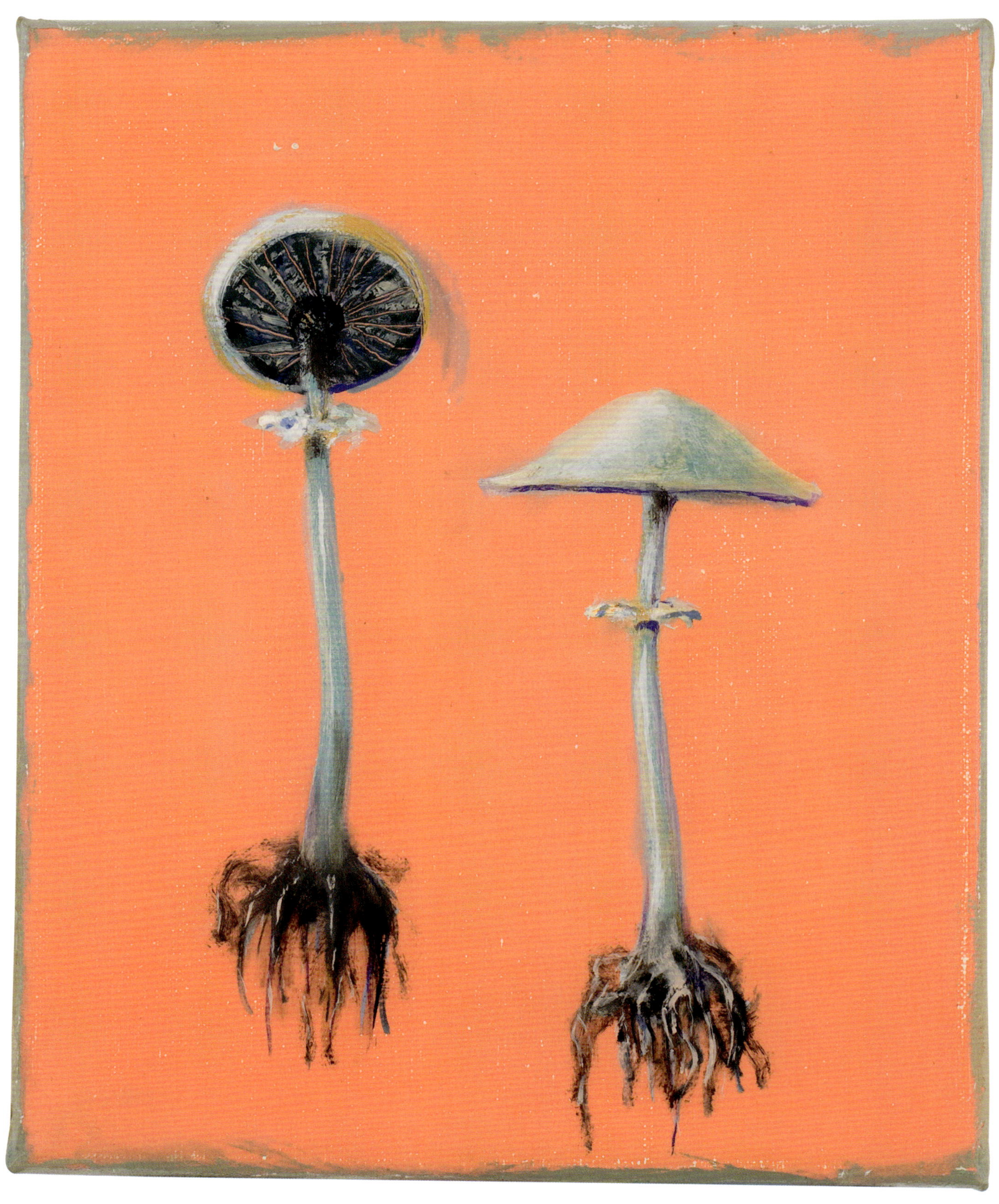

65. Psilocybin   2008

Oil on canvas
30.5 x 25.4 cm (12 x 10 in)
Collection of the artist

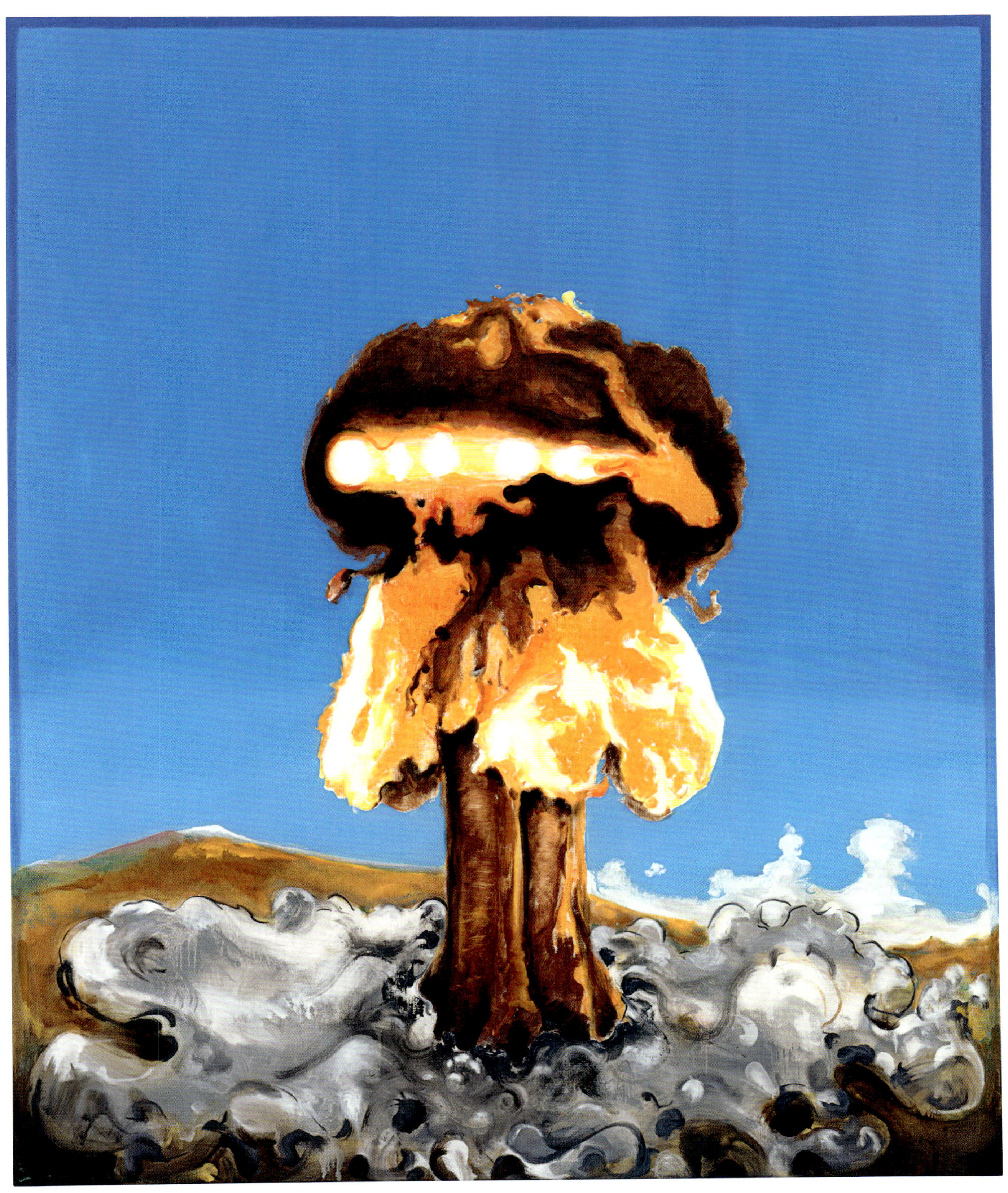

66. Atomic Bomb   2007

Oil on canvas
213.4 x 182.9 cm (84 x 72 in)
Private collection, Switzerland

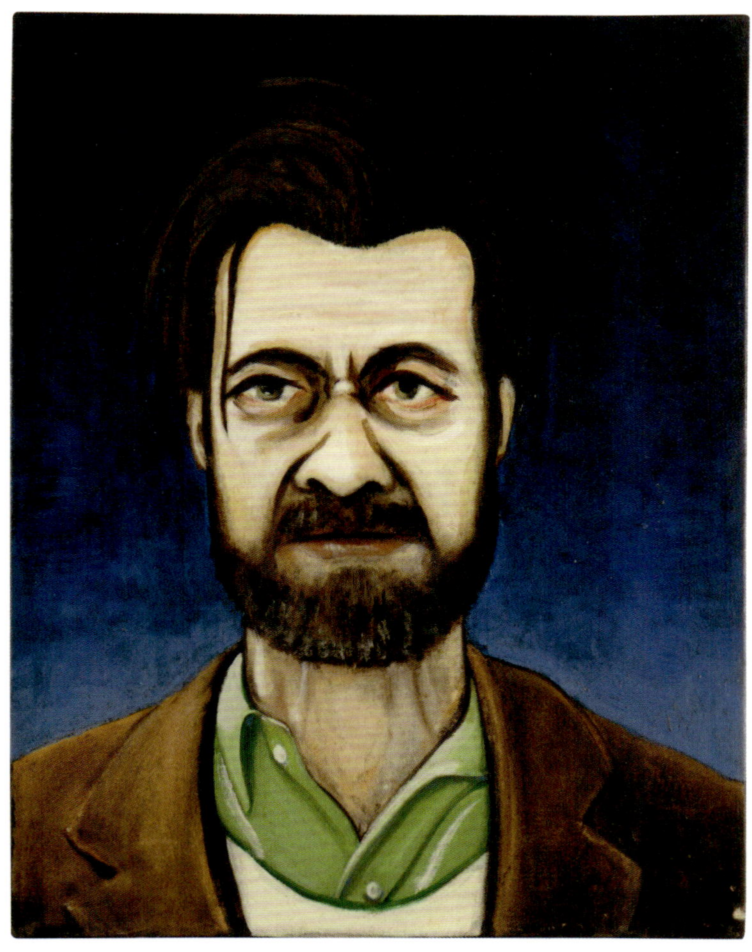

67. Theodore Kaczynski   1998

Oil on canvas
50.8 x 41.3 cm (20 x 16¼ in)
Private collection, New York

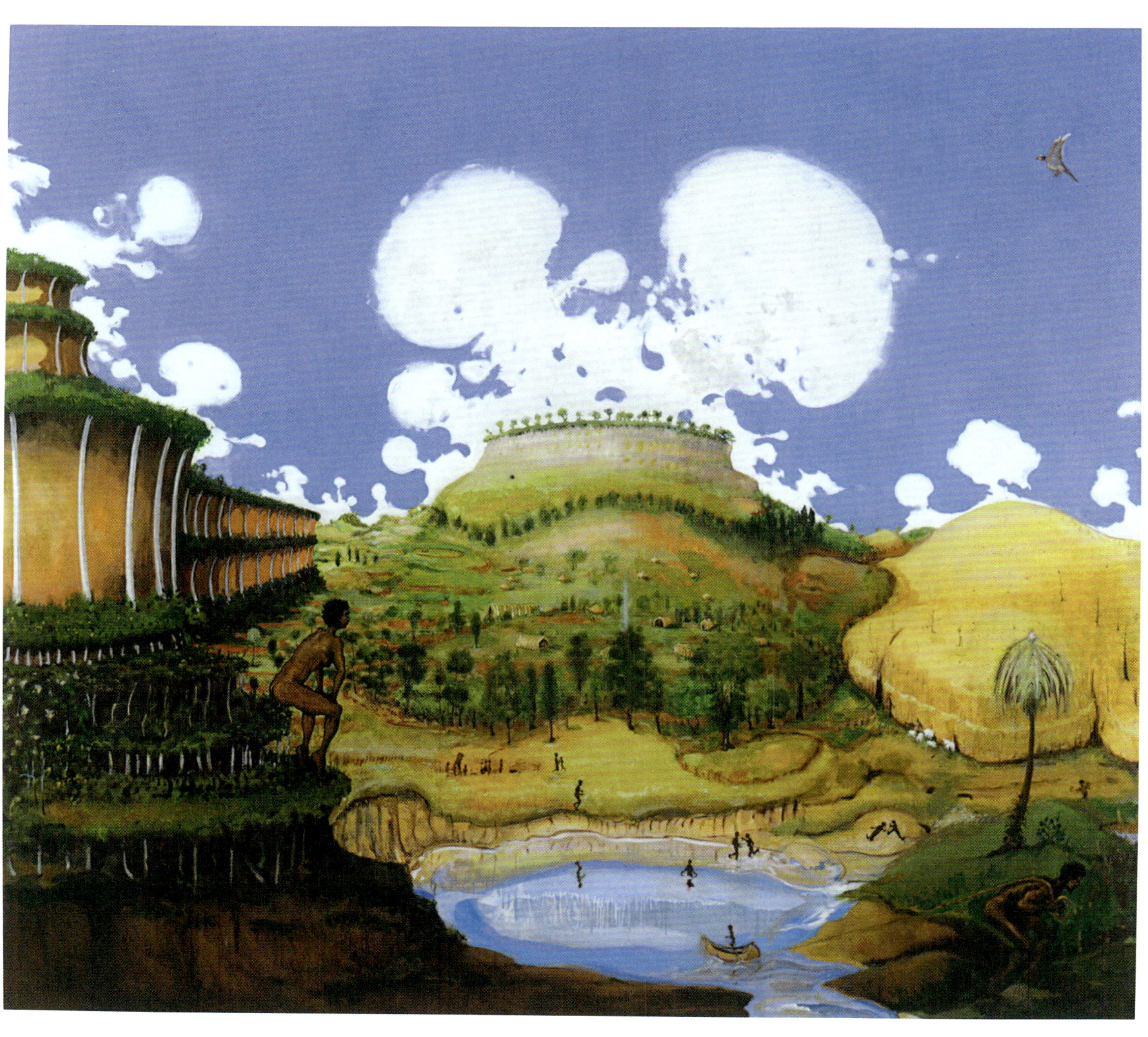

68. Olduvai Gorge 2002

Oil on canvas
320 x 280 cm (126 x 110¼ in)
Courtesy Gavin Brown's enterprise, New York/Rome

research project, and some of the participants who were given high doses of the drug reported extremely odd phenomena.[28] About half of them said that they had visited other worlds and had encountered intelligent beings who seemed to be of another species. Their experiences were so powerful that they were convinced of the reality of their interaction with the other beings, who took on various forms: sometimes they were embodied as elves, imps or dwarves, while on other occasions they appeared as omniscient deities or angelic beings.

Without proposing a direct connection between Dawson's work and McKenna's ideas or drug-induced psychedelia in general, it may not be too far-fetched to see reflections of psychedelic experience in paintings such as *Gnome in the Vines* (fig.71) and *Korrigan on the Run in Brittany* (fig.70). They are also deliberately archaic, to use McKenna's term. Even allowing for their comical aspect, it might be argued that these images are defiantly nostalgic, founded as they are on a belief that modern life has separated us from natural truths, and that old stories and traditions, many of which have come down to us from prehistoric times, are still important and may serve to sustain us. Although in some of Dawson's paintings, such as the huge, uncanny, but hopeful *Earthly Paradise (community house with utilities dome and examples of dematerialized human transport)* (fig.72), the old and new can harmoniously coexist, his view of what is to come is more often doubtful, if not pessimistic. Other than the paintings of the atomic bombs and the ambiguous depiction of *The Future*, with its unnaturally fiery sunset that lights up ruined buildings (fig.73), there is little in his work that is overtly dystopic, but it is precisely the absence of signs of contemporary life in all but his most recent images that reveals his scepticism about the here and now.

In addition to his complicated allegories, Dawson has painted many non-narrative pictures that are hard to categorize or even to understand. They include abstract compositions, some of them based on arcane numerology and others derived from buildings, and a group of semi-figurative images, among them the freely painted *Smith* (fig.75), *Elf in the Alley*, *The War Room* (fig.74) and *Two Figures in a Landscape* (fig.76). Although neither specifically dystopic nor futuristic, these odd pictures are undoubtedly disconcerting – hard to resolve and troubling in their refusal to draw a clear line between fantasy and reality, history and myth, now and then. Not all of Dawson's more recent paintings are as uncomfortable as these, however, though his brushstroke has become increasingly free. His newer work (figs 101–105) has tended to be more grounded, matter-of-fact and literal than before, and he appears to be becoming more and more detached from the idealized or imaginary world that has obsessed him for so many years.

In some respects, his work has become closer to that of his late friend Bill Lynch, whose paintings, rough and lyrical, are also infused with earthy melancholia. Lynch, whom Dawson knew well when they were students at Cooper Union, never exhibited his work during his lifetime. His first show was held in 2013 in New York,

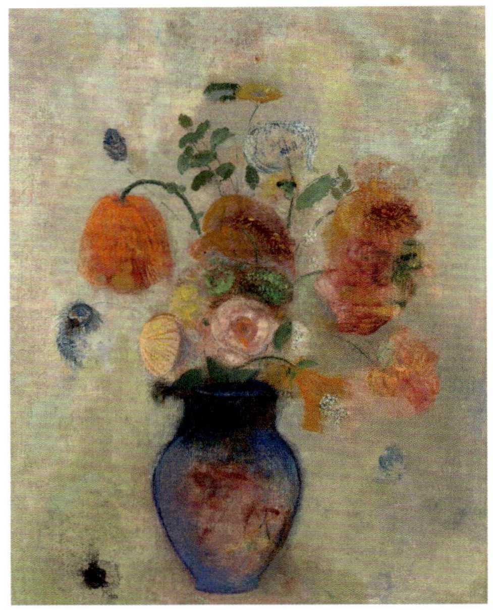

69. Odilon Redon
Large Vase with Flowers   c.1912

Oil on canvas
73 x 54.6 cm (28¾ x 21½ in)
National Gallery of Art, Washington DC

curated by Dawson, who was determined to bring his friend's art into public view. Lynch suffered from mental illness and struggled to find a place for himself in the art world, but he made a lucid body of work that draws on a wide variety of sources, ranging from nature to folk and Chinese art, and which also incorporates religious and mythological motifs. Lynch painted in a simple and immediate manner, usually applying fluid strokes on to plain wood that was often scavenged and recycled; the visible grain added much to the paintings' sense of humility and love for the natural world, qualities that set them apart from the work of most contemporary painters. His paintings are never inflated, pretentious or self-referential; they are quiet and contemplative things, beautiful but also easy to ignore or pass by.

Some of Dawson's paintings of birds (figs 78–81), which are sketchy but vibrant, lonely and lyrical, have elements in common with Lynch's work. Another less obvious connection with Lynch lies in Dawson's strange and almost hallucinogenic images of a French vase (figs 82 and 83), which have a decorative intensity reminiscent of the still lifes of the 19th-century French Symbolist painter Odilon Redon (1840–1916, fig.69). Besides the inherent oddness of the vase itself, Dawson's pictures of it are understated, funny and peculiar – they are very different from his earlier still lifes, which are plain depictions of art materials that are so straight-faced as to be a little unnerving.

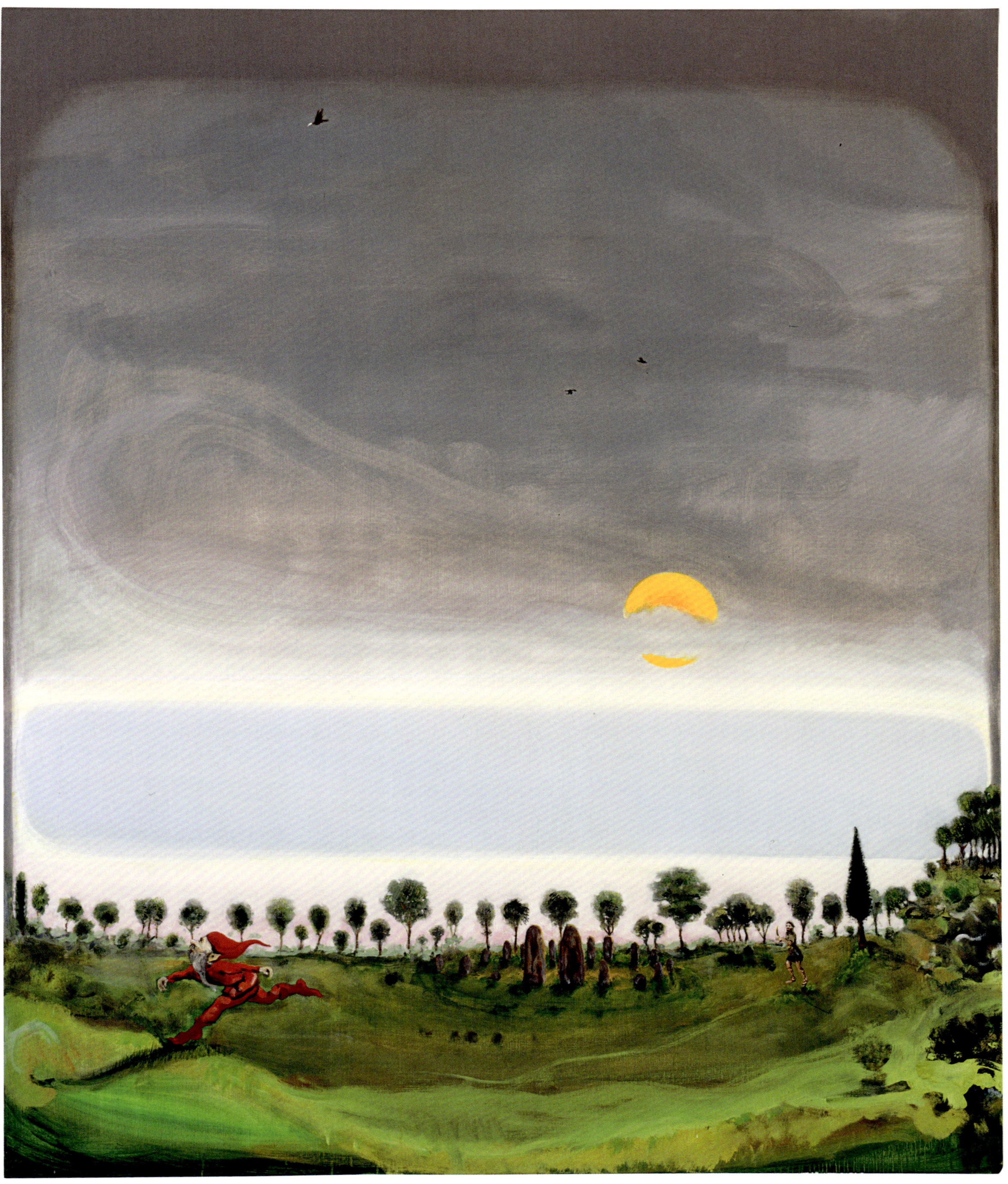

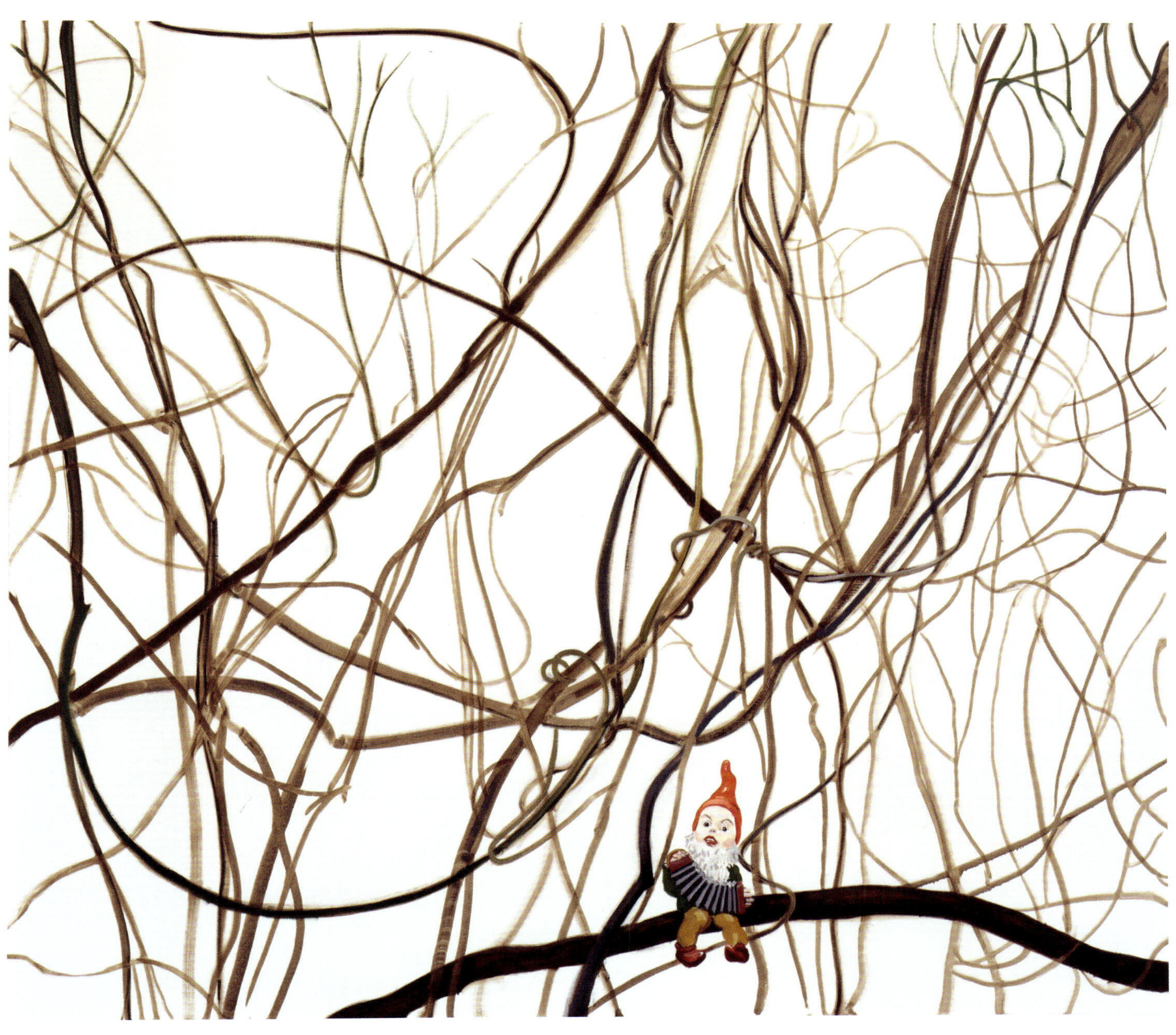

70. Korrigan on the Run in Brittany   2007

Oil on canvas
213.4 x 182.9 cm (84 x 72 in)
Private collection

71. Gnome in the Vines   2007

Oil on canvas
182.9 x 213.4 cm (72 x 84 in)
Burger Collection, Hong Kong

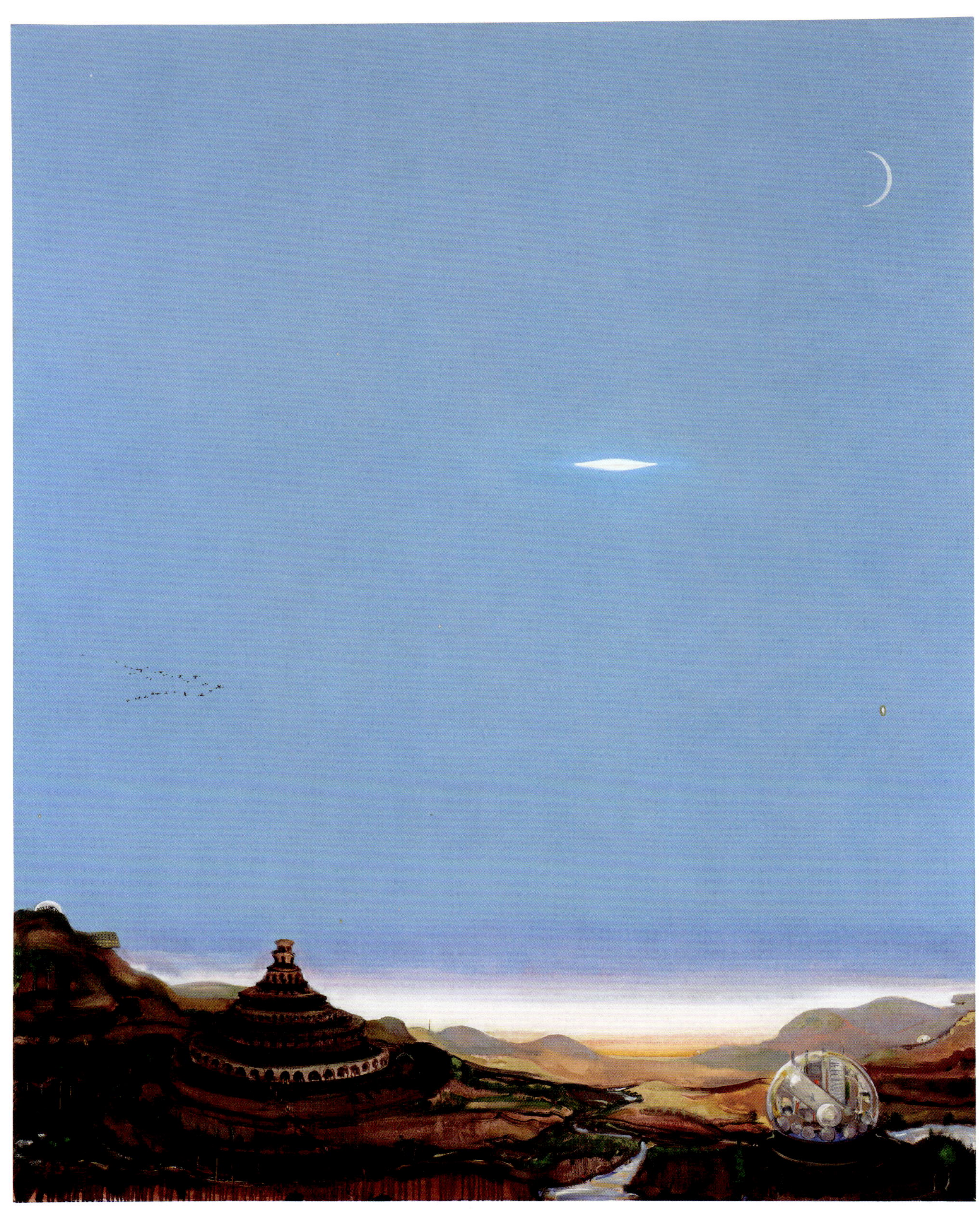

72. Earthly Paradise (community house with utilities dome
and examples of dematerialized human transport)   2003–16

Oil on canvas
218.4 x 177.8 cm (86 x 70 in)
Collection of Martin & Rebecca Eisenberg, USA

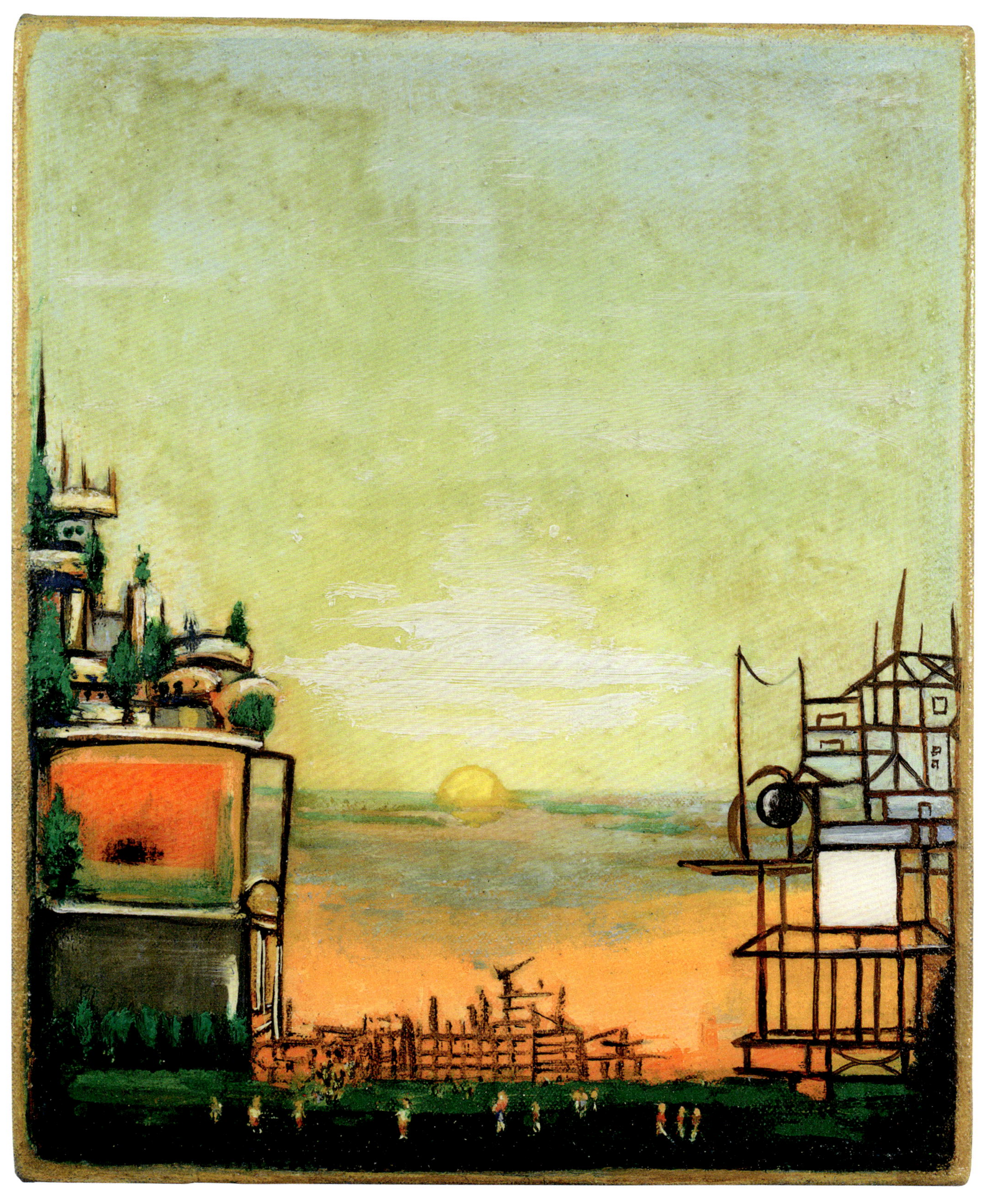

73. The Future   1998

Oil on canvas
30.5 x 25.4 cm (12 x 10 in)
Private collection

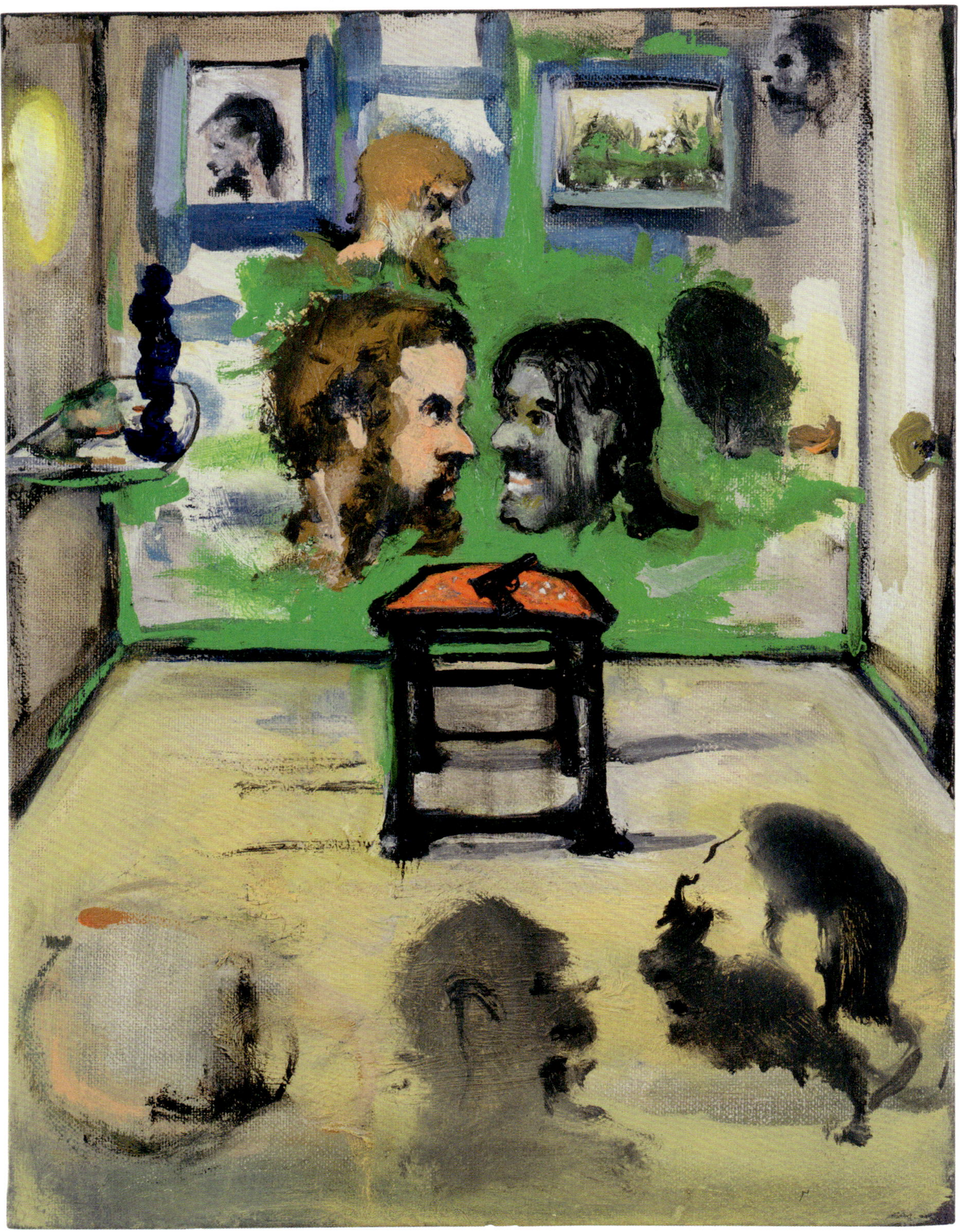

74. The War Room   2003

Oil on board
35.6 x 27.9 cm (14 x 11 in)
Private collection

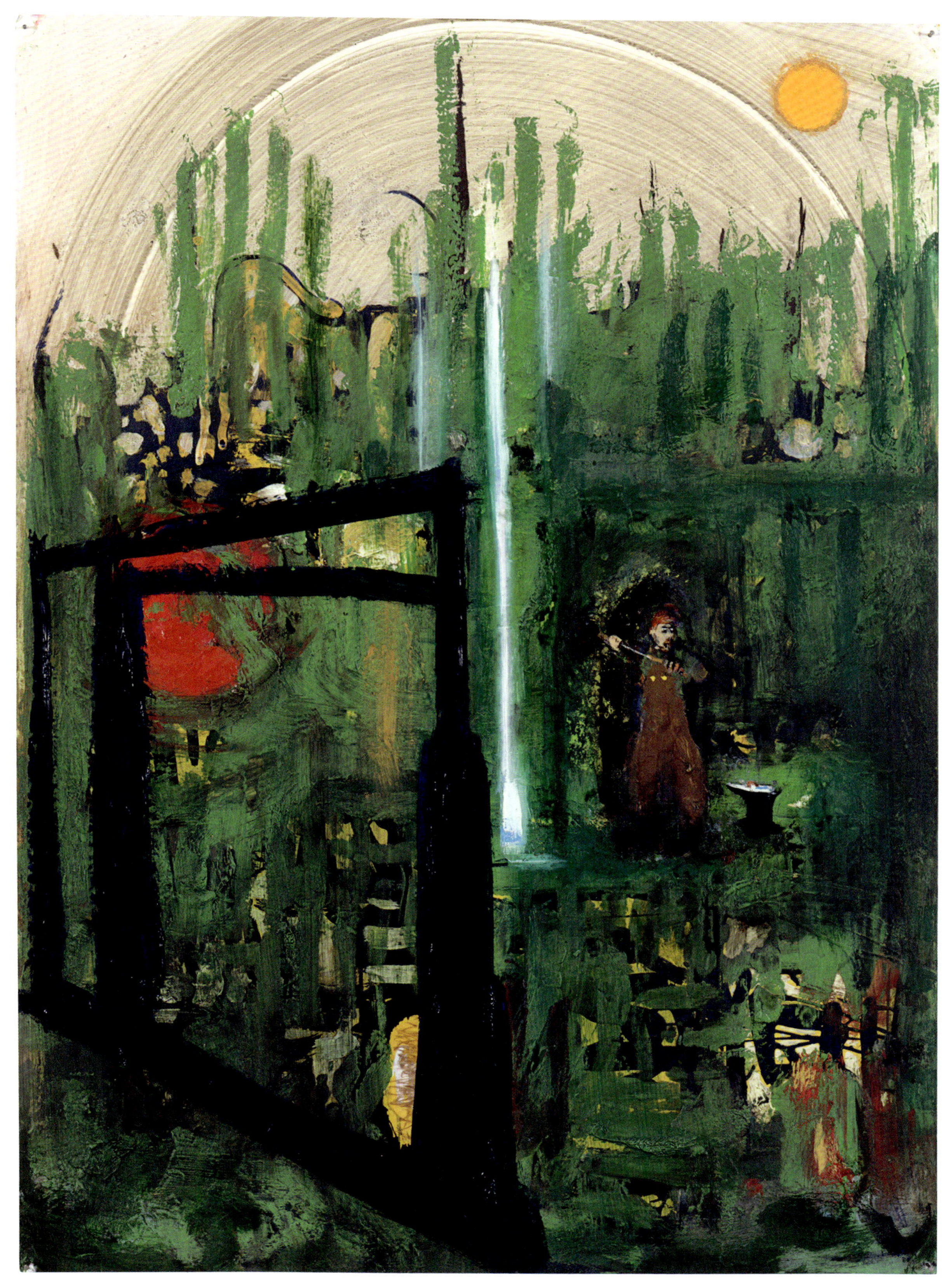

75. Smith   2007

Oil on tin
61 x 45.7 cm (24 x 18 in)
Courtesy Galerie Eva Presenhuber, Zurich, New York

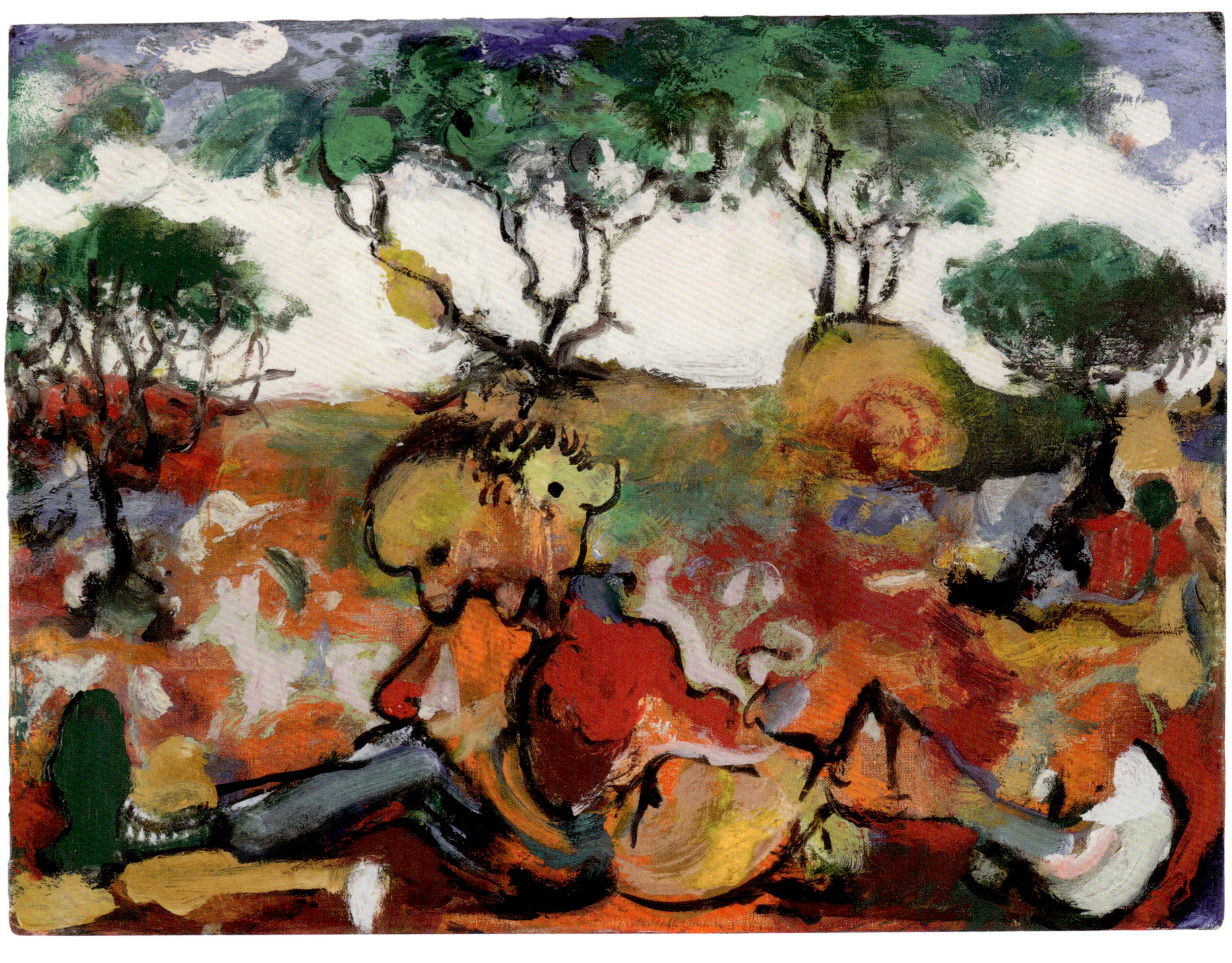

76. Two Figures in a Landscape 2014

Oil on canvas
30.5 x 40.6 cm (12 x 16 in); 34.3 x 45.1 cm framed (13½ x 17¾ in framed)
Collection of the artist

77. Girl Reading a Book 2007

Oil on canvas
50.8 x 40.6 cm (20 x 16 in)
Courtesy Galerie Eva Presenhuber, Zurich, New York

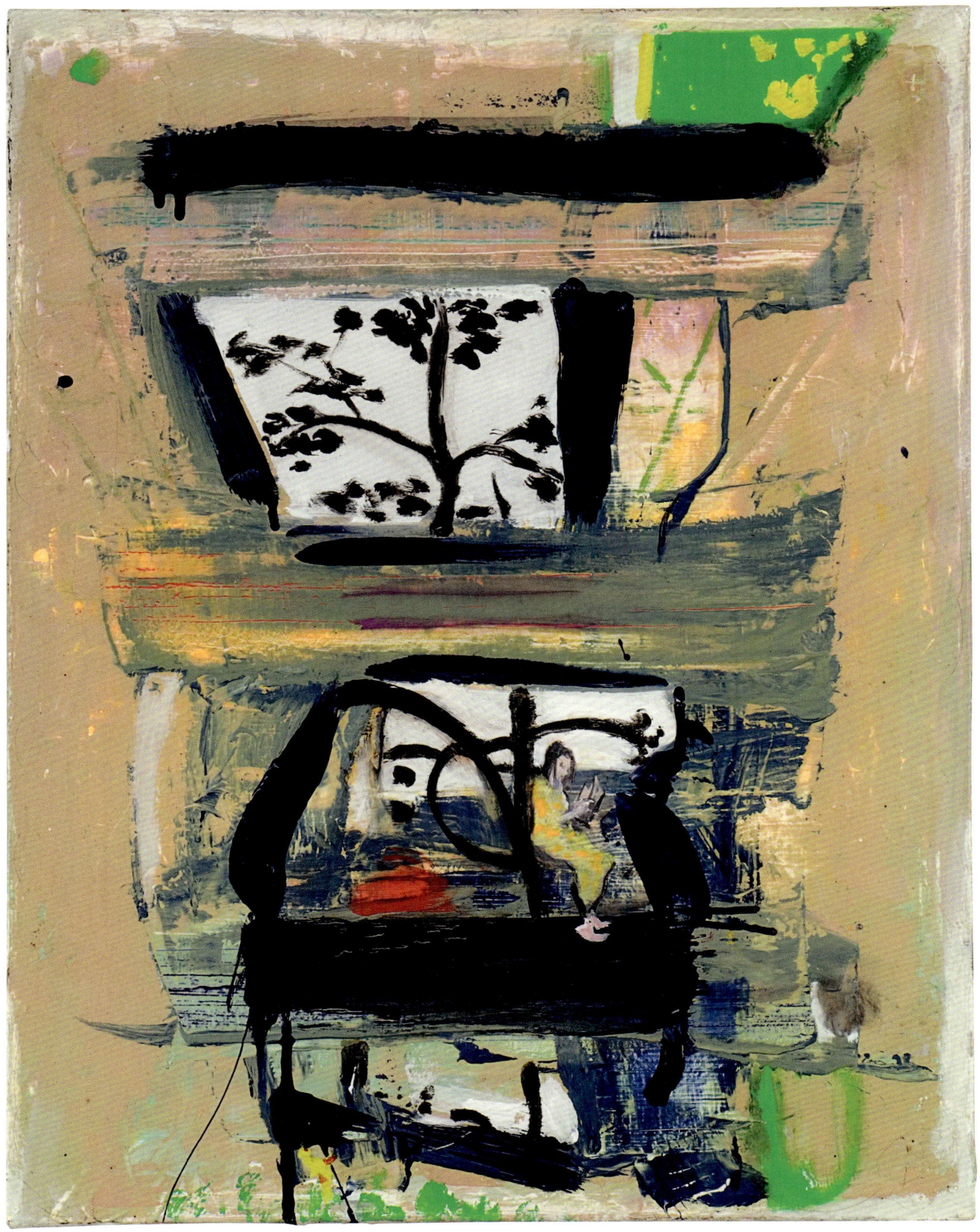

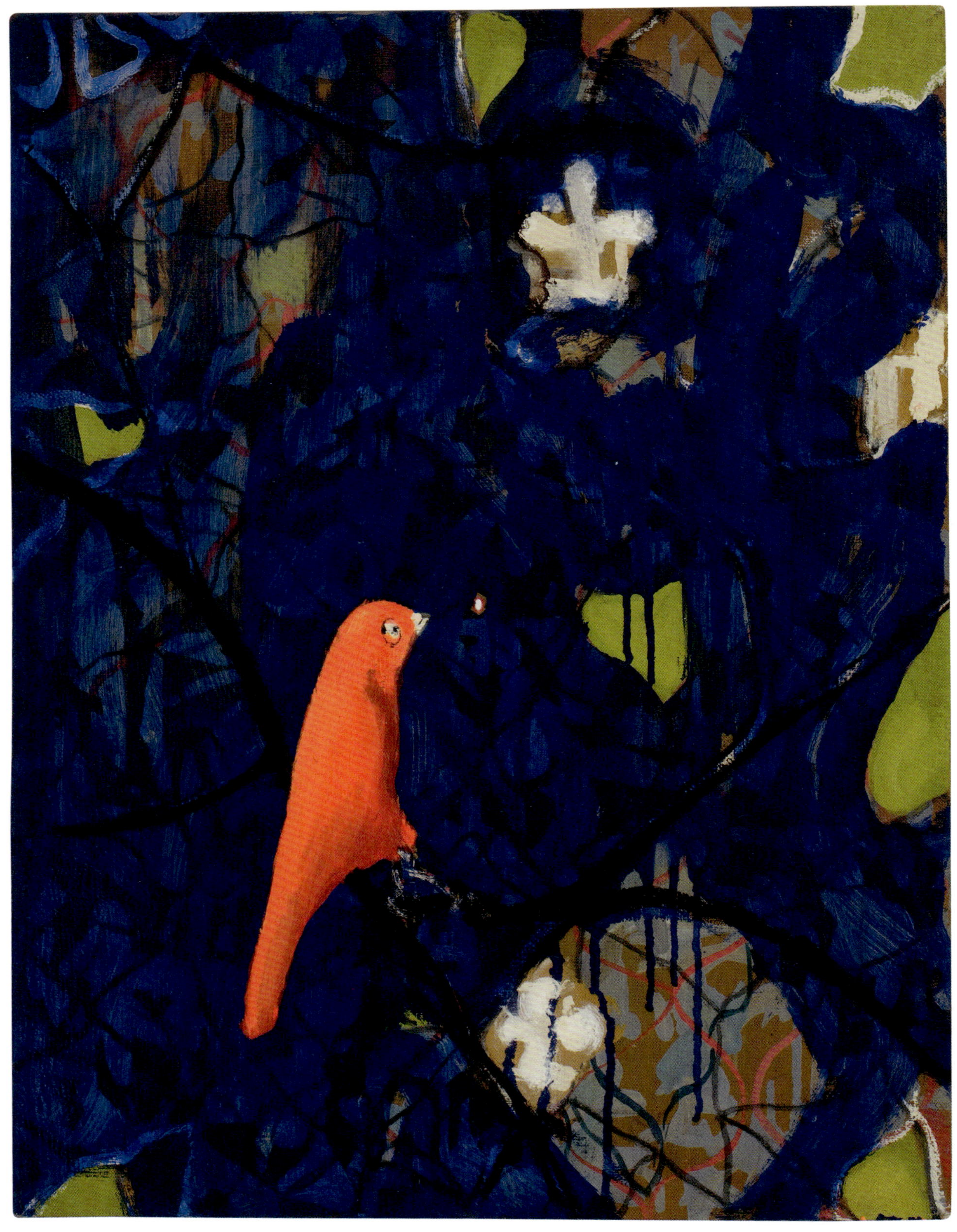

78. Red Bird   2009

Oil on canvas
45.7 x 35.6 cm (18 x 14 in)
Private collection

79. Canary in a Bell Jar   2009

Oil on canvas
50.8 x 40.6 cm (20 x 16 in)
Private collection

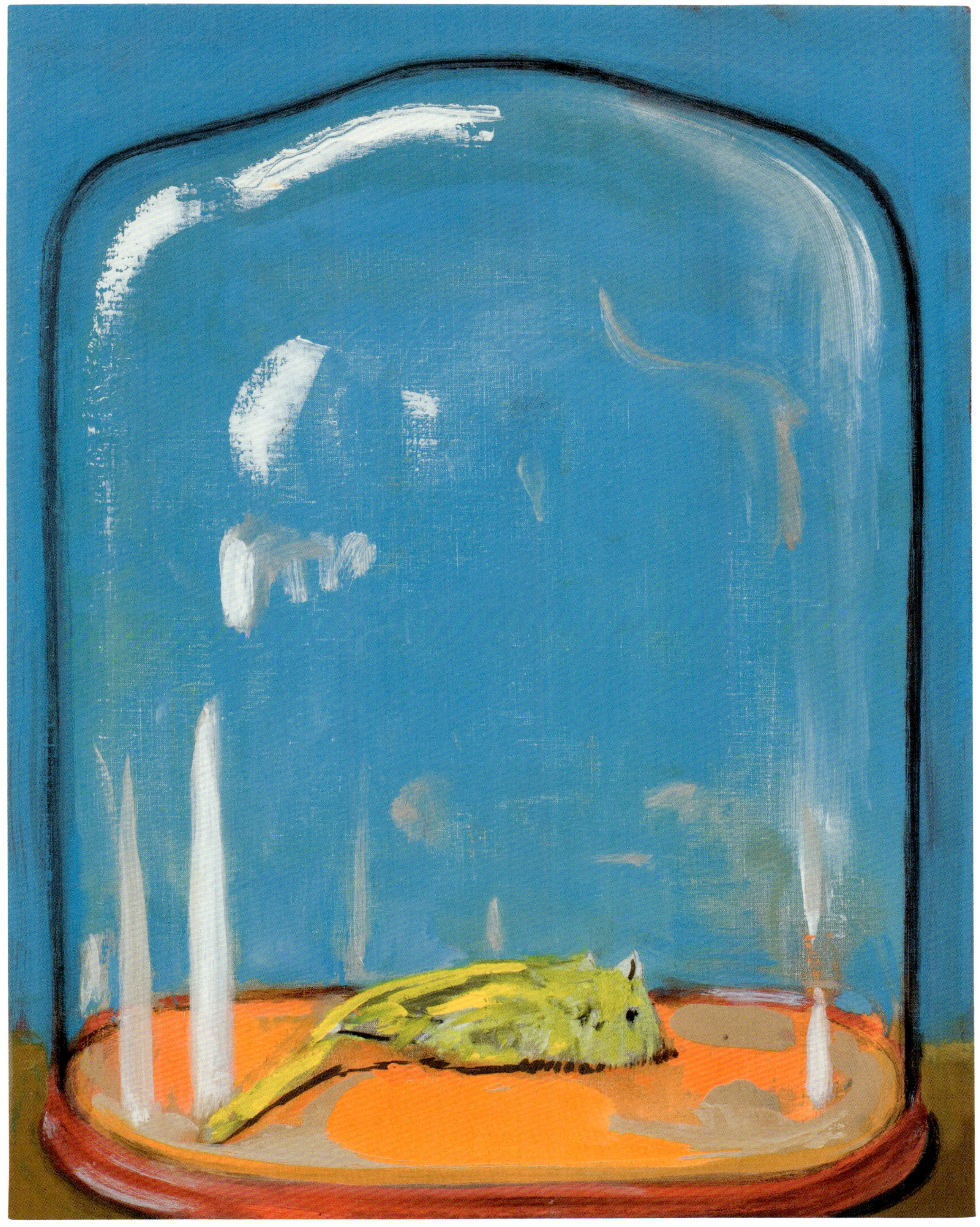

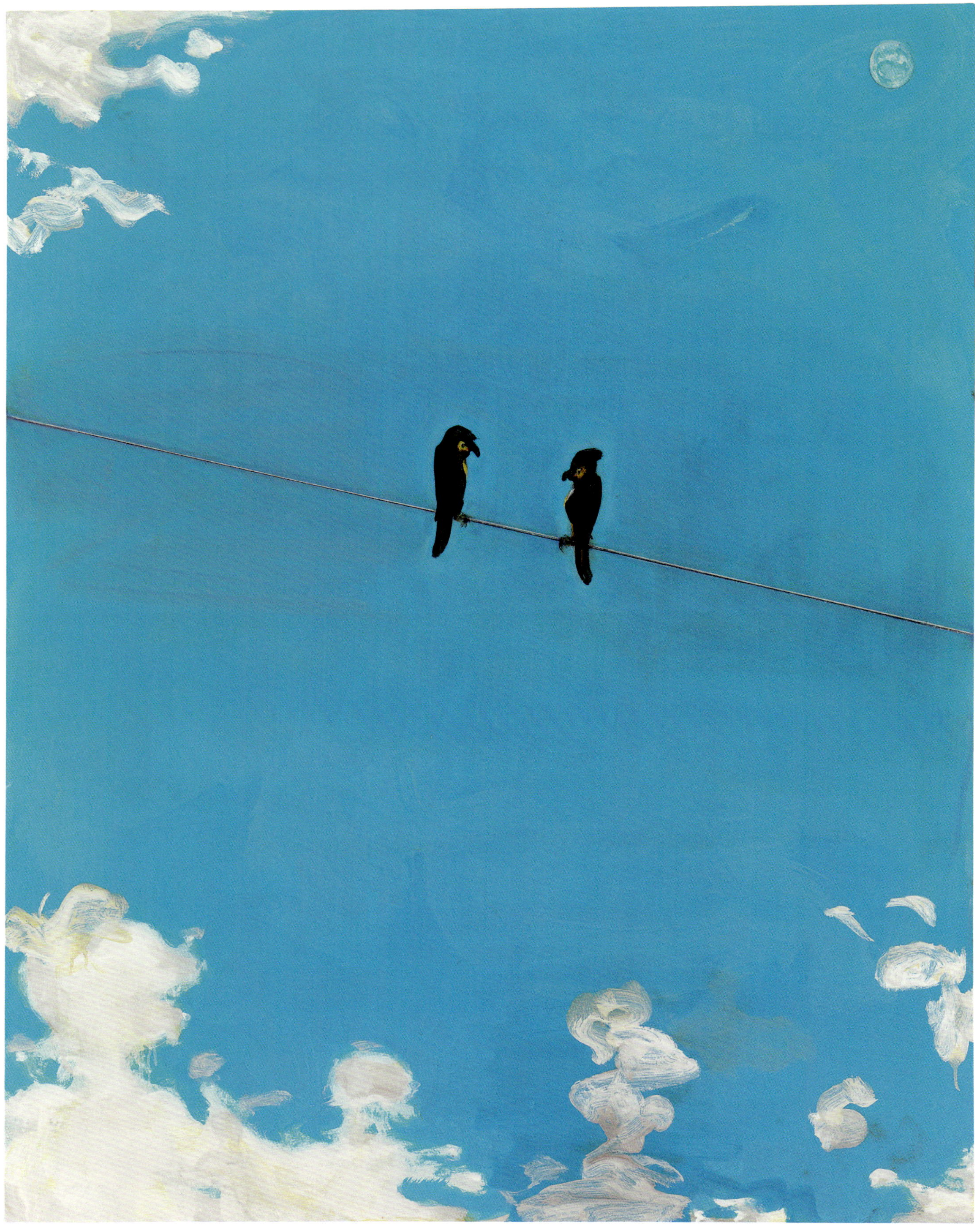

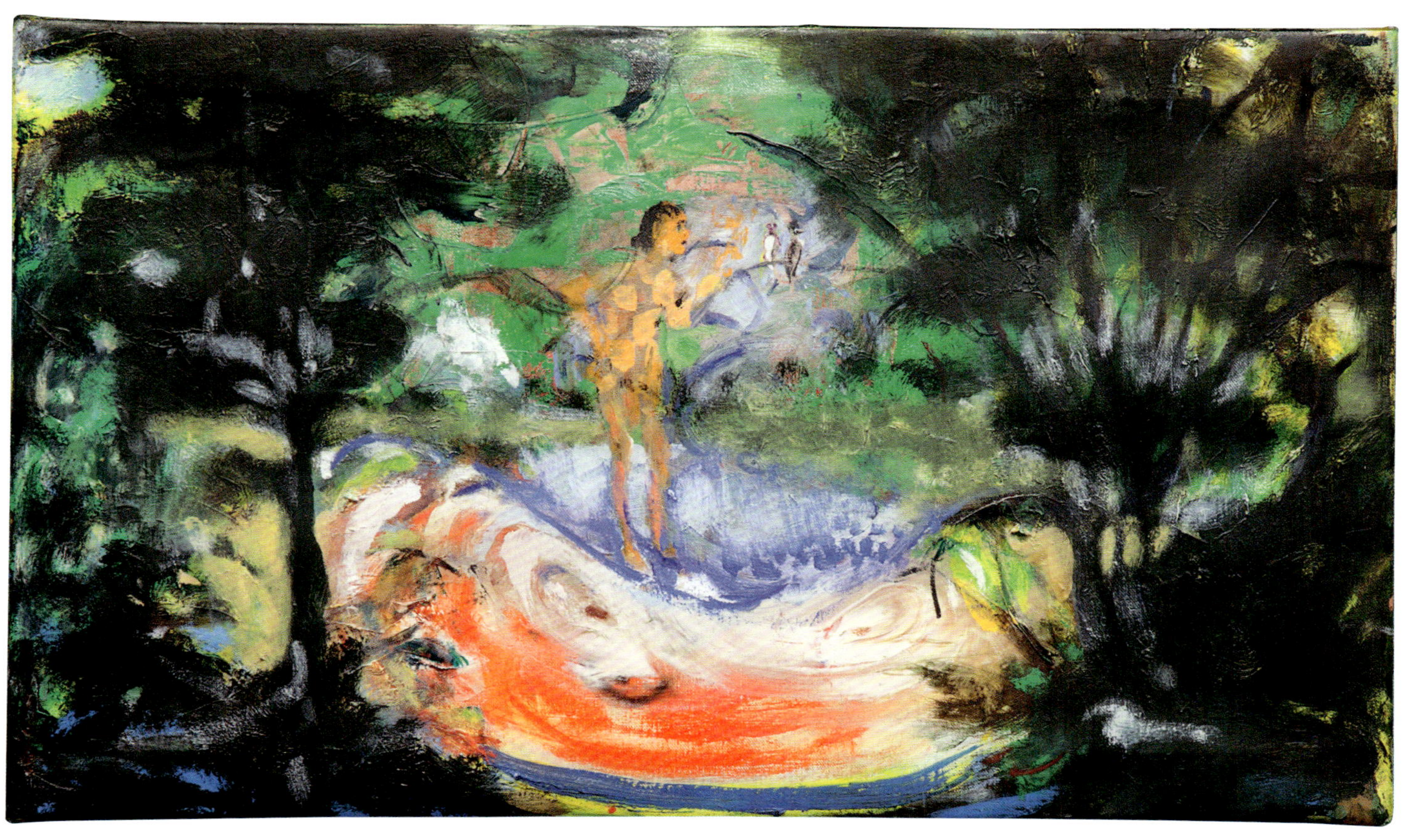

80 . Two Birds on a Wire   2011

Oil on canvas
127 x 101.6 cm (50 x 40 in)
Private collection

81. Man with Two Birds   2015

Oil on canvas
40.6 x 71.1 cm (16 x 28 in)
Courtesy Galerie Eva Presenhuber, Zurich, New York

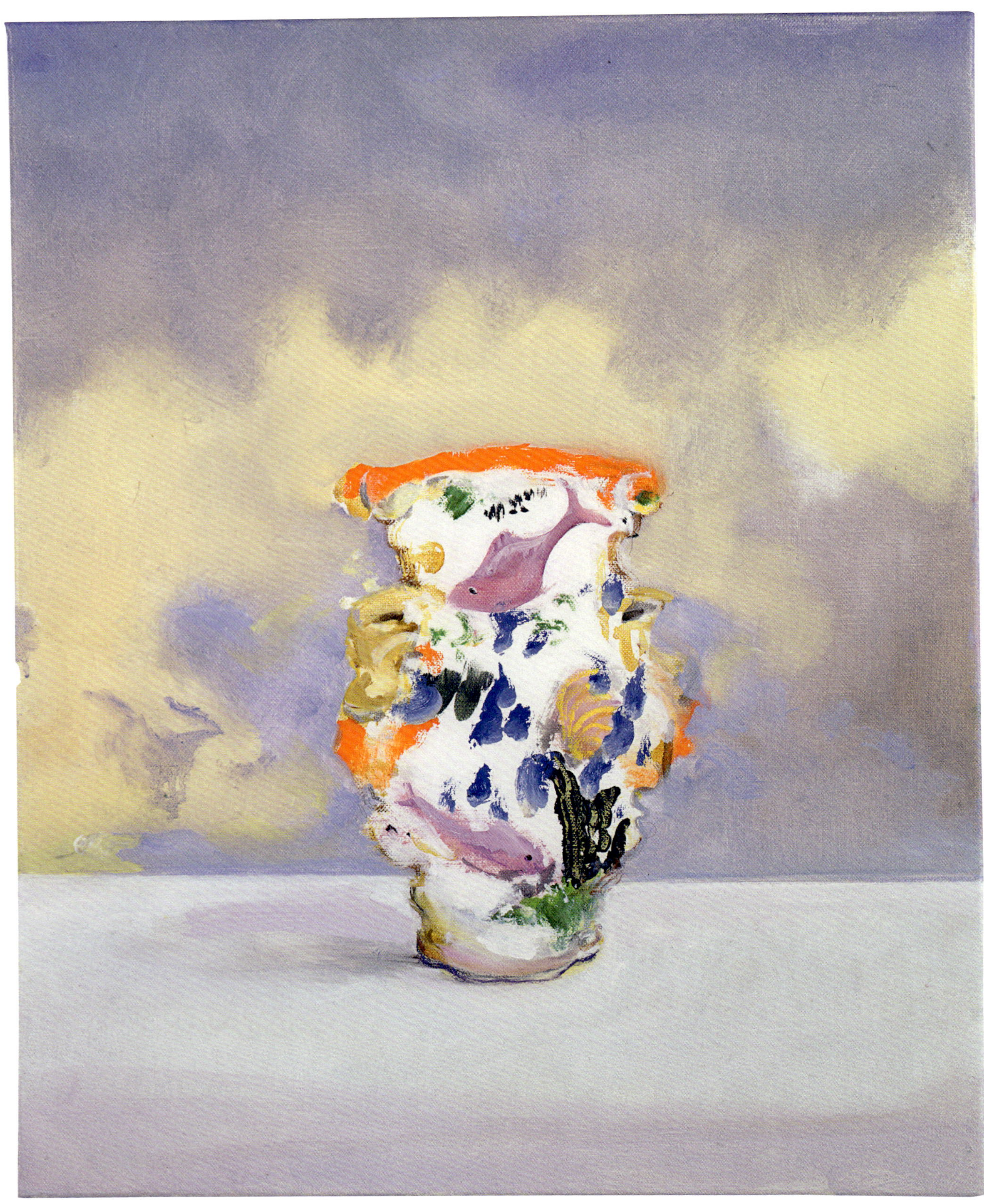

82. French Vase   2002

Oil on canvas
45.7 x 38.1 cm (18 x 15 in)
Collection of Martin and Rebecca Eisenberg, USA

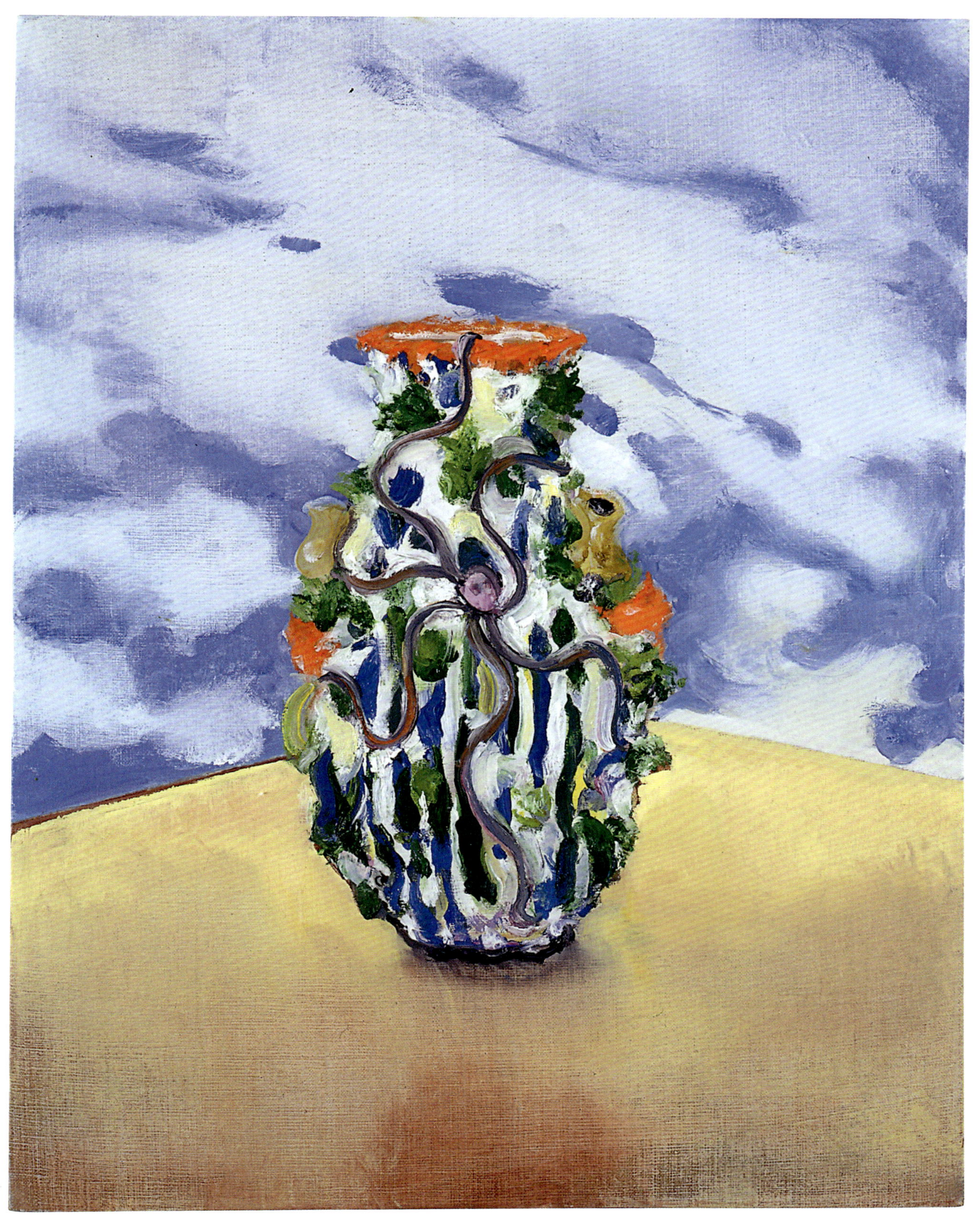

83. French Vase (Octopus Face)   2003

Oil on canvas
50.8 x 40.6 cm (20 x 16 in)
Private collection

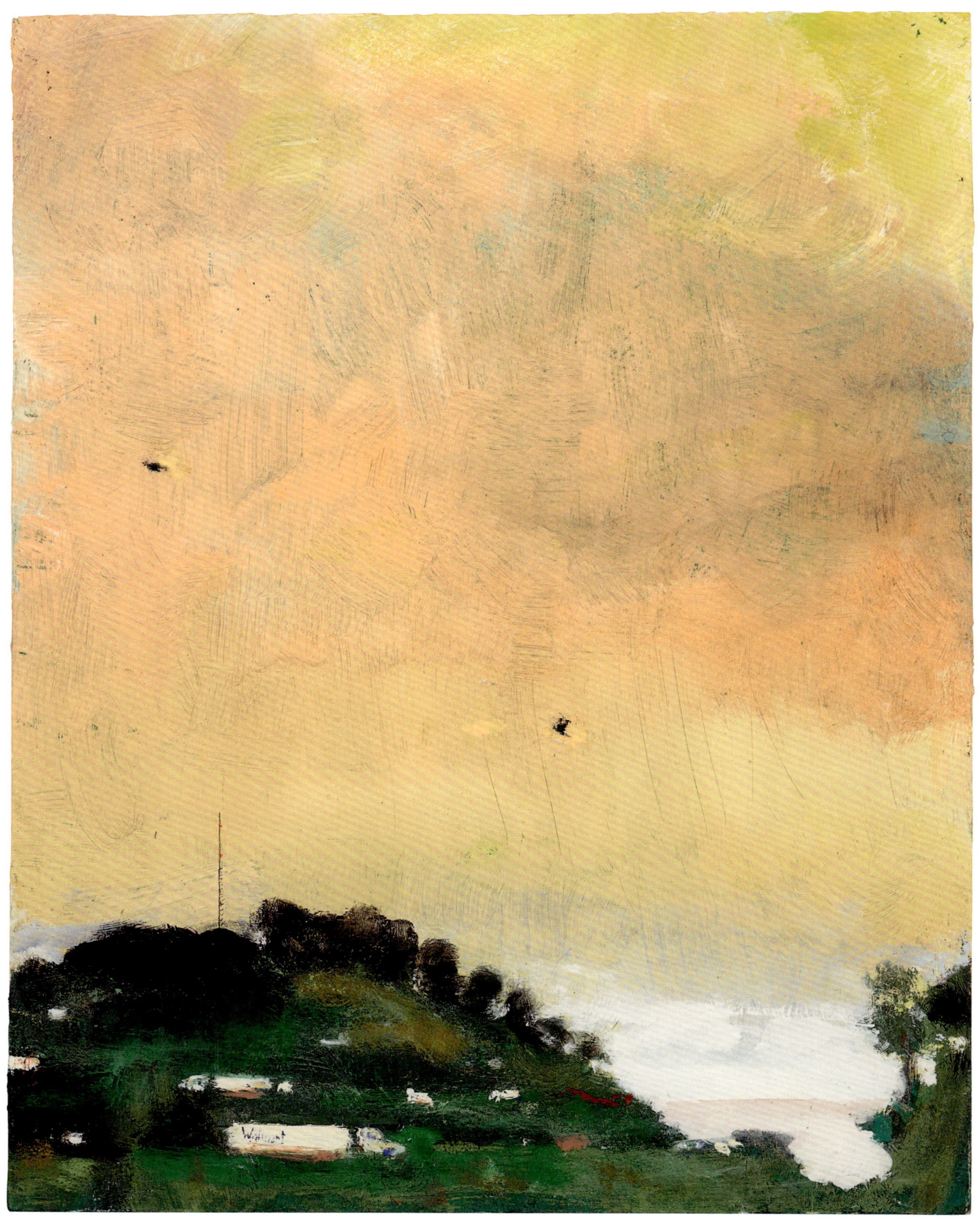

84. I·81   2016–17

Oil on panel
50.8 x 40.6 cm (20 x 16 in)
Courtesy Gavin Brown's enterprise, New York/Rome

3   Arcadia, Innocence and Subversion

As well as being fundamentally Arcadian in tone, American landscape painting of the early decades of the 19th century was marked by a wish to represent nature as the expression and revelation of the divine. Many writers and artists liked to think of America's wild and largely unexplored terrain as the Garden of Eden and the New Jerusalem. Paintings of the landscape, such as those by Thomas Cole, Frederic Church and Alfred Bierstadt (1830–1902), tended to be naturalistic in style, albeit idealized and often configured in classical compositions, but there soon developed another eccentric strand, one with which Verne Dawson also has a certain empathy.

The earliest and most celebrated artist in this more introspective lineage was Albert Pinkham Ryder, whom Dawson identifies as his youthful inspiration to become a painter. Ryder's career, which straddled the late 19th and early 20th centuries, was notable for its poetic and moody allegorical seascapes, which often contained stylized figures in scenes illuminated by pale sunlight or a moon surrounded by dramatic clouds (fig.87). An erratic painter with an odd personality and an unconventional and bizarre technique, Ryder founded his reputation on not many more than a dozen works, most being his famous 'marines', which are dark, intense images of boats struggling against the forces of wind and sea under eerie moonlight. Nevertheless, many American artists, including Marsden Hartley (1877–1943) and Jackson Pollock (1912–56), have admired Ryder as a symbol of aesthetic integrity and authenticity, and also as an artistic prophet who formed a bridge between tradition and modernism.

Another anomaly in early 20th-century American art history, Arthur B. Davies (1862–1928) was a painter whose main artistic interest lay in the visual exploration of dreams – at that time a subject only recently considered by psychologists and rarely tackled by artists. Davies' images are odd, whimsical or intriguingly strange (fig.88); some are attractive and lyrical, while others are arch and awkward. Above all they are visionary and have made him a reputation as a dreamer and an accomplished painter of the inner world. With their fanciful groups of figures in woodland or more expansive landscape settings, Davies' paintings may appear faintly absurd to our eyes, not least because of their ingenuous adoption of fantasy and folklore, but they provide an unexpected parallel with some of Dawson's more unconventional figurative compositions.

Perhaps the oddest of all the painters in this early 20th-century American line was Louis Michel Eilshemius (1864–1941). Academically trained and influenced by the work of Ryder, Eilshemius developed a highly idiosyncratic manner of painting

"

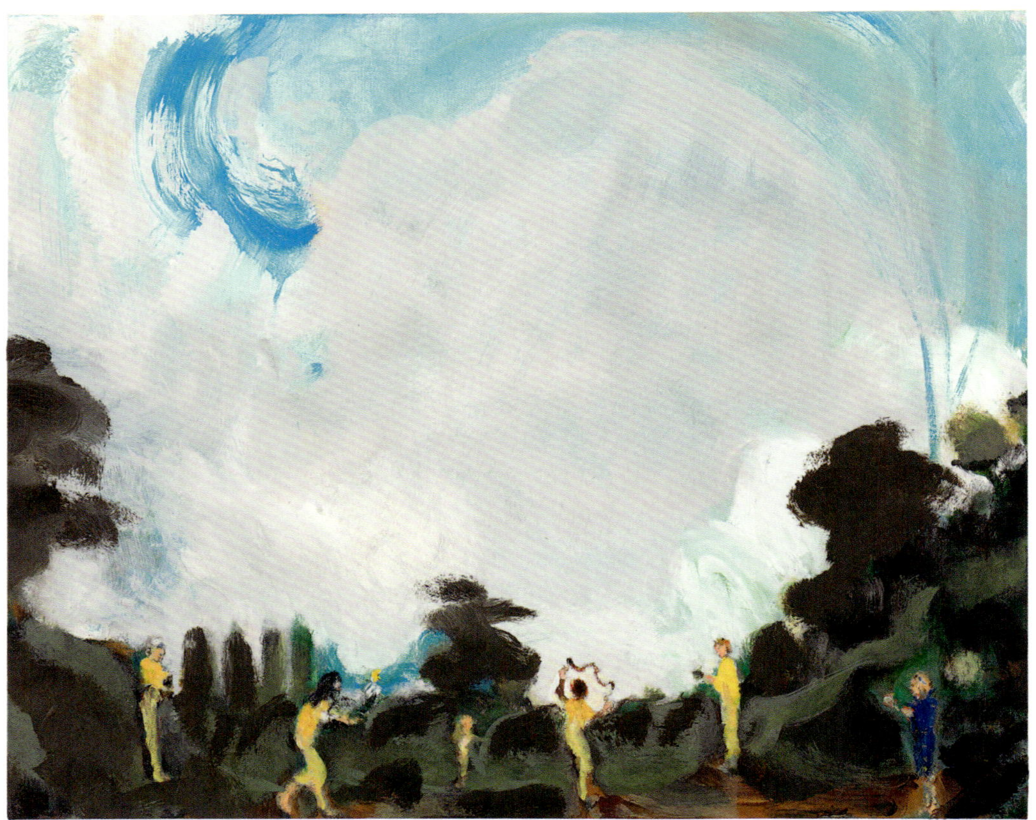

85. Arcadia (1, 2 & 3)   2011

Oil on canvas
55.9 x 71.1 cm (22 x 28 in)
Courtesy Galerie Eva Presenhuber, Zurich, New York

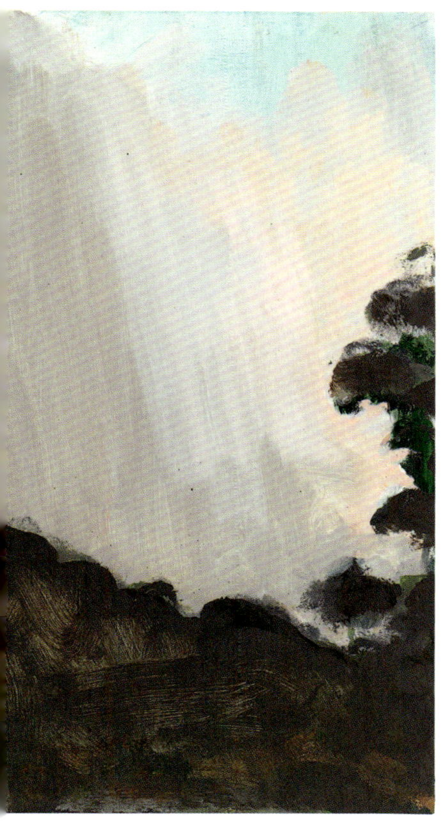
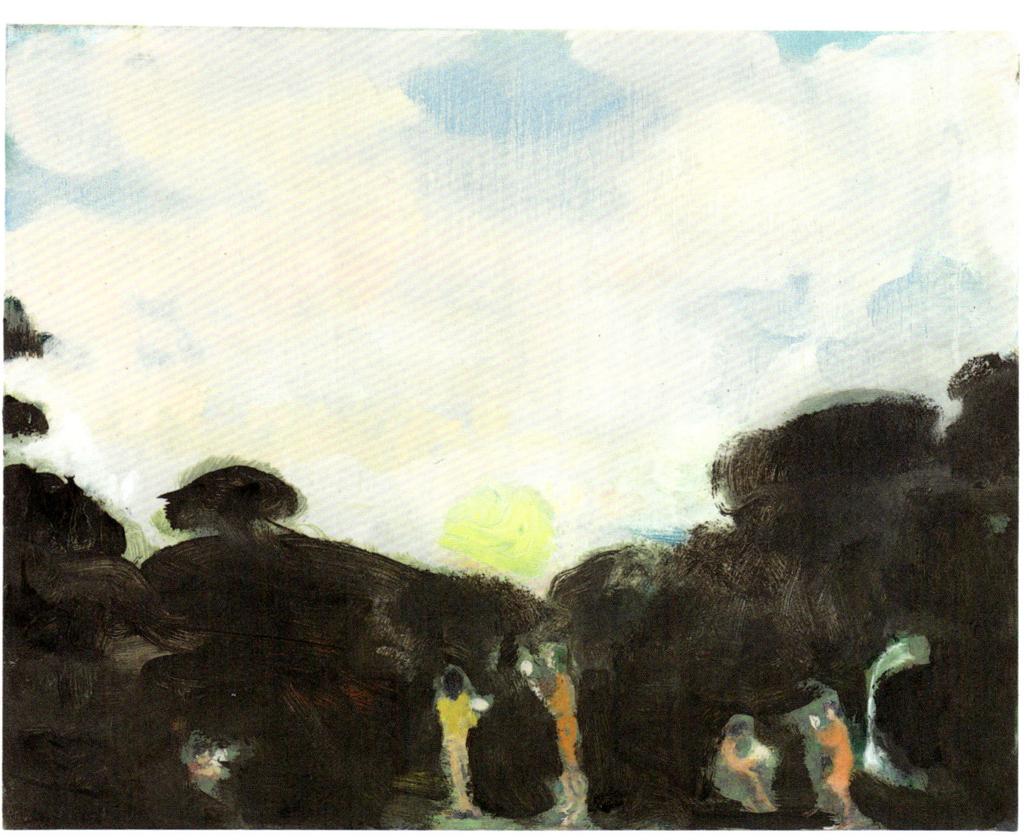

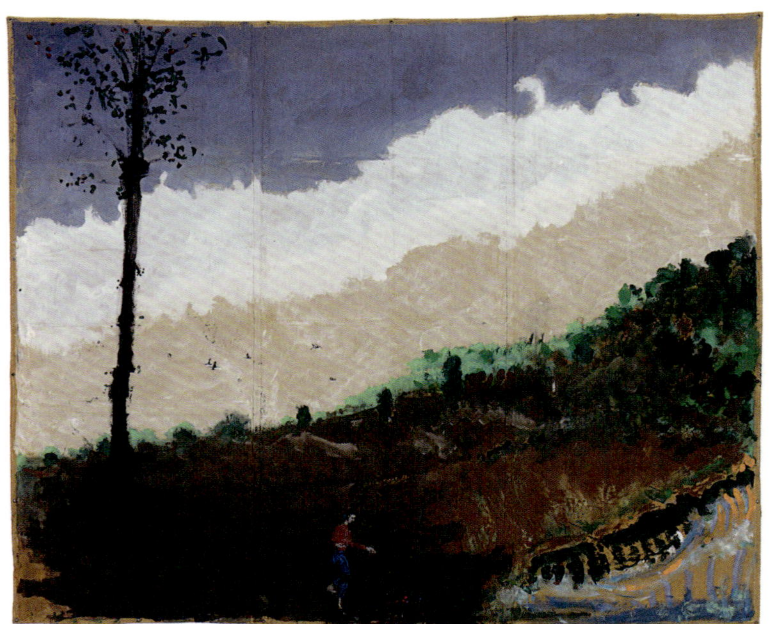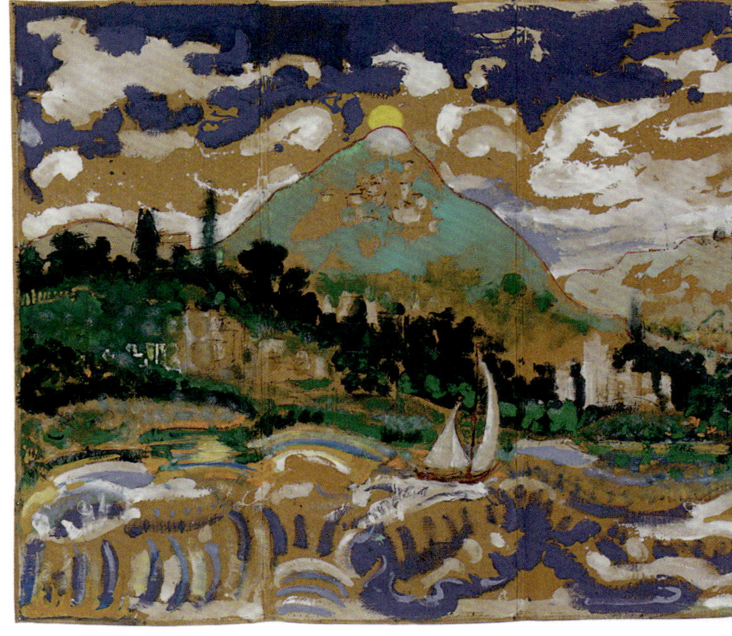

86. The Old Mill Calendar   2011

Acrylic house paint on canvas tarp
Four panels, each 304.8 x 365.8 cm (each 120 x 144 in)
Burger Collection, Hong Kong

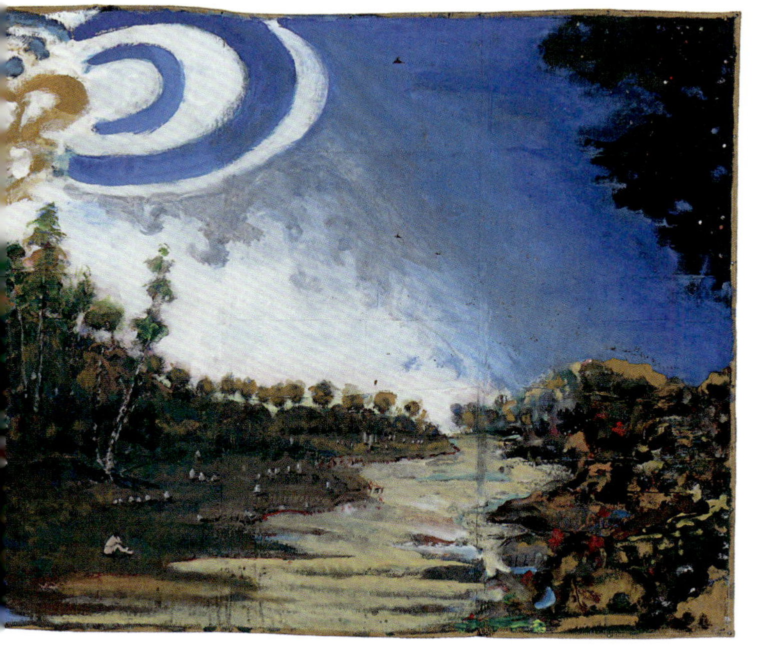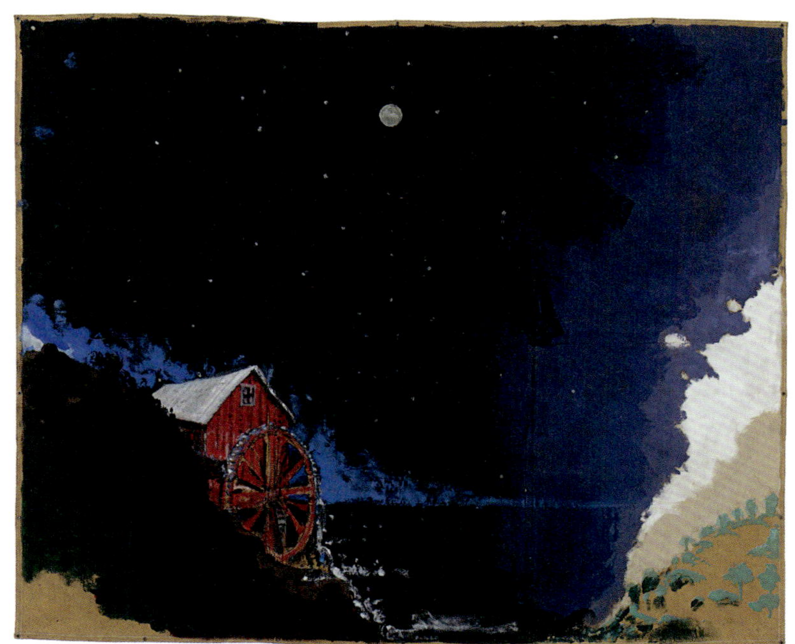

landscape, the figure and genre, his weird style combining elements of the amateur, folk artist, visionary and surrealist (fig.89). Widely collected during his lifetime, his allegorical landscapes populated with nymph-like bathers and dancing fairies were championed by Marcel Duchamp, whose enthusiasm has encouraged a 21st-century reassessment of his prolific oeuvre.

Eilshemius was a dissenter, a deeply unconventional outsider. As recent commentators have put it, he was 'eccentric to the point of mental instability; a quasi-mystic; a self-proclaimed polymath and prolific dabbler in other fields alongside his painting; a shameless self-publicist, self-publisher, self-mythologiser and purveyor of home-spun theory and philosophy'.[29] Eilshemius' gradual abandonment of painting and increased concern with the assertion of his own greatness probably contributed to Duchamp's interest in him, but it does not altogether account for the unexpected appeal of his work to some of his contemporaries. An art critic who saw the show curated by Duchamp in 1924 wrote: 'Suddenly, like another Saint Paul, I see a great light, and the scales drop from my eyes. The pictures at the Anonyme Gallery are completely lovely.'[30] This is echoed today in the growing number of enthusiasts who, in the context of post-modern painting, find his work provocative and engaging. And although his work has little of the beauty and quality of Henri Rousseau's, they do have some things in common. Both artists had great respect for academic painting, were simultaneously avant-garde and vernacular, and in different ways could be thought of as 'outsider' artists. It was Eilshemius' naivety, also a quality of Rousseau's personality, which is often supposed to be the reason for Duchamp's interest in him.

★

'I feel like I'm an outsider artist', Verne Dawson once said,[31] but this is probably only true insofar as he believes that the contemporary world is alienated from the ancient values that have traditionally helped to give life substance and meaning. Most of his work can be understood as the expression of a desire to develop our awareness of the beauty of the natural world, and the stories he tells, so many of them rooted in prehistory, are a way of furthering that aspiration. Nonetheless, his work can have the earnestness and naivety of many self-taught artists, and like them, the world of Dawson's imagination has, at least until recently, almost completely eclipsed his artistic engagement with what would commonly be regarded as 'reality'.

Similarly, although there are resemblances, both superficial and profound, between some of Dawson's paintings and what is known as 'folk art', it would be a mistake to press the comparison very far. It is more useful, perhaps, to make the analogy between Dawson's position in contemporary art discourse and that of Henri Rousseau (1844–1910) (fig.90) in early 20th-century European Modernism, because

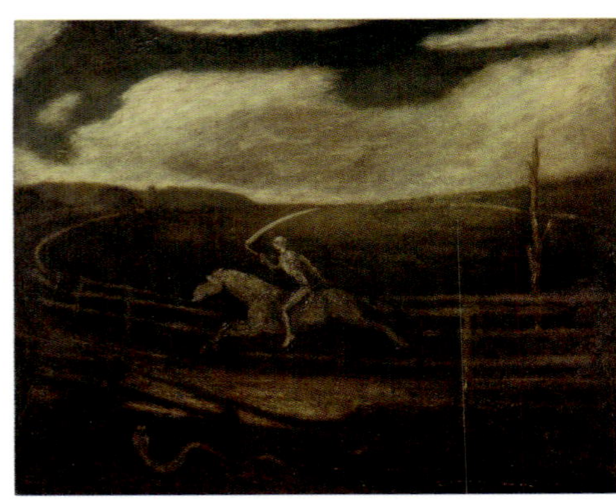

87. Albert Pinkham Ryder
The Race Track (Death on a Pale Horse)   c.1896–1908

Oil on canvas
70.5 x 90 cm (27¾ x 35⅜ in)
The Cleveland Museum of Art, Ohio

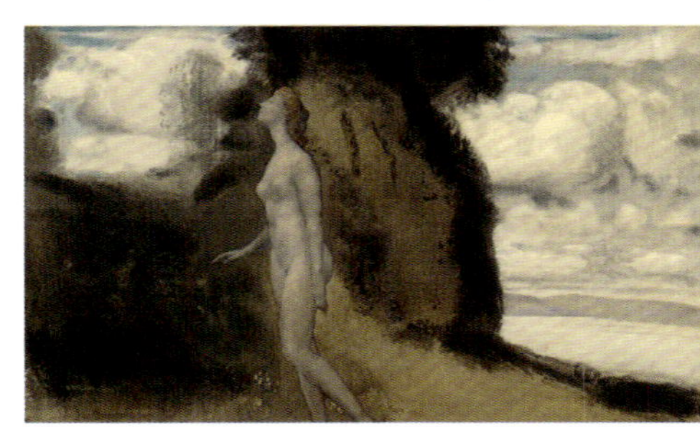

88. Arthur B. Davies
A Measure of Dreams   c.1908

Oil on canvas
45.7 x 76.2 cm (18 x 30 in)
The Metropolitan Museum of Art, New York

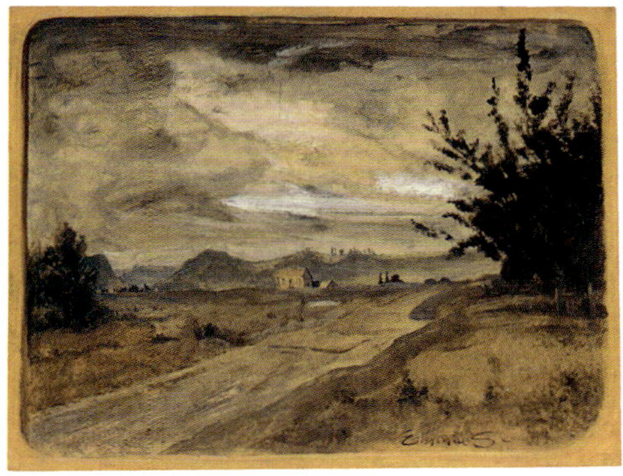

89. Louis Michel Eilshemius
The Haunted House c.1917

Oil on Masonite, 76.2 x 101 cm (30 x 39¾ in)
The Metropolitan Museum of Art, New York

90. Henri Rousseau
The Dream 1910

Oil on canvas
204.5 x 298.5 cm (80½ x 117½ in)
Museum of Modern Art, New York

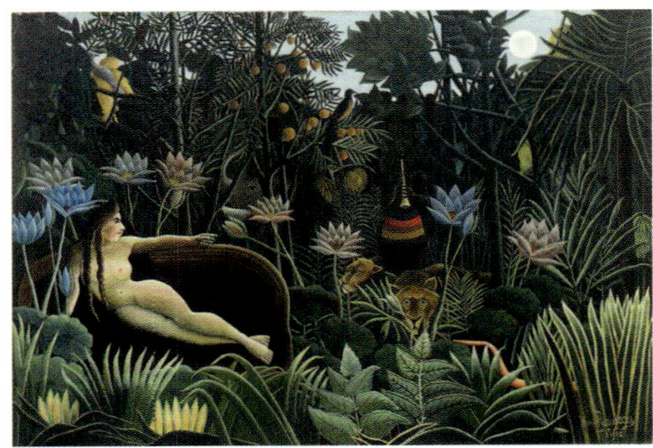

both of their practices reflect elements of outsider and folk art while remaining fundamentally part of the metropolitan art world.

Rousseau became a full-time artist at the age of 49, after retiring from his job at the Paris customs office, or *douane*, hence the reason for his famous nickname 'Le Douanier'. Despite his admiration of academic painters, Rousseau's style had little in common with them, and it was mocked by contemporary critics. However, it was admired by artists such as Picasso, who found in Rousseau's paintings a candour and directness that also formed part of his own work, which was inspired by African tribal masks, Iberian carvings and other 'primitive' and archaic art forms.

Among Rousseau's most celebrated paintings are his exotic jungle scenes, but it is significant that they were not influenced by direct experience of the tropics but were the products of his imagination (and visits to the Paris zoo), just as Dawson's scenes are imaginary. Ambitious and determined to become a famous academic painter, but largely self-taught, Rousseau developed a style that made the most of his lack of conventional training: proportions were incorrect, perspective was peculiar and colours were bright and often unexpected. He became what can only be described as a 'naive' artist, which was far from what he had planned for himself. These characteristics, however, were the source of the idiosyncrasies that infuse his work and which have come to be universally admired. His individualism, however, was not always appreciated. One Paris journalist remarked that 'Monsieur Rousseau paints with his feet with his eyes closed'.[32] Influenced by multiple sources, including classical sculpture, postcards, newspaper illustrations and his jaunts around Paris, Rousseau created unorthodox modern interpretations of traditional painting genres such as landscape, portraiture and allegory. Their dreamlike moods and offbeat juxtapositions may seem simple, but they are often extremely clever.

Rousseau's art was 'primitive' in form but not in intention; he wanted to achieve 'natural' appearances and liked 'finishing' pictures. He had an enthusiasm for verisimilitude, but was loathe to exclude interesting objects from his pictures simply because they were far away. He used perspective only to create a minimum of order in space; the paintings rarely have a single focal point. Rousseau's art, like Dawson's, was far from literal. Guided by a personal vision of reality, he arbitrarily changed natural appearances to suit his own purpose. The crux of Rousseau's work lies in his inability, or unwillingness, to paint the world as he saw it but rather as his mind reconfigured it. In its freedom from theory and in submission to an innocent vision, Rousseau's magic realism is based on the remembered or dream image, 'the image seeking not to outrage the optical arrangement of the world, but to complete it', as writer Roger Shattuck puts it.[33] Interestingly, Shattuck also sees a connection between Rousseau's work and the animal paintings of Lascaux, 'themselves masterpieces of direct statement', which were, of course, influential on the development of Dawson's own artistic vision.

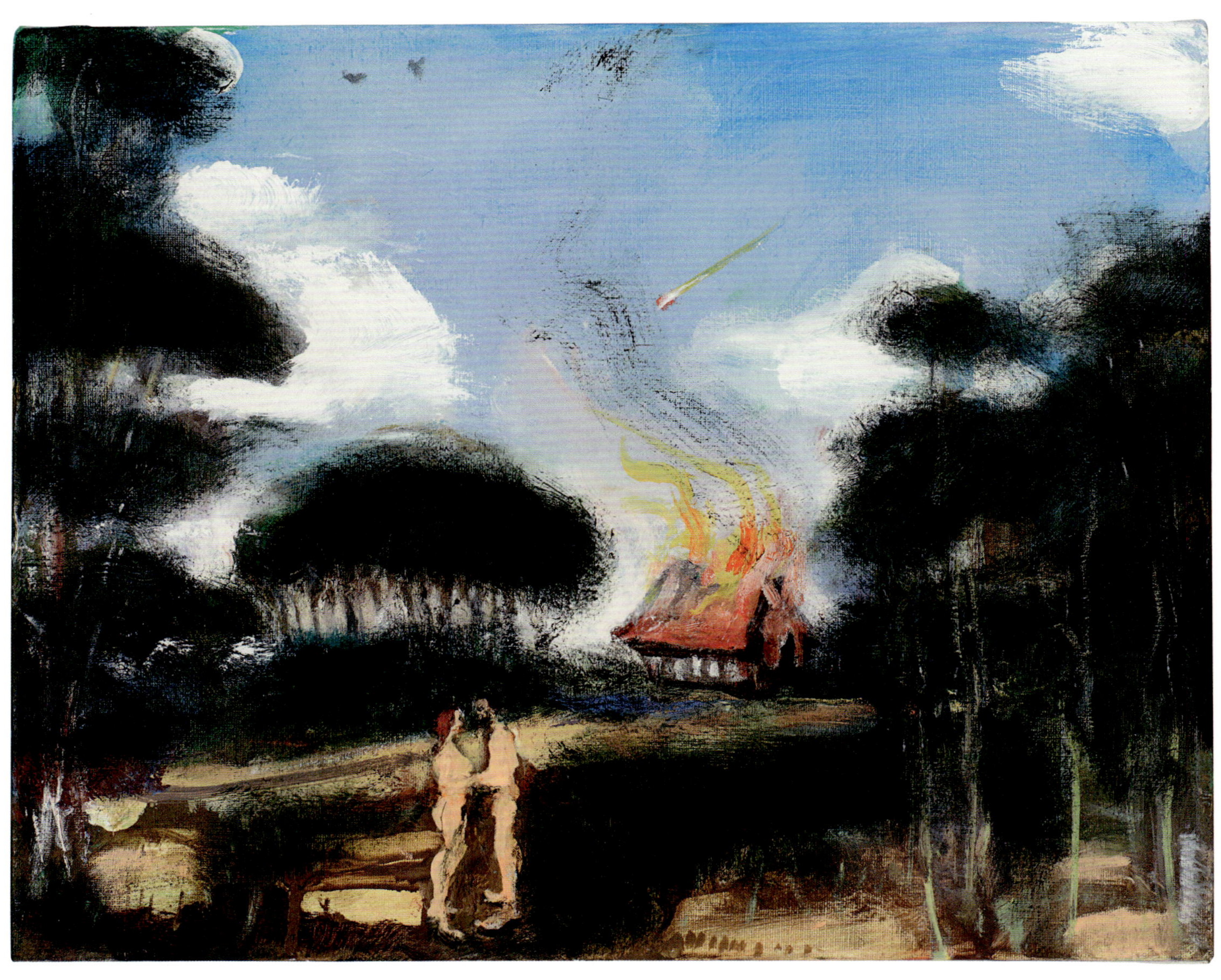

91. House on Fire   2013–16

Oil on canvas
35.6 x 45.7 cm (14 x 18 in)
Kent-Nicoll & Nicoll, USA

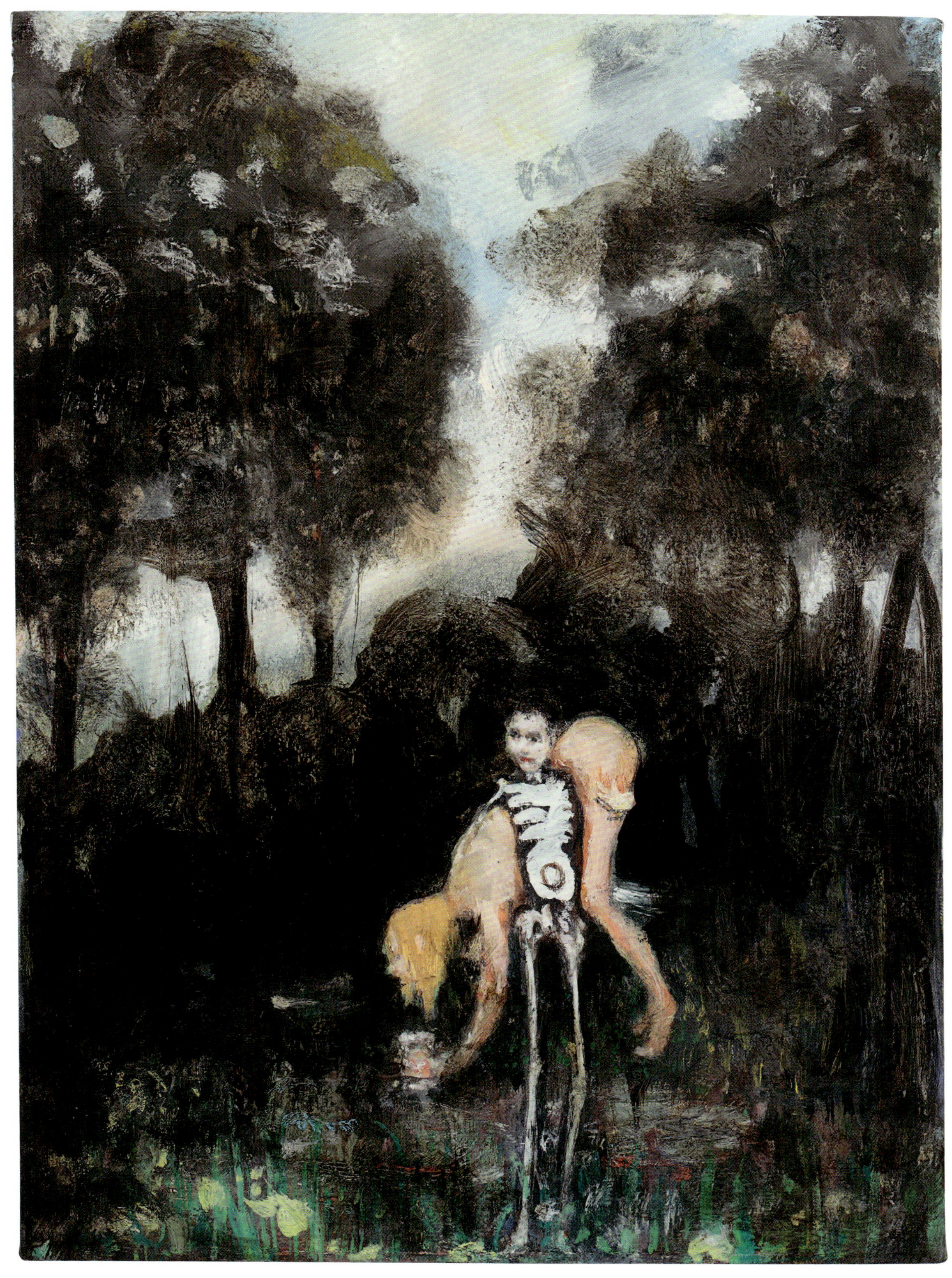

92. Tallahassee   2011

Oil on canvas
40.6 x 30.5 cm (16 x 12 in)
The Bailey Collection

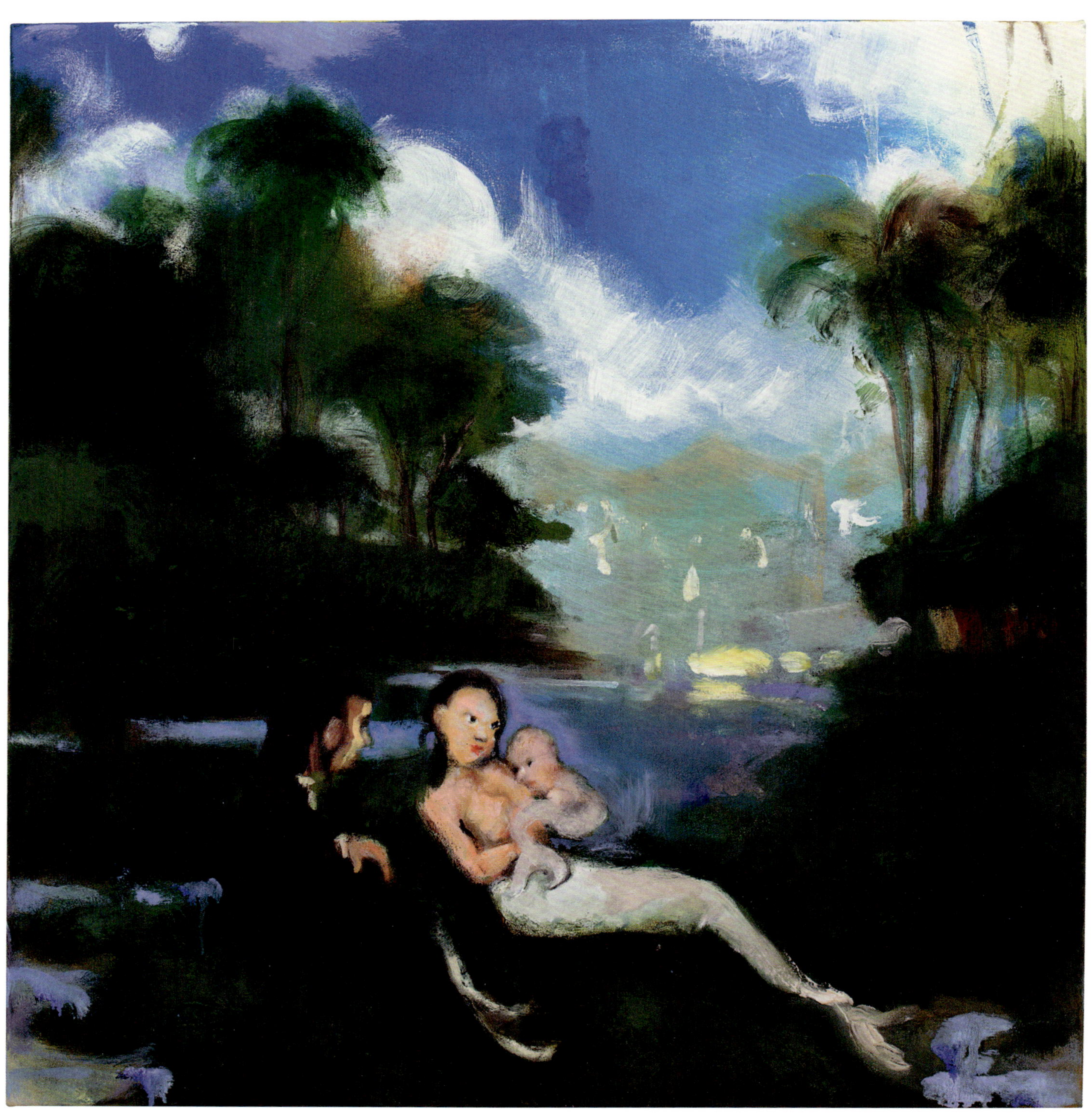

93. Mermaids   2015

Oil on canvas
91.4 x 91.4 cm (36 x 36 in)
Courtesy Gavin Brown's enterprise, New York/Rome

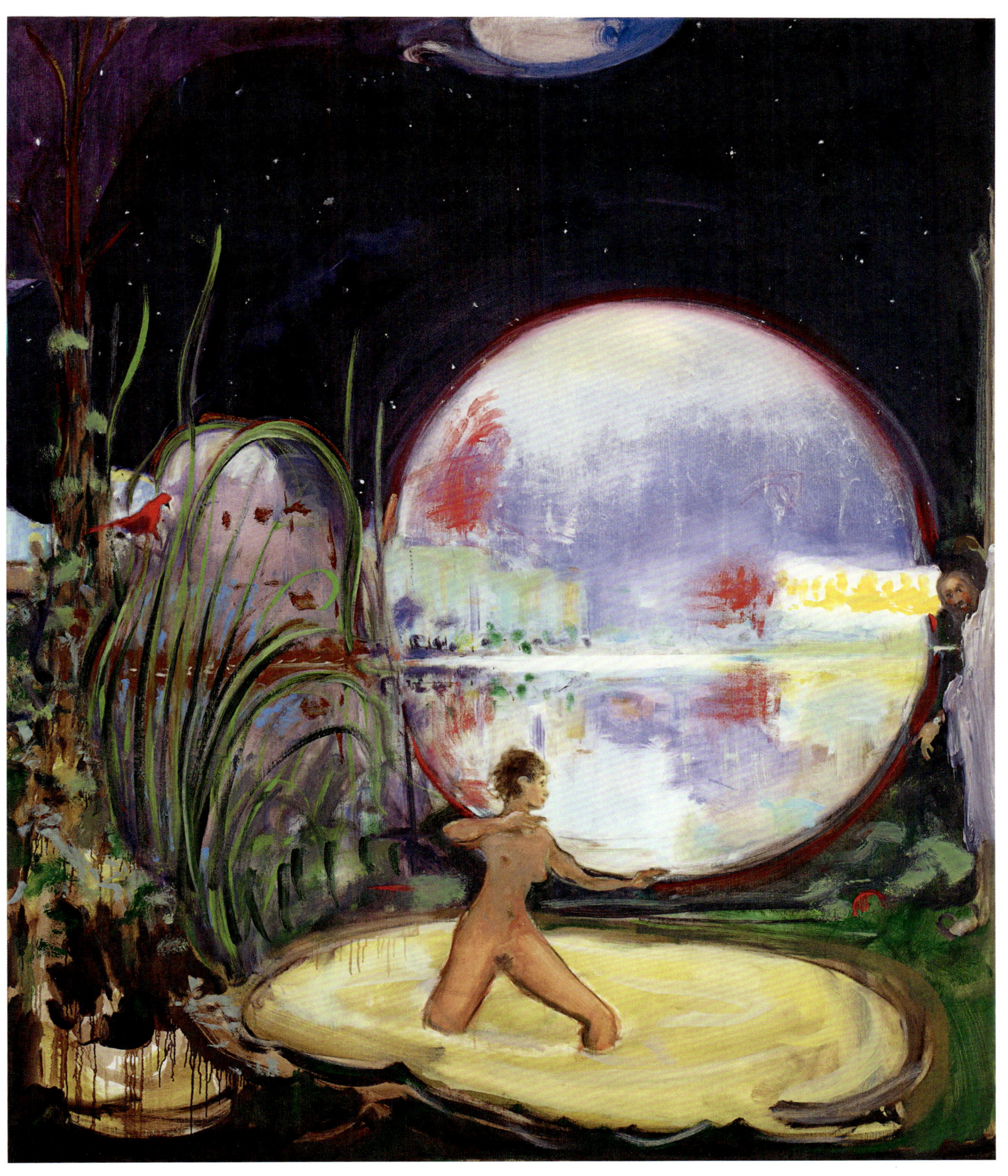

94. Mariana   2013

Oil on linen
208.3 x 177.8 cm (82 x 70 in)
Courtesy Galerie Eva Presenhuber, Zurich, New York

★

Like Rousseau, Dawson paints in a manner that might be described as both
innocent and subversive. His paintings are neither confrontational nor deliberately
provocative, and despite their sometimes portentous subject matter, they are never
intended to impress or overwhelm the viewer. Nonetheless, they go against the grain
of most contemporary art. Dawson distances the seriousness of his art with hints
of humour, frequent arcane references to the past and wry exaggerations. Charles
LaBelle has astutely observed that his work could be an example of what Gilles
Deleuze and Felix Guattari have called a 'minor' art form, a cultural production that
rejects major or dominant artistic languages in favour of a less familiar alternative.[34]
'Minor' art, according to Deleuze and Guattari, functions within a dominant culture,
and involves 'becoming a stranger' in one's own tongue, using the same words, but in
a different way. In the global language of contemporary art, for example, this might
mean a focus on the local and vernacular.

'Operating firmly within the territory of our cultural majority', LaBelle writes,
'Dawson's speech, while stuttering, strangled, is never impolite or improper. It does
not call attention to its rebellious nature but gently goes its own way, quietly disobeys
. . . His work has not so much progressed as remained entrenched in its digressive
tendencies. Dawson is a stranger within painting. He is without peers, an exile.'
Going on to remark that part of the function of 'minor forms' is to 'deterritorialize',
LaBelle remarks that it should come as little surprise that much of Dawson's work
is concerned with the land and questions about how we can preserve it. 'For him',
he concludes, individual interests 'are always tied to the greater concerns of society,
nature, and the cosmos.'[35]

Not everybody agrees with LaBelle's assessment of Dawson's ideology and social
consciousness. It could be argued that his ideas are eccentric, his paintings simply odd
and his earnestness and lack of irony more beguiling than convincing. Nonetheless,
there are elements in his paintings that engage even a sceptic's attention, and
although they eschew mainstream contemporary art discourse, they contain ample
references to art history. Like Rousseau, he deliberately breaks the rules, often subtly,
in terms of perspective, composition, palette and pattern. It is the tension between
their apparent innocence and their less obvious depth of knowledge of history,
science and myth that so often brings these pictures to life. Something similar might
be said about Dawson's use of paint. In his early work, particularly, the technique is
painstaking, almost awkward in its careful deliberation; recently, it has become freer,
less self-conscious and more spontaneous. The contrast is striking.

Dawson has an offbeat and intense imagination that has given rise to an array of
strange and compelling paintings. Notably, it is often their unexpected juxtaposition
that gives sinew to his exhibitions, and it is perhaps their determined heterogeneity
that has found him a niche in the today's art world. It is no accident that the viewer

is not impelled to settle on any one perspective or conclusion, and that the impact
of Dawson's images depends greatly on their context. His paintings, if used as
illustrations in children's books, would read and be understood in a particular way.
In the contemporary art world, their effect is radically different, especially as his
seemingly naive or folkish style is clearly a matter of choice. After learning something
about the artist's intentions and cultural context, the sophistication of the paintings'
references and allusions becomes evident.

And yet, as is to be expected, Dawson's work is changing. In the paintings made
and exhibited in the last few years, much of his innocence has disappeared. For the
best part of three decades, Dawson's subject matter has remained the contemporary
world's failure to recognize the importance of the integration of humanity with nature.
He elaborates:

> What interests and concerns me most becomes the subject of my paintings, and
> although painting may not initially allow the widest broadcast of ideas it can
> be an extremely efficacious means for an individual without wealth, without
> community support, without conformity to present norms, to craft and sing a
> beautiful song that has the potential to be sung by others in the future . . .
>
> As our physical world becomes less habitable, the means to abandon it are
> advanced and promoted. It seems that much of the most ubiquitous, valued and
> touted art of our time is helpful in fostering the acceptance of the degradation
> and desensitization of humanity. My own position is to try to resist this. Almost
> every work is intended to be a paean to the paradise we live in, a long goodbye
> to what the world was and could have been. I'm always going back in time, and
> sometimes I find that the further back I go, the more I turn up in the future; as
> a painter I became interested in vernacular styles of painting because I wanted
> to communicate something, and I didn't want it to be about art, but about the
> vanishing cultures, extant for thousands of years, that are disappearing like rare
> species, and about the birds, insects, and animals that are also under threat.
> From my use of paint and brushes, which are of course an antique medium, to
> my attempts to conserve attributes of maths and astronomy in mythology, to my
> interest in trying to keep alive the 'long time', to my efforts to employ as much
> love as possible for the glories of the natural world – in so many ways the work
> has been a prolonged farewell to the world of nature, to beauty, to sentiment,
> memory, and even to nostalgia.[36]

Since his last major exhibition, held in 2017 in New York, it might appear that
Dawson's idealistic impetus has begun to fade. His newer paintings look different and
are perhaps less charming than before, but their refusal to fit in, be fashionable and
impress, is stronger than ever. He is adamant that his ideas are relevant and important
today, and that while many of his convictions have parallels in the counterculture of

the 1960s, they are independent and not especially influenced by them. Dawson's understanding of the world is unconventional and Quixotic; he is something of a maverick, driven onwards by the sharpness of his curiosity and a commitment to the values in which he passionately believes.

It is nonetheless true, though, that outside influences, not chosen but unconsciously assimilated, become internalized and are reflected in artists' work; their practices will inevitably reveal shifts in the concerns of the world around them as well as their own sensibilities. In Dawson's case, this may account for much of the disenchantment in his recent work. There is little optimism to be found in the paintings in his last exhibition, just reflections of the difficulty of finding harmony in contemporary life and allusions to the melancholy side of human existence.

The recent painting *I-81* (fig.84) depicts Interstate Highway 81, which runs diagonally through Virginia along the Shenandoah Valley, forming the main part of the route that Dawson takes on his frequent drives from New York to North Carolina. 'It is very spectacular, rural, with grand heights and views,' he explains. 'But what is wilderness now? Here? A paradise crossed by a gash of highway with a steady flow of lorries and cars? Is this what contemporary rural life looks like?'[37] But then he turns to recollections of the way things once were, to his childhood days. Asked to comment on *Pair of Cardinals* (fig.95), a key painting in the 2017 exhibition that shows a trailer home, surveyed by the birds of its title, with a fantasy figure scene painted on one of its sides, he answers with lines from a song by Stephen Foster (1826–64), the so-called father of American music:

> I dream of Jeanie with the light brown hair,
> Borne, like a zephyr, on the summer air;
> I see her tripping where the bright streams play,
> Happy as the daisies that dance on her way.
> Many were the wild notes her merry voice would pour.
> Many were the blithe birds that warbled them o'er:
> Oh! I dream of Jeanie with the light brown hair,
> Floating, like a vapor, on the soft summer air.

'I was working out a memory, which dates from the age of four,' Dawson goes on to explain. 'It was about living for nine months in a trailer in Pascagoula, Mississippi, while my father was in the army, studying at aviation school. You see landscaping, shrubs, and flowers around trailers, which are often well established and beautified. Like some birds, humans can't stop beautifying their nests.' His vision may now be taking new form, but Verne Dawson's quest for Arcadia and the establishment of an 'archaic future' continues, just as his body of work remains a striking and necessary counterbalance to the dominant forces in our cultural world.

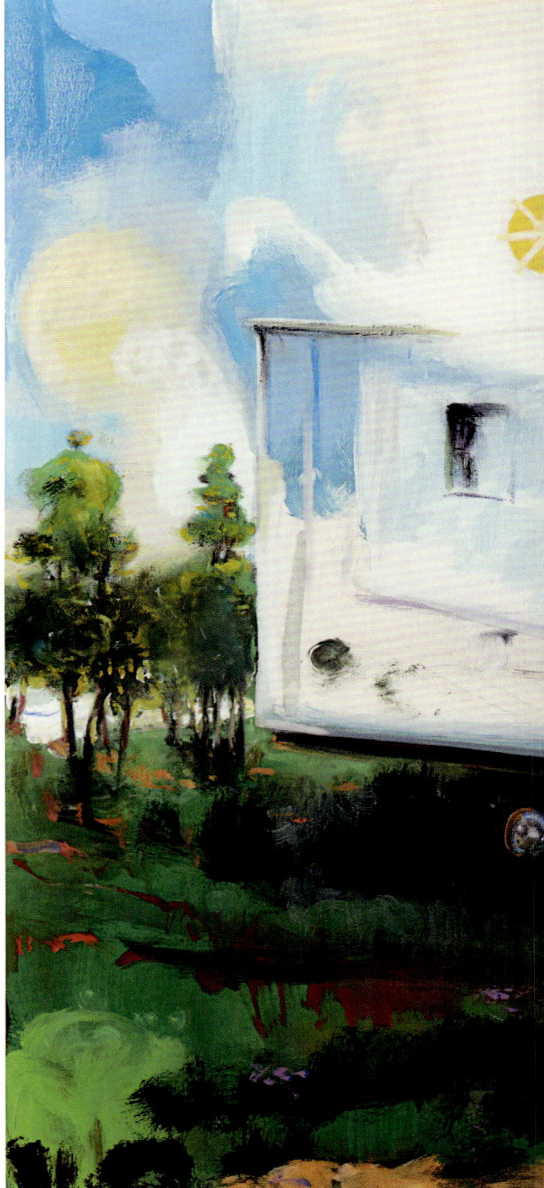

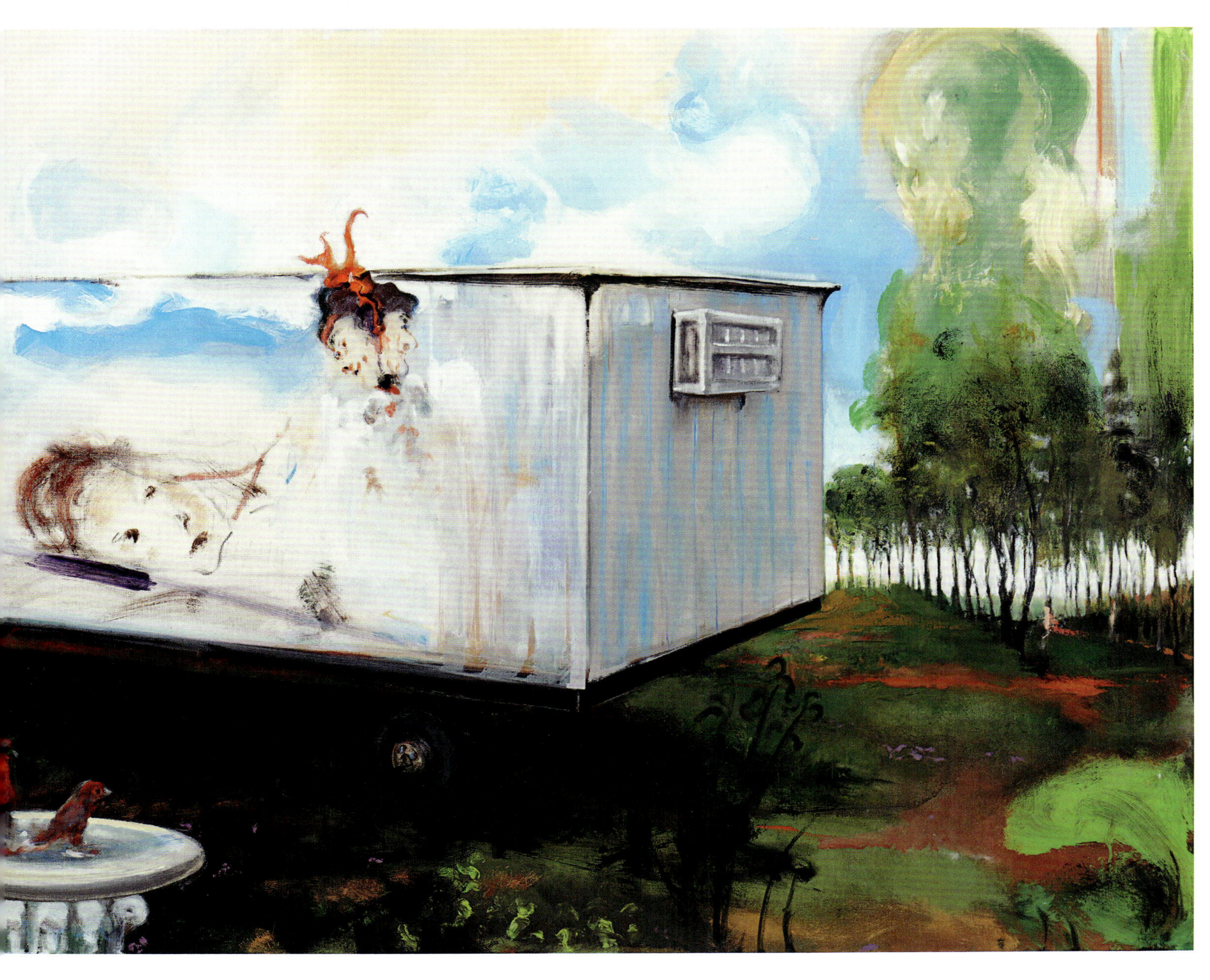

95. Pair of Cardinals   2017

Oil on wood panel
114.3 x 215.9 cm (45 x 85 in)
Courtesy Gavin Brown's enterprise, New York/Rome

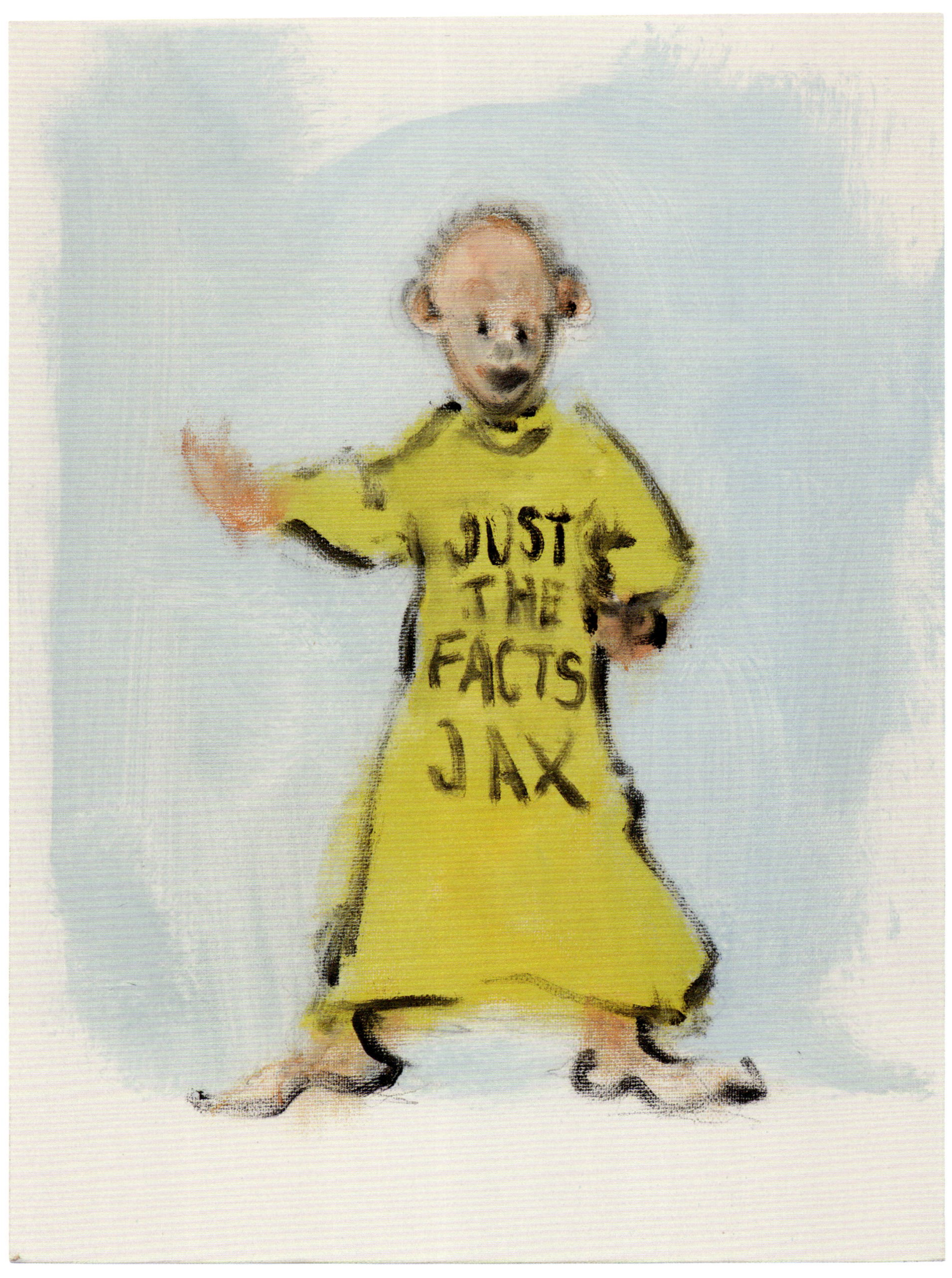

96. Just the Facts Jax (Yellow Kid) 2017

Oil on panel
40.6 x 30.5 cm (16 x 12 in)
Courtesy Gavin Brown's enterprise, New York/Rome

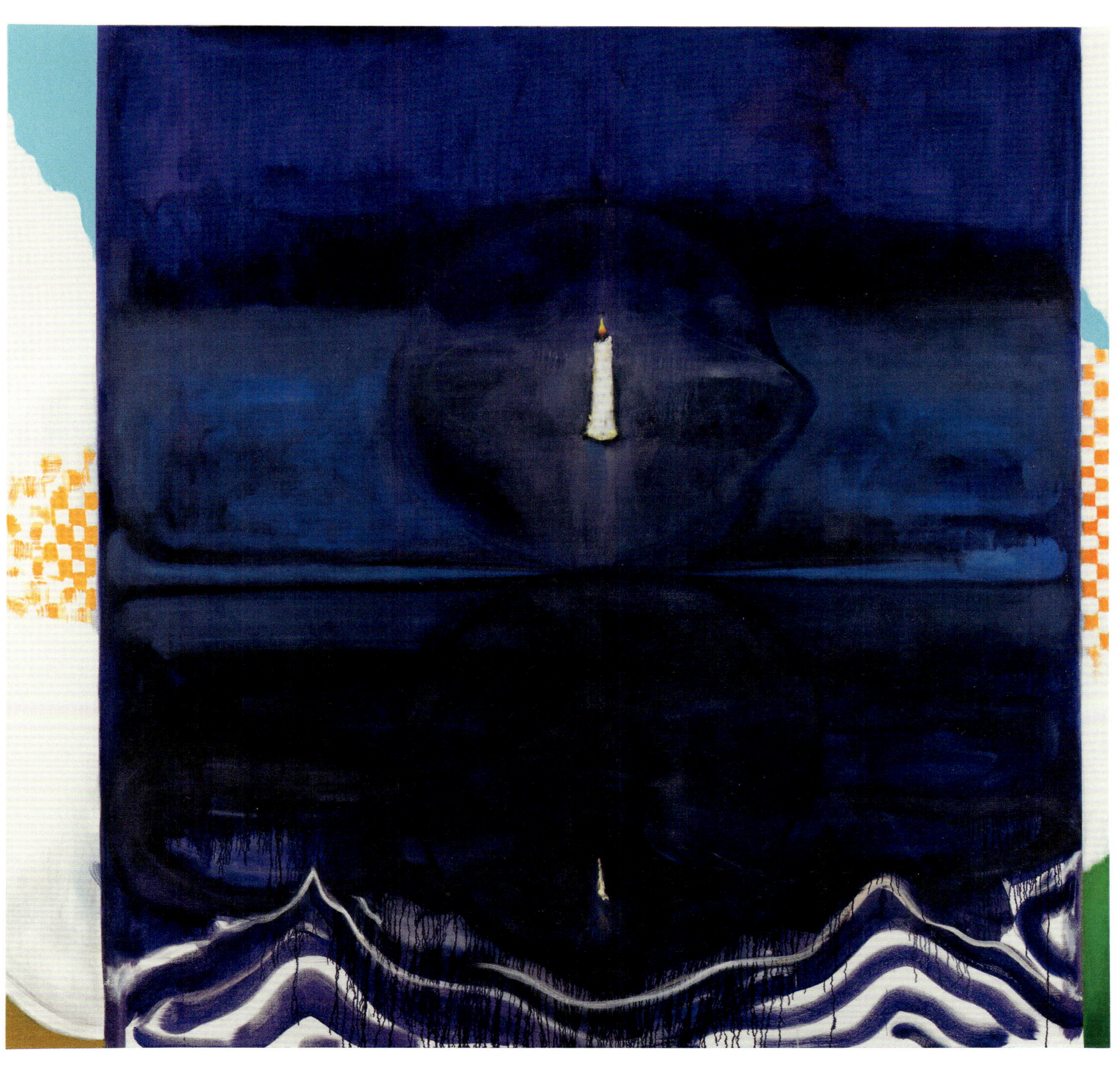

97. Violet Candle   2011

Oil on canvas
279.4 x 254 cm (110 x 100 in)
Courtesy Galerie Eva Presenhuber, Zurich, New York

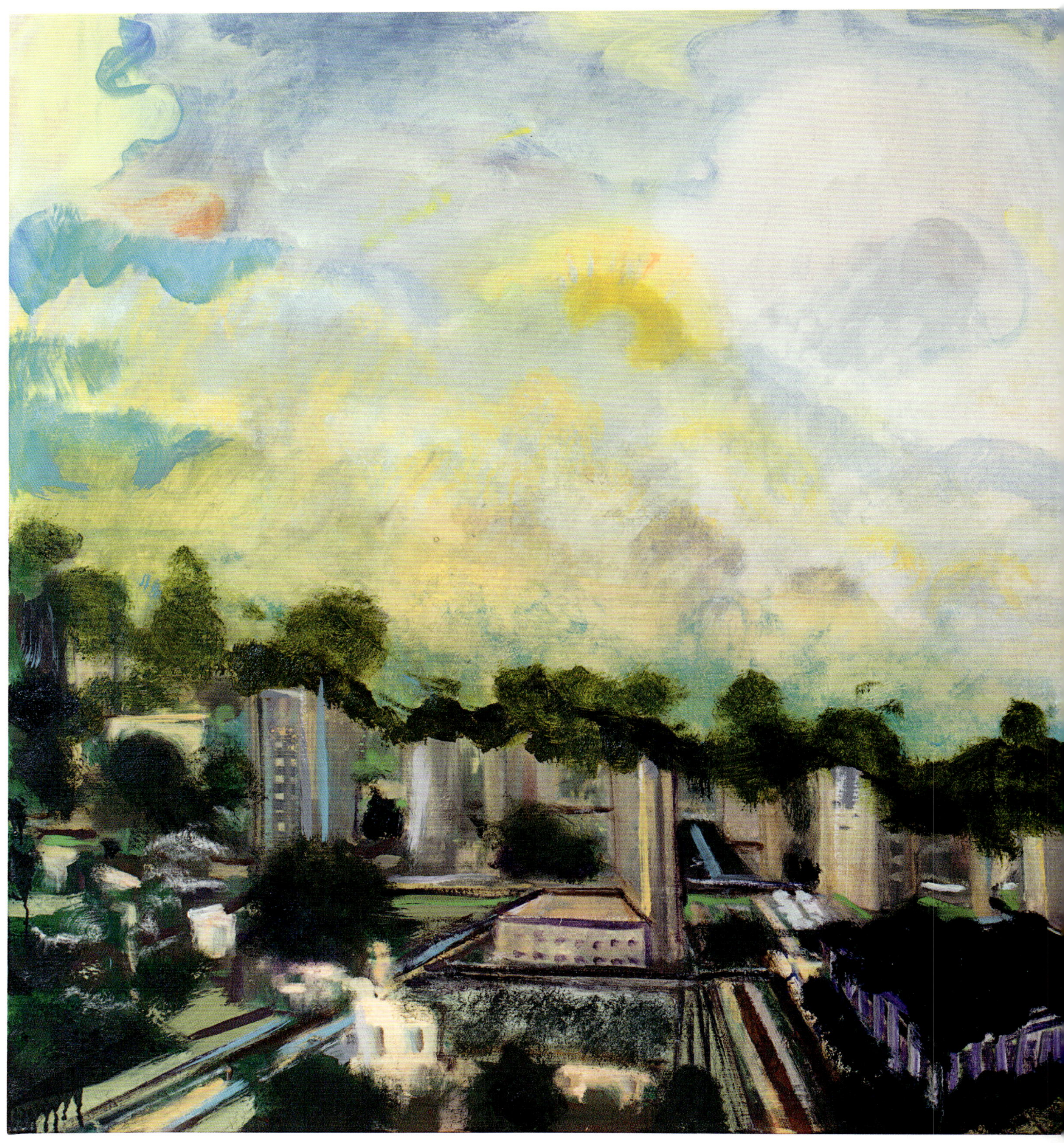

98. Harbor Town   2015

Oil on canvas
104.1 x 205.7 cm (41 x 81 in)
Courtesy Galerie Eva Presenhuber, Zurich, New York

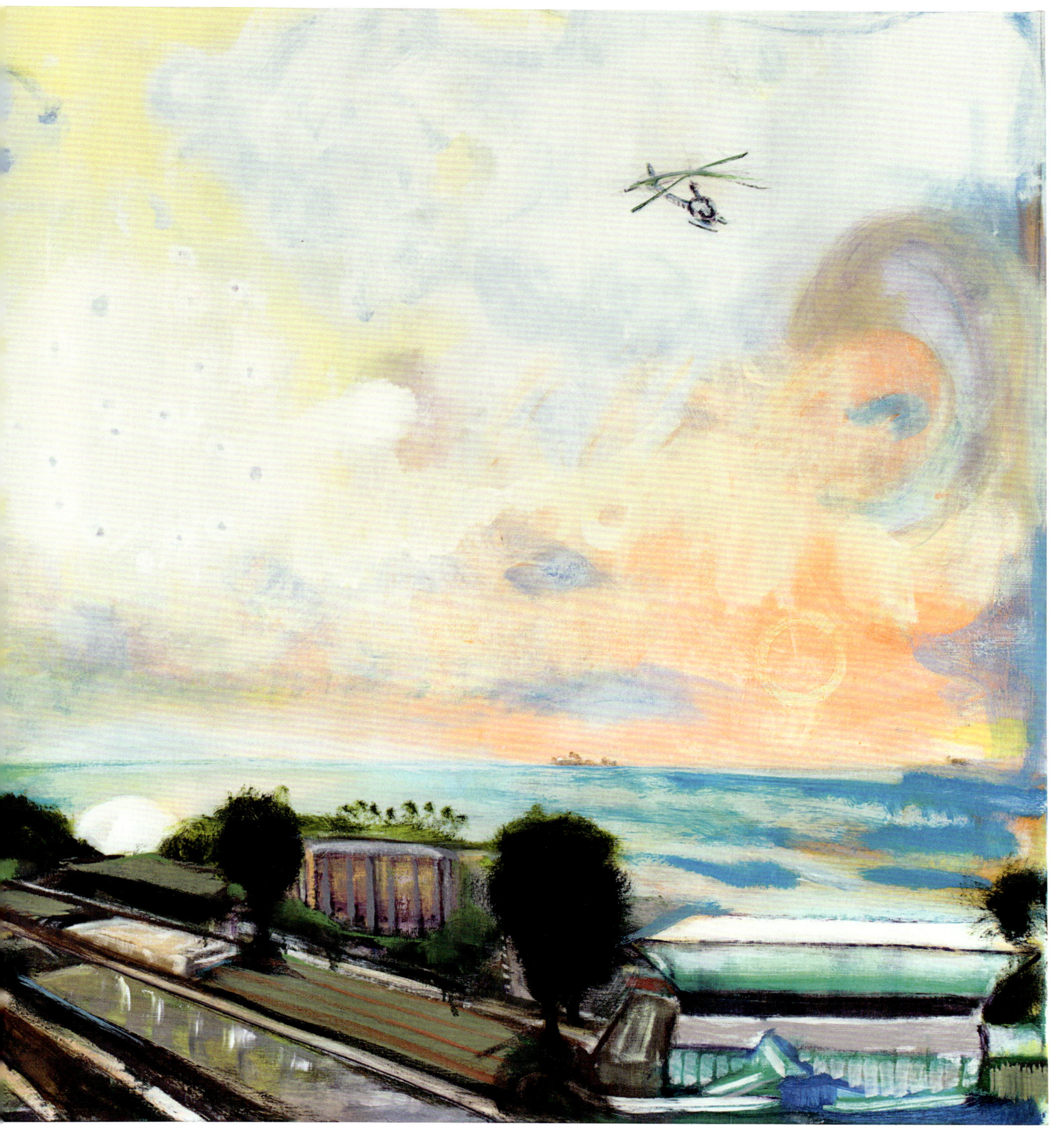

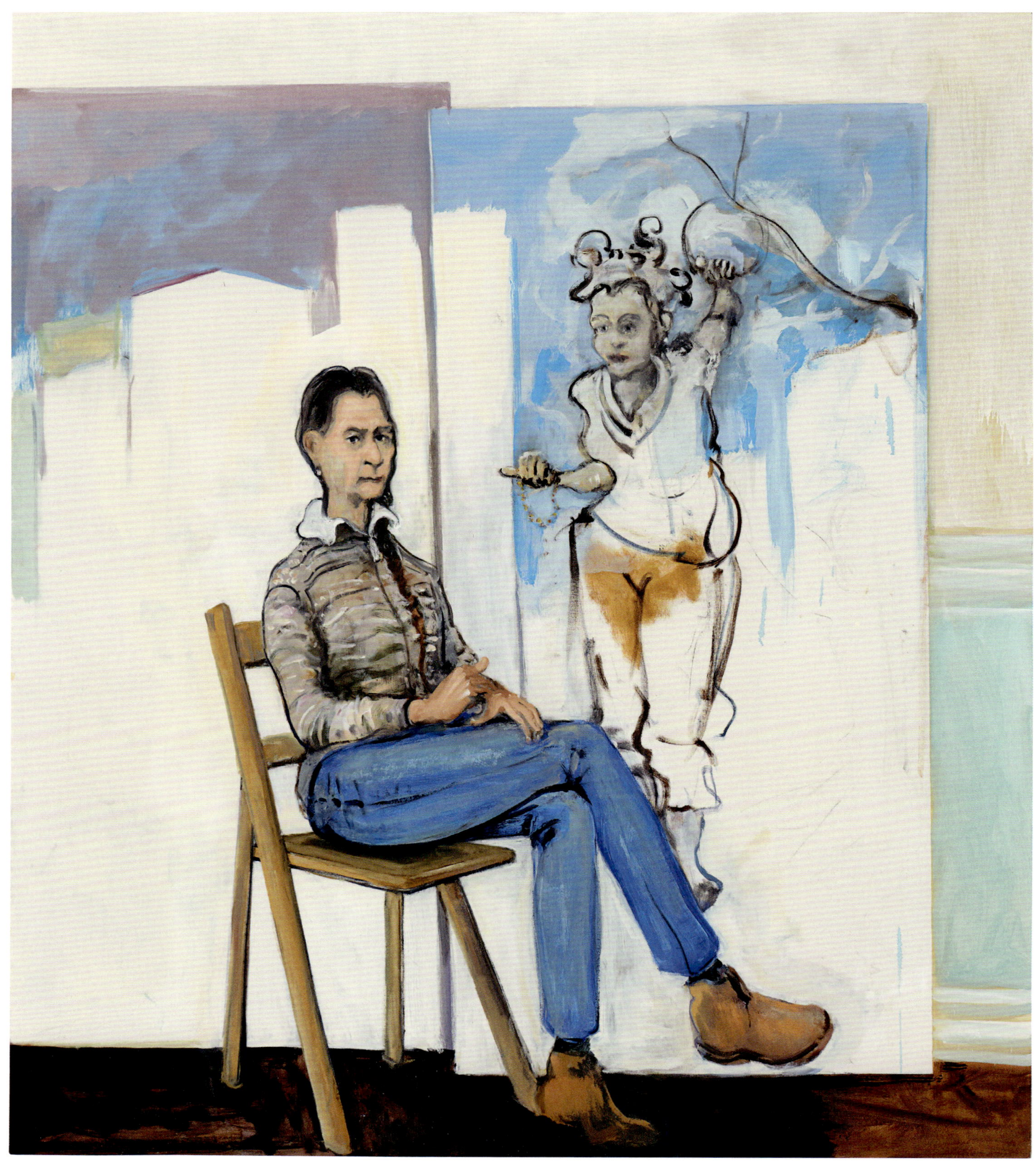

99. Portrait of Sermin Kardestuncer   2017

Oil on canvas
215.9 x 193 cm (85 x 76 in)
Detroit Institute of the Arts, Gift of the Alex Katz Foundation

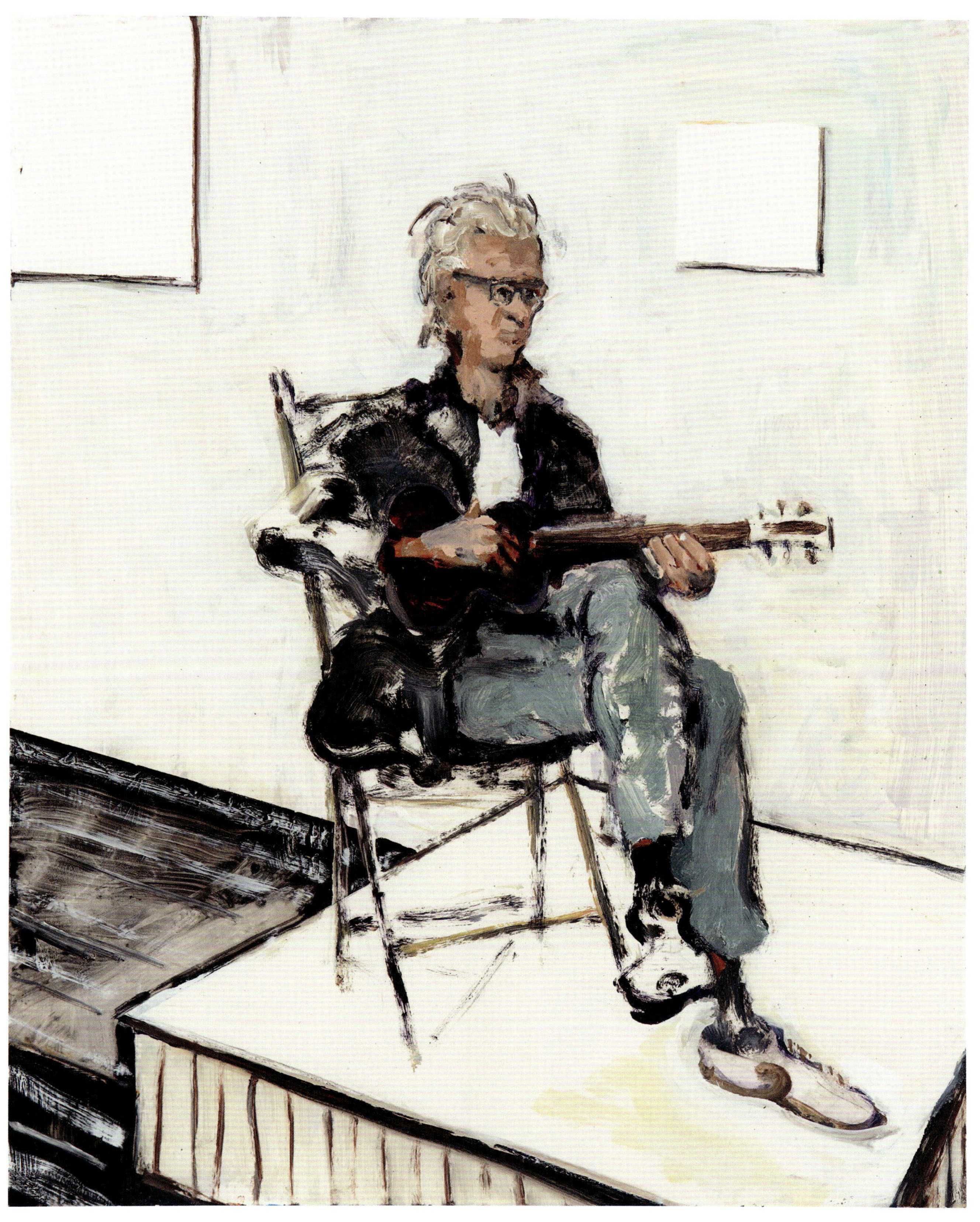

100. Tej Hezarika 2017

Oil on panel
50.8 x 40.6 cm (20 x 16 in)
McEvoy Famiy Collection

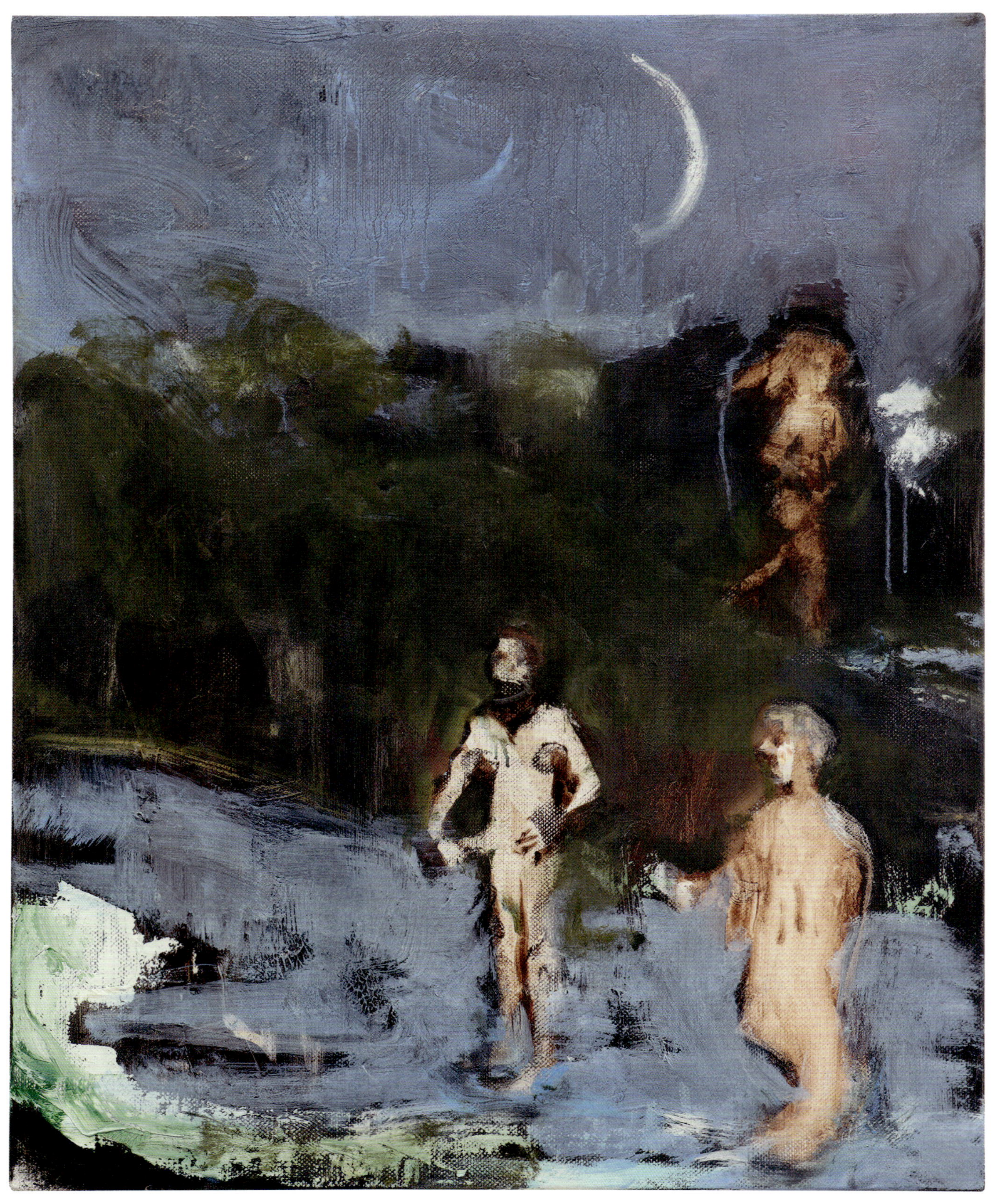

101. Penniless   2018

Oil on canvas
61 x 50.8 cm (24 x 20 in)
Collection of the artist

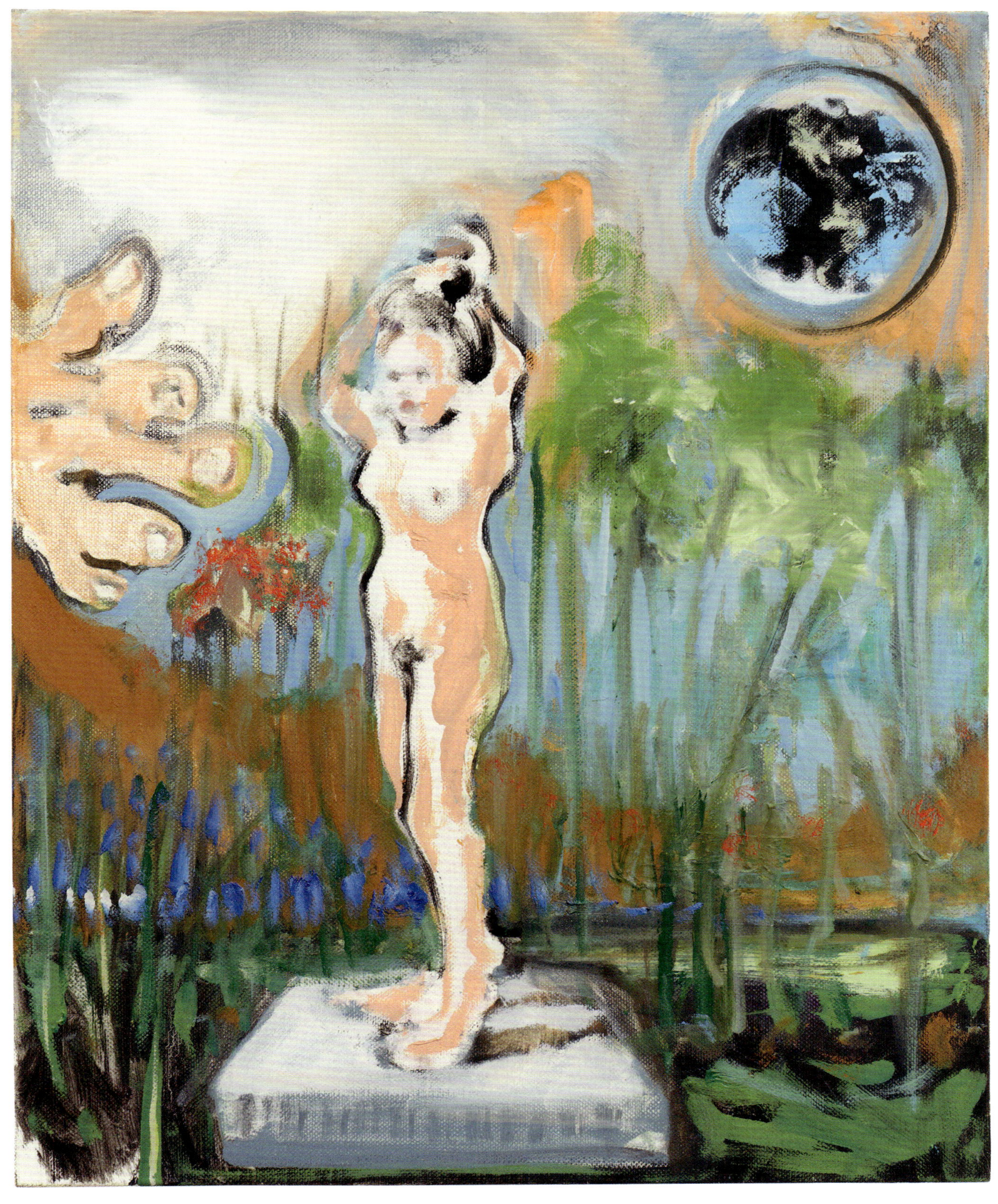

102. Aphrodite   2018

Oil on canvas
61 x 50.8 cm (24 x 20 in)
Collection of the artist

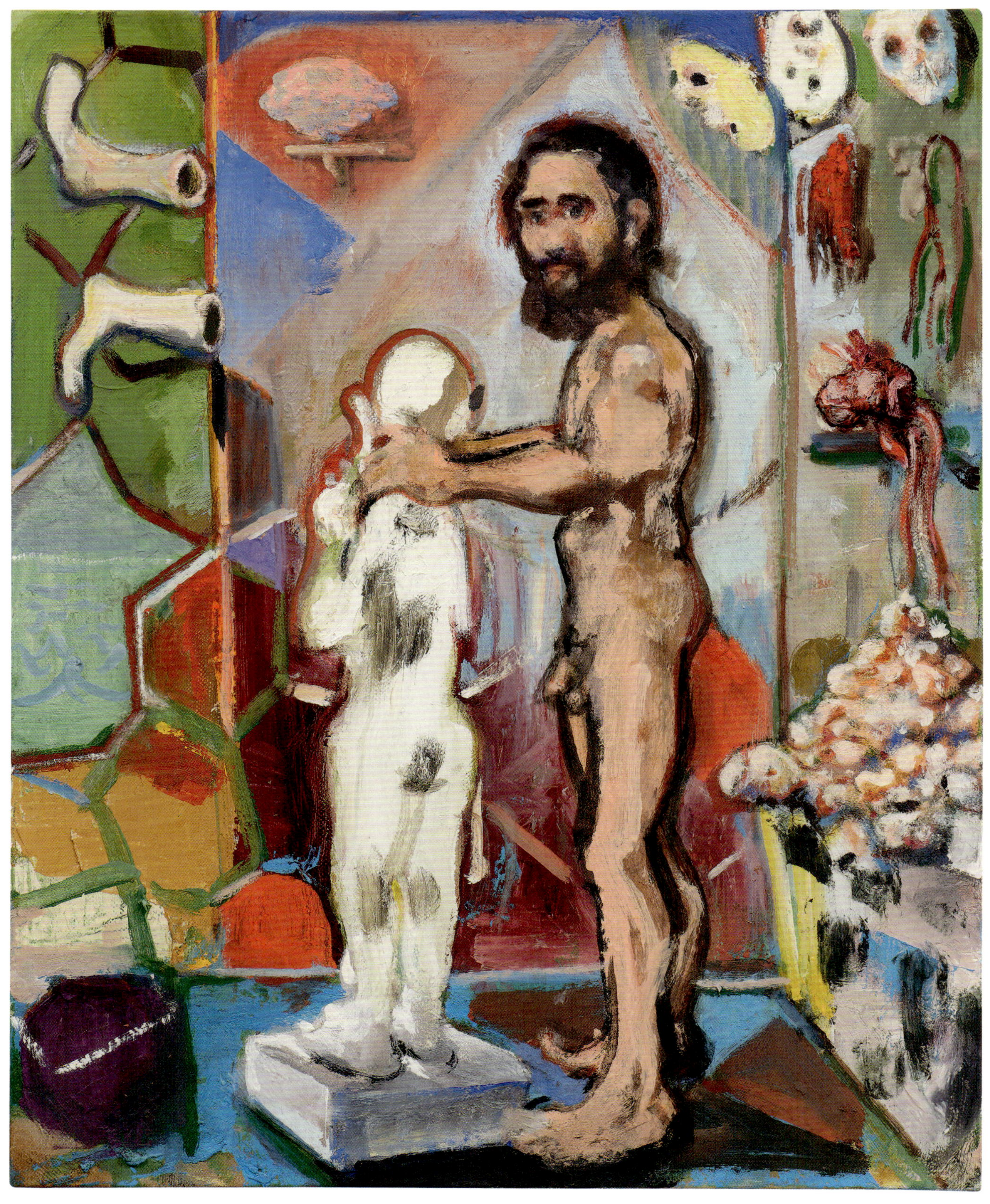

103. Prometheus in the Studio   2018

Oil on canvas
61 x 50.8 cm (24 x 20 in)
Collection of the artist

134

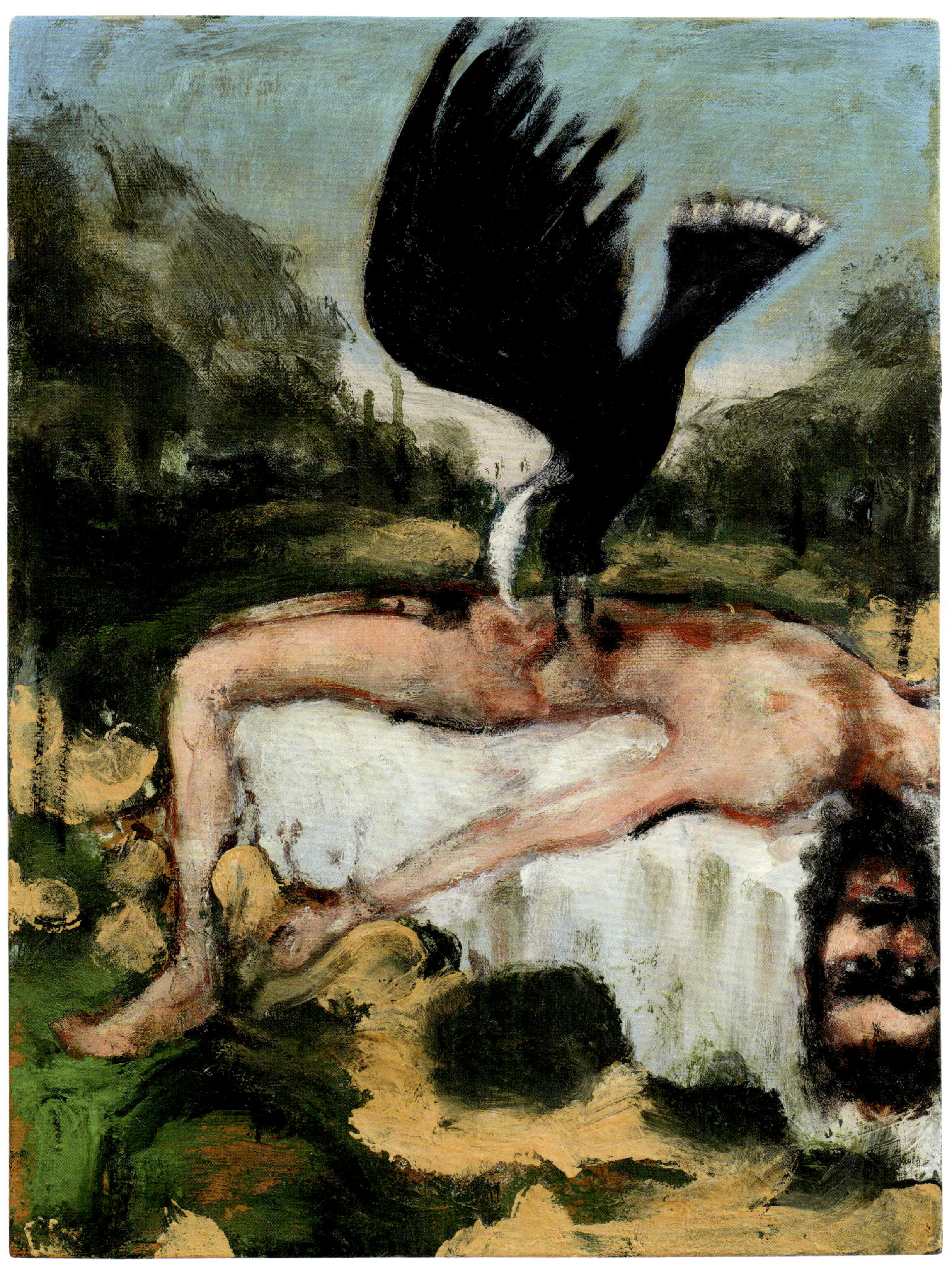

104. PrometheusBound   2018

Oil on canvas
40.6 x 30.5 cm (16 x 12 in)
Collection of the artist

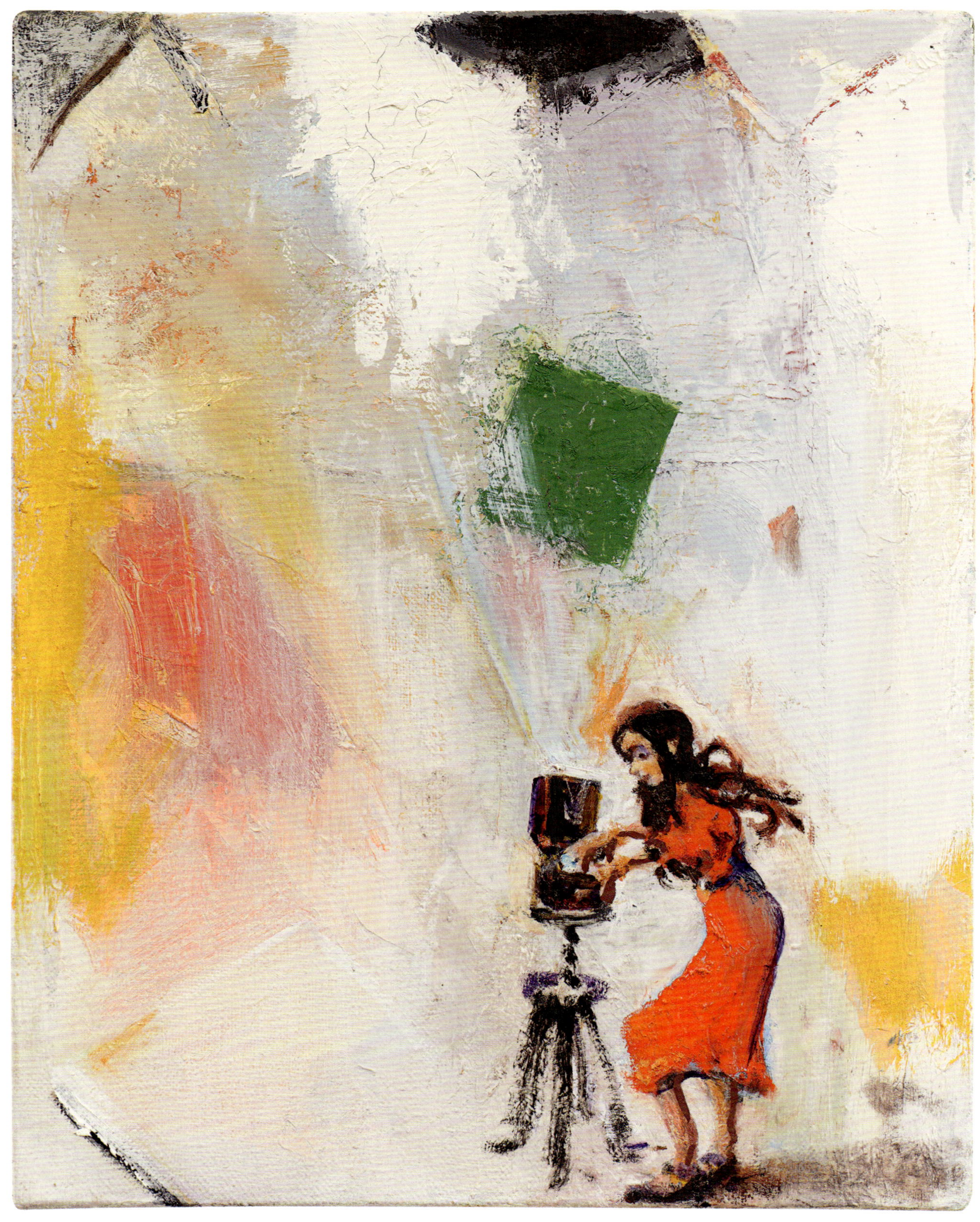

105. *Pandora*   2018

Oil on canvas
50.8 x 40.6 cm (20 x 16 in)
Collection of the artist

Notes

Unless otherwise credited, all quotes from the artist are from communications between the author and the artist in 2018.

1. Verne Dawson in conversation with Sinziana Ravini, *Annual Magazine*, 2013.
2. Walter Benjamin, 'Experience and Poverty', published in *Die Welt im Wort* (Prague) in December 1933, and taken from *Gesammelte Schriften, II* (Collected Writings, II), translated by Rodney Livingstone, pp 213–19: atlasofplaces.com/Experience-and-Poverty-Walter-Benjamin.
3. Walter Benjamin, 'The Storyteller: Reflections on the Works of Nikolai Leskov' (1968), in *Walter Benjamin: Illuminations*, Hannah Arendt (ed.), Jonathan Cape, London, 1970.
4. Bruno Bettelheim, *The Uses of Enchantment: The Meaning and Importance of Fairy Tales*, Penguin, London, 1991.
5. Ibid., p.3.
6. Quoted in Wikipedia article on 'Hillbilly': Julian Hawthorne, 'Mountain Votes Spoil Huntington's Revenge', *New York Journal*, 23 April 1900, p.2.
7. Fiona Ritchie and Doug Orr, *Wayfaring Strangers: The Musical Voyage from Scotland and Ulster to Appalachia*, The University of North Carolina Press, 2014, p.194.
8. Verne Dawson and Genesis Breyer P-Orridge, *Bomb* magazine, Spring 2013, bombmagazine.org/articles/genesis-breyer-p-orridge-and-verne-dawson/
9. Communication with the author, 2018.
10. Verne Dawson, 'A Recollection', in *Verne Dawson: Precession of the Equinoxes. Paintings 1994–2010*, les presses du réel, 2012. This is a fundamental source of information on the artist's early life, and he was happy to have it quoted so extensively in this text. The book also includes a significant essay on the artist by Caoimhín Mac Giolla Léith.
11. Verne Dawson in conversation with Sinziana Ravini, 2013.
12. 'Outside In: The Art of Verne Dawson', *At Cooper Union* magazine, 2008.
13. Bob Nickas, 'Eternal Returns: The Art of Verne Dawson', *Artforum*, November 2001.
14. 'Verne Dawson and Genesis Breyer P-Orridge', Spring 2013.

15. Arthur Koestler, *The Sleepwalkers: A History of Man's Changing Vision of the Universe*, Hutchinson, London, 1959.
16. Alexander Marshack, *The Roots of Civilization: the Cognitive Beginnings of Man's First Art, Symbol and Notation*, McGraw-Hill, New York, 1972.
17. See, for example, Iain Davison's review of the revised edition of 'The Roots of Civilization' in *American Anthropologist*, December 1993.
18. Giorgio de Santillana and Hertha von Dechend, *Hamlet's Mill: An Essay Investigating the Origins of Human Knowledge and Its Transmission through Myth*, David R. Godine, Boston, Massachusetts, 1977.
19. 'Outside In: The Art of Verne Dawson', 2008.
20. Communication with the author, 2018.
21. Ibid.
22. Andrew Wilton, 'The Sublime in the Old World and the New', in *American Sublime: Landscape Painting in the United States 1820–1880*, Tate Publishing, London, 2002. This catalogue has provided much of the information on the American landscape painters mentioned in the text.
23. For more information on this subject, see Gordon Kennedy, *Children of the Sun: A Pictorial Anthology from Germany to California, 1883–1949*, Nivaria Press, 1998.
24. 'Outside In: The Art of Verne Dawson', 2008.
25. See Jacques F. Vallée, 'Five Arguments against the Extraterrestrial Origin of Unidentified Flying Objects', in *Journal of Scientific Exploration*, vol.4, no.1, 1990: 105–17; and Ross Douthat, 'Flying Saucers and Other Fairy Tales', *The New York Times*, 23 December 2017.
26. For more information, see the exhaustive Wikipedia entry on Terence McKenna.
27. Terence McKenna, *The Archaic Revival*, HarperCollins, New York, 1991.
28. See Caroline Christie, 'The psychedelic drug that could explain our belief in life after death', *Little Atoms* magazine: littleatoms.com/science/psychedelic-drug-could-explain-our-belief-life-after-death.
29. Merlin James and Carol Rhodes in a digital leaflet accompanying 'E(i)lshem(i)us', an exhibition at 42 Carlton Place, Glasgow, 2016.

30. Ibid.
31. 'Outside In: The Art of Verne Dawson', 2008.
32. Quote by a Parisian journalist in 1891.
33. Roger Shattuck, *The Banquet Years*, rev. ed., Vintage Books, New York, 1968, from which much of the information on Rousseau in this text has been taken.
34. Charles LaBelle, 'Celestial Bodies', *Frieze* magazine, June 2002, p.101.
35. Ibid.
36. Verne Dawson in conversation with Sinziana Ravini, 2013.
37. Communication with the author, 2018.

Bibliography

Articles

Adams, Brooks, 'Report from Lyon: Time After Time', *Art in America*, February 2006, pp 56–63

Ash, John, *Art in America*, March 1990, p.207

Campbell-Johnson, Rachel, 'Best London Exhibitions', *The Times*, 15 February 2003

Cattelan, Maurizio, 'Interstellar Overdrive', *Flash Art*, October 2002, pp 62–5

Colard, Jean-Max, 'Enquêtes sur le Réel', *L'Officiel Art*, no.2, June 2012, pp 280–2

Dawson, Verne and Genesis Breyer P-Orridge, *BOMB*, issue 123, Spring 2013, pp 26–37

Denny, Ned, 'Infinitely Fabulous', *New Statesman*, 10 March 2003

Dunne, Aidan, 'Scene Stealing?', *The Irish Times*, 16 April 2004

Finel Honigman, Ana, Review, *Time Out*, London, 19 March 2003

Ford, Felicity, Review, *CIRCA Art Magazine*, March–May 2004

Guner, Fishun, Review, *Metro London*, 19 February 2003

Halle, Howard, Review, *Time Out*, New York, 11 June 2009

———, Review, *Time Out*, New York, 14 January 1999

Harper's, September 2002, p.26 (illustration)

Hase, Bettina von, 'A Monument to Passion', *ArtReview*, vol.2, no.6, 2004, pp 90–3

Herbert, Martin, 'Round and Round Again', *Time Out*, London, 25 May 2005, p.66

Hubbard, Sue, Review, *The Independent*, 25 February 2003

'Interview: John Giorno by Verne Dawson', *BOMB*, issue 140, Summer 2017

Iremonger, Anne, Review, *The Dubliner*, 2004

Johnson, Ken, Review, *The New York Times*, 12 June 2009

———, Review, *The New York Times*, 24 March 2000

———, Review, *The New York Times*, 8 January 1999

Jones, Ronald, Review, *Frieze*, issue 46, May 1999

Kort, Pamela, 'Verne Dawson: Eva Presenhuber', *Artforum*, vol.54, no.7, March 2016

LaBelle, Charles, 'Celestial Bodies', *Frieze*, issue 68, June 2002, pp 98–101

Montague, Jemima, 'Urgent Painting', *Frieze*, issue 66, April 2002, pp 88–9

Moufarrage, Nicolas, *Flash Art*, March 1983, p.32

'News and Around: Biennale de Lyon', *Tema Celeste*, July–August 2005, p.96

Nickas, Bob, *Dutch*, January–February 2001

———, 'Eternal Returns: The Art of Verne Dawson', *Artforum*, vol.40, no.3, November 2001, pp 132–5

———, 'People Take Pictures of Each Other', *Influence*, issue 2, 2004, pp 90–109

'Outside In: The Art of Verne Dawson', *At Cooper Union* magazine, 2008

Ratcliff, Carter, 'Prehistory Man', *Tate Etc.*, January–February 2003, pp 34–41

Reust, Hans Rudolf, Review, *Artforum*, vol.42, no.9, May 2004, p.221

Review, *Paper*, June 2001, p.104

Review, *The New Yorker*, 4 June 2001

Saltz, Jerry, 'Primordial Seasonings', *Village Voice*, 19 June 2001, p.61

Smith, Roberta, Review, *The New York Times*, 1 June 2001

———, Review, *The New York Times*, 18 February 2000

———, *The New York Times*, 20 October 1989, p.28

Supplement, *Flash Art*, May–June 1989, p.3

'Verne Dawson comes to Victoria Miro this month', Phaidon online, March 2015: uk.phaidon.com/agenda/art/articles/2013/march/07/verne-dawson-comes-to-victoria-miro-this-month/

Verne Dawson in conversation with Sinziana Ravini, *Annual Magazine*, issue 5, 2013, pp 164–5

'Verne Dawson: Mermaid Money', *Mousse Magazine*, issue 51, December 2015–January 2016

Vincent, Steven, Review, *Art in America*, April 2005, pp 142–3

Westcott, James, Review, *ArtReview*, December 2004–January 2005, vol.14, p.105

White, Barry, 'A Round of Golf on the Moon: The Art of Verne Dawson', *Trinity News*, 13 April 2004

Williams, Eliza, Review, *Flash Art*, issue 248, May–June 2006, p.128

Yablonsky, Linda, Review, *Time Out*, New York, 31 May 2001

Books

432, Douglas Hyde Gallery, Dublin, Ireland, 2004

Dawson, Verne, *Verne Dawson: Precession of the Equinoxes. Paintings 1994–2010*, les presses du réel, Dijon, France, 2012

Hutchinson, John and Tal R, *Huts*, Douglas Hyde Gallery, Dublin, 2005

Nickas, Bob, *After the Observatory*, exh. cat., Paula Cooper Gallery, New York, 2003

Obrist, Hans Ulrich, *Vitamin P*, Phaidon Press, London, 2002, pp 76–9

Obrist, Hans Ulrich, Laurence Bossé, et al., *Urgent Painting*, Paris-Musées, Paris, 2002

Ruf, Beatrix, *Verne Dawson, Heaven and Earth: Twenty-One Paintings*, exh. cat., Kunsthalle Zurich, 2002

Translation, a commemorative publication by M/M (Paris) celebrating the exhibition 'Translation', Deste Foundation for Contemporary Art, Athens, 2006

Biography

1955 Born in Meridianville, Alabama, USA

1976 Moves to New York, enrols at Art Students League, and then the Cooper Union School of Art

1980 Graduates from the Cooper Union School of Art

1983 Returns to New York after travel in Europe. Opens and runs 'Portrait Studio' in New York

1988 First important group exhibition, at White Columns, New York

1989 First solo exhibition in New York, at Althea Viafora Gallery

1994 First exhibition at Gavin Brown's enterprise, New York

1999 Marries Laura Hoptman

2002 First exhibition at public space in Europe, Kunsthalle Zurich, Switzerland

2003 Exhibition at Galerie Hauser & Wirth and Galerie Eva Presenhuber, Zurich, Switzerland

2003 First exhibition at Victoria Miro Gallery, London, UK

2010 Exhibits at the Whitney Biennial, Whitney Museum of American Art, New York

Exhibitions

Solo Exhibitions

2017
Tinnitus, Gavin Brown's enterprise, New York, USA

2016
The Douglas Hyde Gallery, Dublin, Ireland

2015
Mermaid Money, Galerie Eva Presenhuber, Zurich, Switzerland

2013
Galleria Il Capricorno, Venice, Italy
Apalachicola to Zirconia, Victoria Miro Gallery, London, UK

2011
Galerie Eva Presenhuber, Zurich, Switzerland

2009
Gavin Brown's enterprise, New York, USA

2008
Paradise, Douglas Hyde Gallery, Dublin, Ireland

2007
Paintings, Galerie Eva Presenhuber, Zurich, Switzerland

2006
Le Consortium, Dijon, France
Sunday, Monday, Tuesday, Wednesday, Thursday, Friday, Saturday, Gavin Brown's enterprise, New York, USA
Victoria Miro Gallery, London, UK

2005
Camden Arts Centre, London, UK

2004
The Days of the Week and other Paintings, Gavin Brown's enterprise, New York, USA
Douglas Hyde Gallery, Dublin, Ireland

2003
Wheel of Fortune, Victoria Miro Gallery, London, UK
Aerialists, Galerie Hauser & Wirth and Galerie Eva Presenhuber, Zurich, Switzerland

2002
Kunsthalle Zurich, Switzerland

2001
Gavin Brown's enterprise, New York, USA

2000
Galleria Monica de Cardenas, Milan, Italy

1999
Gavin Brown's enterprise, New York, USA

1997
Gavin Brown's enterprise, New York, USA

1995
Gavin Brown's enterprise, New York, USA

1989
Althea Viafora Gallery, New York, USA

1985
The Portrait Studio, New York, USA

Group Exhibitions

2017
Get Outta That Spaceship and Fight Like a Man, Franklin Parrasch Gallery, New York, USA
Ugo Rondinone: I ♥ John Giorno, a 13-venue exhibition in New York, USA

2016
Outside, Karma, Amagansett, New York, USA

2015
Ugo Rondinone: I ♥ John Giorno, Palais de Tokyo, Paris, France
Works on Paper, Galerie Eva Presenhuber, Zurich, Switzerland

2014
Paesaggio mon amour, Museum of Modern and Contemporary Art (MART) of Trento and Rovereto, Italy
Somos Libres II: Works from the Mario Testino Collection, Pinacoteca Giovanni e Marella Agnelli, Torino, Italy

2013
Paisaje 1969–2013, Museo del Palacio de Bellas Artes, Mexico City, Mexico

2012
Art Unlimited, Art Basel, Basel, Switzerland
Le Monde comme volonté et comme papier peint (*The World as Will and Wallpaper*), Le Consortium, Dijon, France
Painting Now, Galerie Eva Presenhuber, Zurich, Switzerland

2011
Our Magic Hour, Yokohama Triennale, Yokohama, Japan

2010
2010, Whitney Biennial, Whitney Museum of American Art, New York, USA
At Home/Not at Home, Hessel Museum of Art, New York, USA
In the Company of Alice, Victoria Miro Gallery, London, UK
Shut Your Eyes in Order to See, Galerie Praz-Delavallade, Paris, France

2009
Cave Painting, Gresham's Ghost, New York, USA
Cave Painting, PSM Gallery, Berlin, Germany
Hello, Mrs. MacGruder, Benson Keyes Arts, Southampton, New York, USA
We are Sun-kissed and Snow-blind, Galerie Patrick Seguin, Paris, France, with Galerie Eva Presenhuber

2008
ESTRATOS Art Festival, Murcia, Spain
Future Tense: Reshaping the Landscape, Neuberger Museum of Art, Purchase College, New York, USA
Gallery Hyundai/doART, Seoul, South Korea
Gallery Hyundai/doART, Beijing, China

2007
Painting as Fact, Fact as Fiction, de Pury & Luxembourg, Zurich, Switzerland
The Third Mind, Palais de Tokyo, Paris, France

2006
Panic Room, Deste Foundation for Contemporary Art, Athens, Greece

2005
Expérience de la durée, Lyon Biennale, Lyon, France
Interested Painting, Gallery 400, University of Illinois, Chicago, USA
Translation, Palais de Tokyo, Paris, France

2004
Huts, Douglas Hyde Gallery, Dublin, Ireland

2003
20th Anniversary – Welcome Home, Gavin Brown's enterprise, New York, USA
Breathing Under Water, Galerie Hauser & Wirth and Galerie Eva Presenhuber, Zurich, Switzerland
Dirty Pictures, The Approach, London, UK
Game Over, Grimm Rosenfeld, Munich, Germany
Utopia Station, Venice Biennale, Venice, Italy

2002
Five Years, Jousse Enterprise, Paris, France
From the Observatory, Paula Cooper Gallery, New York, USA
Urgent Painting, Musée d'Art Moderne de la Ville de Paris, Paris, France

2001
Best of the Season, The Aldrich Contemporary Art Museum, Ridgefield, USA
Extended Painting, Galleria Monica de Cardenas, Milan, Italy
How is Everything? Everything's Going to Be . . . Alright, Elizabeth Cherry Contemporary Art, Tuscon, Arizona, USA
Invisible Museum, Memphis, USA
London Painting 2001, Victoria Miro Gallery, London, UK
Works on Paper: From Acconci to Zittel, Victoria Miro Gallery, London, UK

2000
Collected (in Mind), Sandra Gering Gallery, New York, USA
Cosmobiology, Bellweather, New York, USA
Ghosts, Invisible Museum, Memphis, USA
There Is no Spirit in Painting, Le Consortium, Dijon, France

1999
Another Country, Lawrence Rubin Greenberg Van Doren Fine Art, New York, USA
Titles for Drawings, AC Project Room, New York, USA

1998
Pets, Bronwyn Keenan Gallery, New York, USA

1997
Landscape USA, Bronwyn Keenan Gallery, New York, USA

1996
AC Project Room, New York, USA
Gavin Brown's enterprise, New York, USA

1993
Art in General, Randolph Street Gallery, Chicago, USA
Delta Axis, Memphis, USA
Little Things, Feseque (Municipal Art Museum), Budapest, Hungary

1990
Nicole Klagsbrun Gallery, New York, USA

1987
Ridge Street Gallery, New York, USA

1986
Ridge Street Gallery, New York, USA

1985
The Portrait Studio, New York, USA

1984
King Street Gallery, New York, USA
Sharpe Gallery, New York, USA

1983
Olsen Gallery, New York, USA

1982
Olsen Gallery, New York, USA

1981
Columbia Museum of Art, South Carolina, USA
Greenville County Museum of Art, South Carolina, USA
High Museum of Art, Atlanta, USA
The Mint Museum, Charlotte, North Carolina, USA

Selected Public Collections

Albright-Knox Art Gallery, Buffalo, NY
Birmingham Museum of Art, Birmingham, AL
Broad Art Foundation, Santa Monica, CA
Colby College Museum of Art, Waterville, ME
Des Moines Art Center, Des Moines, OH
Deste Foundation for Contemporary Art, Athens, Greece
The Eli and Edythe L. Broad Collection
Essl Museum, Klosterneuburg, Germany

Hamburger Kunsthalle, Hamburg, Germany
Kemper Museum of Contemporary Art, Kansas
    City, MO
Kunstmuseum Wolfsburg, Wolfsburg, Germany
Museo Nacional Centro de Arte Reina Sofía,
    Madrid, Spain
Museum der Moderne Salzburg, Salzburg,
    Austria
Museum Moderner Kunst Stiftung Ludwig Wien,
    Vienna, Austria
Museum of Fine Arts, Boston, MA
Museum of Modern Art, New York, NY
Philadelphia Museum of Art, Philadelphia, PA
Rose Art Museum, Brandeis University,
    Waltham, MA
San Francisco Museum of Modern Art,
    San Francisco, CA
Solomon R. Guggenheim Museum of Art,
    New York, NY
Whitney Museum of American Art, New York,
    NY

Acknowledgements

During my time as Director of the Douglas Hyde Gallery in Trinity College, Dublin, I had the opportunity of working with Verne Dawson on several occasions. We came to know each other well, as we had many interests and tastes in common. This friendship has further developed through the process of writing this book; we have been in constant touch, and our uninhibited communication has been a great pleasure. I am most grateful for his warm interest and support.

It was Barry Schwabsky who first encouraged me to embark on this project, and I am thankful to him for the opportunity, which has turned out to be an enjoyable privilege. Everyone at Lund Humphries has been extremely helpful, especially Lucy Clark, to whom I offer my warm gratitude for her patience and detailed advice. I also thank Catherine Hooper for her editorial work on the text. Gavin Brown, of Gavin Brown's enterprise, has been very supportive, as have his colleagues Emily Bates and Sonny Noladiv. Finally, I would like to thank William Firebrace, who has much more experience than me in dealing with publishing projects, for his occasional wise words.

Image Credits

First published in 2019 by Lund Humphries

Lund Humphries
Office 3, Book House
261A City Road
London EC1V 1JX
UK
www.lundhumphries.com

ISBN: 978–1–84822–298–4

A Cataloguing-in-Publication record for this book is available from the
British Library

Copy-edited by Catherine Hooper
Designed by Mark Thomson
Typeset by Crow Books
Set in Custodia (Fred Smeijers)
Printed in Italy

Frontispiece: Verne Dawson photographed by Thomas Müller
Cover: *Pagans*, 2009–10, oil on canvas